ISBN 978-1-5280-8910-4
PIBN 10163785

1917
FEDERAL COUNCIL
YEAR BOOK

COVERING THE YEAR 1916

H. K. CARROLL, LL.D.

FEDERAL COUNCIL YEAR BOOK

AN ECCLESIASTICAL AND STATISTICAL
DIRECTORY OF THE FEDERAL COUNCIL,
ITS COMMISSIONS AND ITS CONSTITUENT
BODIES, AND OF ALL OTHER RELIGIOUS
ORGANIZATIONS IN THE UNITED STATES

COVERING THE YEAR 1916

PREPARED UNDER THE AUSPICES OF THE FEDERAL COUNCIL
OF THE CHURCHES OF CHRIST IN AMERICA

By

H. K. CARROLL, LL.D.
ASSOCIATE SECRETARY IN WASHINGTON

PUBLISHED BY

MISSIONARY EDUCATION MOVEMENT
OF THE UNITED STATES AND CANADA
156 FIFTH AVENUE, NEW YORK

1917

CONTENTS

Contents

A PREFATORY WORD

Benefiting by suggestions received, this second issue of the YEAR BOOK has been improved for purposes of reference by an index, by changes in type, by a better classification, and by the addition of new tables of statistics of Sunday-schools, of the distribution of communicants of many denominations by states, and of the chief Protestant bodies of the world. Other denominations would have been included in the distribution by states, but they were unable to make the compilation. It is hoped that they may provide for this hereafter.

The general tables of statistics include, as heretofore, those organizations recognized as religious bodies by the United States Census Bureau. No attempt has been made to classify the denominations as evangelical, orthodox, non-evangelical, etc. With the statistical information given for all, any one can make for himself such lists as his judgment may determine. Those who want to ascertain the strength of the evangelical churches may begin with the constituent bodies of the Federal Council, for which a separate table is given at the end of the Directory of the Constituent Bodies, and add such other denominations thereto as, in his opinion, belong properly to the evangelical group.

Hundreds of denominational statisticians and other correspondents have freely furnished information, and the editor hereby makes grateful acknowledgment of their favors.

H. K. CARROLL, Editor.

HISTORY AND ORGANIZATION OF THE FEDERAL COUNCIL

HISTORICAL SKETCH

The Federal Council held its first meeting at Philadelphia in 1908 and was largely the culmination of previous voluntary federative movements, the chief of which had been the Evangelical Alliance and the National Federation of Churches and Christian Workers. The important preliminary work leading up to the organization was accomplished by the Interchurch Conference on Federation held in Carnegie Hall, New York City, in 1905, a body composed of official delegates from thirty denominations convened through the initiative of the National Federation of Churches and Christian Workers. This conference adopted the Constitution of the Federal Council and transmitted it to the various denominations with the understanding that approval by two thirds of them would give it full effect. This approval was secured early in 1908.

THE FEDERAL COUNCIL—AN ORGANIZED BODY

The difference between the Federal Council and the previous movements is that it is not an individual or voluntary agency, or simply an interdenominational fellowship, but is an officially and ecclesiastically constituted body.

It is differentiated from other general movements for the manifestation of Christian unity in the fact that it is the cooperation of the various denominations for service rather than an attempt to unite them upon definitions of theology and polity.

It does not interfere with the autonomy of these bodies and its Constitution specifically states that "The Federal

Council shall have no authority over the constituent bodies adhering to it; but its province shall be limited to the expression of its counsel and the recommending of a course of action in matters of common interest to the churches, local councils, and individual Christians. It has no authority to draw up a common creed or form of government or of worship, or in any way to limit the full autonomy of the Christian bodies adhering to it."

The basis and limitations of its constituency are indicated by the preamble to the Constitution, which reads as follows: "In the providence of God, the time has come when it seems fitting more fully to manifest the essential oneness of the Christian churches of America, in Jesus Christ as their Divine Lord and Savior, and to promote the spirit of fellowship, service, and cooperation among them."

ORGANIZATION

The Federal Council meets quadrennially and consists of about four hundred qualified members officially elected by the various denominational assemblies or other constituted authorities.

Its Executive Committee consists of about ninety of these delegates and acts for the Council during the quadrennium between its sessions, holding regular annual meetings.

The Executive Committee has an Administrative Committee, holding regular monthly meetings which acts for the Executive Committee between its sessions.

The national office and its executives, under the Administrative Committee, carry on the continuous work of the Council.

THE NATURE OF ITS WORK

The united work undertaken by the Council is indicated by the titles of its commissions and committees. Among these are the Commissions on Evangelism, Social Service, Christian Education, Temperance, International Justice and Good-will (formerly Peace and Arbitration), Church and Country Life, Interchurch Federations (State and Local), and Relations with the Orient (formerly Relations with Japan); and Committees on Foreign Missions, on Home

Missions, on Family Life and Religious Rest Day, and on Ministerial Relief and Sustentation.

The Home Missions Council is a cooperating body of the Federal Council. The Commission on Temperance is in alliance with the National Temperance Society. The Commission on International Justice and Good-will cooperates with the World Alliance for Promoting International Friendship through the Churches.

The Commission on the Church and Social Service was the first to be effectively organized, as its work seemed to offer a larger immediate field for common action. The Commissions on International Justice and Good-will, on Evangelism, on the Church and Country Life, and on Interchurch Federations also have offices and executive secretaries.

Other special commissions or committees are appointed from time to time to take up special activities calling for action upon the part of the churches.

THE FUNCTIONS OF THE COUNCIL

One of the important results of the work during the first quadrennium was the development of a more intimate acquaintance and a better understanding between the great bodies in the Council through working together and through the larger view which each has gained of the other's work by means of this mutual relation. This bond of fellowship has constantly and rapidly become stronger. One of the chief tasks of the Council is that of educating the churches in the interest of united action.

Its general functions require careful development, owing to the wide variety in ecclesiastical polity among its various constituent bodies. It is generally conceded, however, that it should represent and declare the common conscience of the Christian churches upon important questions with regard to which the common consciousness of Christianity is practically unanimous. This is best illustrated by its declarations on the problems of the social order and concerning the moral life of the nation. For example, upon such questions as international peace no concerted action can be taken except by such a comprehensive representative body as the Council.

One of its important functions is the constant creation on

the part of the churches of a state of mind which has deepened their sense of fellowship. This it accomplishes by bringing together upon every possible occasion its widely varying elements for consultation and common action. This is illustrated by such a movement as the coordination of the religious forces of the nation for work together during the Panama-Pacific Exposition.

The national office of the Council is creating a large body of literature calculated to increase and deepen the sense of fellowship and develop united action upon the part of the churches and to set forth their common obligations.

STATE AND LOCAL FEDERATIONS

While the Federal Council is constituted solely of the national denominations, it has a cooperative relationship with state and local federations.

The weakness or effectiveness of local federations is determined for the most part by local situations and is largely dependent upon the community sense of unity and fraternity.

The Commission on Interchurch Federations (State and Local) by correspondence, literature, and secretarial visitation, is continuously engaged in propagating this work.

The various denominations are called upon for a small apportionment which, however, even if fully met, would cover less than half the expenses of the national office.

The Council has instructed the treasurer to seek for the remaining amount from individual subscriptions, and from appropriations in the budgets of individual churches.

Correlation and unification unquestionably mean efficiency and economy. The work which the various denominations are brought to do in common costs very much less than it does when each denomination attempts it independently.

The subscriptions in the main are sought for the national office and the Washington office of the Council itself. The Commission on the Church and Social Service is maintained by a large number of sustaining memberships of small and moderate amounts. The Commission on the Church and Country Life is sustained by special contributions. The Commission on International Justice and Good-will is maintained by a special gift for the purpose, and the Commission on Interchurch Federations is responsible for the maintenance of its particular work.

OFFICES OF THE FEDERAL COUNCIL
National Offices of the Federal Council
612 United Charities Building
105 East 22d Street
New York City

Office of the Printing and Publication Department
(Has an up-to-date list of more than 90,000 ministers of all denominations)
604 United Charities Building
105 East 22d Street
New York City

Washington Office of the Federal Council,
and the Religious Welfare League for the Army and Navy
1114 Woodward Building
Washington, D. C.

Office of the Commission on the Church and Social Service
105 East 22d Street, New York City

Office of the Commission on Temperance and National
Temperance Society
51 United Charities Building
105 East 22d Street
New York City

Office of the Commission on Interchurch Federations
105 East 22d Street
New York City

Office of Commission on International Justice and Good-will
105 East 22d Street
New York City

Office of Commission on Relations with the Orient
105 East 22d Street
New York City

Office of Commission on Christian Education
105 East 22d Street
New York City

Branch Office of the Commission on the Church and Country Life
Commercial Building
104 North 3d Street
Columbus, Ohio

OFFICERS OF THE FEDERAL COUNCIL

President—Rev. Frank Mason North.
Honorary Secretary—Rev. Elias B. Sanford.
Recording Secretary—Rev. Rivington D. Lord.
Treasurer—Alfred R. Kimball.

EXECUTIVES

General Secretary of the Council—Rev. Charles S. Macfarland.
Field Secretary for Special Service—Rev. Charles Stelzle.
Associate Secretary—Rev. Worth M. Tippy.
Assistant Secretary—Rev. E. W. Rankin.

VICE-PRESIDENTS

Baptist Churches, North
Rev. W. C. Bitting.............................St. Louis, Mo.
Free Baptist Churches
Hon. Carl E. Milliken........................Augusta, Me.
National Baptist Convention (Colored)

Christian Church
Rev. Frank G. Coffin..........................Albany, N. Y.
Congregational Churches
Rev. G. Glen Atkins..........................Providence, R. I.
Disciples of Christ
Pres. E. M. Bowman..........................Chicago, Ill.
German Evangelical Synod of North America
Rev. John Baltzer............................St. Louis, Mo.
Evangelical Association

Friends
Joseph John Mills............................Pasadena, Cal.
Lutheran Church, General Synod
Prof. Victor Tressler........................Springfield, O.
Mennonite Church, General Conference
Rev. A. S. Shelly............................Upland, Cal.
Methodist Episcopal Church
Bishop Luther B. Wilson...................New York City

Methodist Episcopal Church, South
Bishop Edwin D. Mouzon........................Dallas, Tex.

African Methodist Episcopal Church
Bishop L. J. Coppin..........................Philadelphia, Pa.

African Methodist Episcopal Zion Church
Bishop L. W. Kyles............................St. Louis, Mo.

Colored Methodist Episcopal Church in America
Bishop C. H. Phillips........................Nashville, Tenn.

Methodist Protestant Church
Rev. Charles H. Beck..........................Pittsburgh, Pa.

Moravian Church
Rt. Rev. C. L. Moench........................Bethlehem, Pa.

Presbyterian Church in the U. S. A.
Rev. John A. Marquis........................Cedar Rapids, Ia.

Presbyterian Church in the U. S. (South)
Rev. William Crowe..........................Memphis, Tenn.

Protestant Episcopal
 Commissions on Christian Unity and Social Service
Very Rev. Carroll M. Davis....................St. Louis, Mo.

Reformed Church in America
Rev. John E. Kuizenga........................Holland, Mich.

Reformed Church in the U. S.
Rev. J. M. G. Darms..........................Allentown, Pa.

Reformed Episcopal Church
Rev. Joseph D. Wilson......................Philadelphia, Pa.

Reformed Presbyterian Church, General Synod

Seventh Day Baptist Church
Rev. A. L. Davis............................North Loup, Neb.

United Brethren Church
Bishop William M. Bell......................Los Angeles, Cal.

United Evangelical Church
Rev. H. B. Hartzler..........................Harrisburg, Pa.

United Presbyterian Church
Rev. D. F. McGill............................Ben Avon, Pa.

Welsh Presbyterian Church
Rev. W. E. Evans............................Mankato, Minn.

Alternates:

Not yet named.

Christian Church

Rev. Martyn Summerbell, Lakemont, N. Y.
Rev. Oliver W. Powers, Dayton, Ohio.

Alternates:

President William A. Harper, Elon College, N. C.
Hermon Eldredge, Erie, Pa.

Congregational Churches

Hamilton Holt, New York City.
Rev. Hubert C. Herring, Boston, Mass.
Rev. W. T. McElveen, Evanston, Ill.

Alternates:

Rev. H. F. Holton, St. Louis, Mo.
Rev. E. T. Root, Boston, Mass.
Rev. R. A. Beard, Fargo, N. D.

Disciples of Christ

Rev. Peter Ainslie, Baltimore, Md.
Rev. Finis S. Idleman, New York City.
Rev. Graham Frank, Liberty, Mo.
Rev. F. W. Burnham, Cincinnati, Ohio.

Alternates:

Rev. J. H. Garrison, St. Louis, Mo.
Rev. W. F. Richardson, Kansas City, Mo.
Rev. John R. Ewars, St. Louis, Mo.
Rev. B. A. Abbott, St. Louis, Mo.
Rev. A. B. Philput, Indianapolis, Ind.

Friends

President David M. Edwards, Oskaloosa, Ia.
Walter C. Woodward, Richmond, Ind.

Alternates:
Rev. Willard O. Trueblood, Indianapolis, Ind.
Mrs. Harriet S. G. Peelle, Sabina, Ohio.

German Evangelical Synod
Rev. William E. Bourquin, Brooklyn, N. Y.
Professor S. D. Press, St. Louis, Mo.

Alternates:

Evangelical Association
Bishop S. C. Breyfogel, Reading, Pa.

Alternate:

Lutheran Church, General Synod
Rev. George U. Wenner, New York City.
President William Granville, Gettysburg, Pa.

Alternates:
Rev. Frederick Knubel, New York City.
Rev. Luther De Yoe, Philadelphia, Pa.

Mennonite Church, General Conference
President S. K. Mosiman, Bluffton, Ohio.
Professor S. M. Rosenberger, Philadelphia, Pa.

Alternates:
Rev. Jacob Snyder, Roaring Springs, Pa.
Professor G. A. Haury, Newton, Kans.

Methodist Episcopal Church
George Warren Brown, St. Louis, Mo.
Bishop Thomas Nicholson, Chicago, Ill.
Rev. David G. Downey, New York City.
Rev. George Elliott, Mt. Clemens, Mich.
Rev. D. D. Forsyth, Philadelphia, Pa.
Thomas R. Fort, Philadelphia, Pa.
Rev. William I. Haven, New York City.
Rev. C. F. Rice, West Lynn, Mass.
G. M. Spurlock, York, Neb.
Pres. Charles M. Stuart, Evanston, Ill.

Alternates:
Bishop W. F. McDowell, Washington, D. C.
James R. Joy, New York City.
Rev. J. C. Arbuckle, Columbus, Ohio.
Rev. Edgar Blake, Chicago, Ill.
Rev. A. J. Nast, Cincinnati, Ohio.
J. D. Bluffton, Kansas City, Mo.
Rolla V. Watt, San Francisco, Cal.
Rev. E. S. Ninde, Providence, R. I.
J. Frank Hanly, Indianapolis, Ind.

Methodist Episcopal Church, South
Rev. John M. Moore, Nashville, Tenn.
Rev. Frank M. Thomas, Louisville, Ky.
Rev. Paul H. Linn, Fayette, Mo.
Rev. Hoyt M. Dobbs, Dallas, Texas.
Rev. L. C. Branscomb, Birmingham, Ala.
D. B. Coltrane, Concord, N. C.

Alternates:
Rev. B. P. Taylor, Kansas City, Mo.
Rev. R. E. Dickenson, Colorado Springs, Col.
Rev. James W. Lee, St. Louis, Mo.
Dean Wilbur F. Tillett, Nashville, Tenn.
W. D. Bradfield, Dallas, Tex.
Judge John S. Candler, Atlanta, Ga.

African Methodist Episcopal Church
Bishop H. B. Parks, Chicago, Ill.
Professor John R. Hawkins, Washington, D. C.
Rev. R. C. Ransom, Ocean Port, N. J.

Alternates:
Bishop C. T. Shaffer, Chicago, Ill.
Rev. S. P. Felder, Mound Bayou, Miss.
Rev. J. Q. Johnson, Columbia, Tenn.

African Methodist Episcopal Zion Church
Bishop Alexander Walters,* New York City.
Rev. Henry J. Callis, Washington, D. C.
Professor S. G. Atkins, Winston-Salem, N. C.
Rev. James E. Mason, Washington, D. C.

*Deceased.

Alternates:
Bishop George C. Clement, Charlotte, N. C.
Rev. John Martin, St. Louis, Mo.

Colored Methodist Episcopal Church in America
Bishop N. C. Cleaves, Memphis, Tenn.
Rev. J. A. Hamlett, Jackson, Tenn.
Rev. John W. Gilbert, Augusta, Ga.

Alternates:
Dr. G. W. Noble, Louisville, Ky.
G. F. Porter, Jackson, Tenn.
Rev. T. A. Bowers, Paxico, Kans.

Methodist Protestant Church
Rev. Lyman E. Davis, Pittsburgh, Pa.
Hon. F. C. Chambers, Steubenville, Ohio.

Alternates:
President H. L. Elderdice, Westminster, Md.
Sylvester Pearsall, Lynbrook, N. Y.

Moravian Church
Allen W. Stephens, New York City.
Rt. Rev. Morris W. Leibert, New York City.

Alternates:
E. G. Hoyler, Philadelphia, Pa.
Rev. Arthur D. Thaeler, Bethlehem, Pa.

Presbyterian Church in the U. S. A.
Rev. C. L. Thompson, New York City.
Rev. Henry Collin Minton, Trenton, N. J.
Rev. William H. Black, Marshall, Mo.
William H. Scott, Philadelphia, Pa.
James Yereance, New York City.

Alternates:
Rev. George Reynolds, New Rochelle, N. Y.
Rev. John T. Bergen, Minneapolis, Minn.
Rev. James E. Clarke, Nashville, Tenn.
R. L. Rees, New York City.
J. Lewis Twaddell, Devon, Pa.

Presbyterian Church in the U. S.

Rev. J. F. Cannon, St. Louis, Mo.
F. T. Glasgow, Lexington, Va.

Alternates:

Rev. Russell Cecil, Richmond, Va.
W. F. Stevenson, Cheraw, S. C.

Protestant Episcopal Commissions on Christian Unity and Social Service

Rt. Rev. Ethelbert Talbot, South Bethlehem, Pa.
Rt. Rev. Charles P. Anderson, Chicago, Ill.
Robert H. Gardiner, Gardiner, Maine.
John M. Glenn, New York City.

Alternates:

Rt. Rev. Theodore I. Reese, Columbus, Ohio.
Rev. Samuel Tyler, Rochester, N. Y.
Rev. Floyd Tomkins, Philadelphia, Pa.
George Wharton Pepper, Philadelphia, Pa.

Reformed Church in America

Rev. Albertus T. Broek, Newark, N. J.
Rev. Isaac W. Gowen, North Bergen, N. J.

Alternates:

Rev. Ame Vennema, Holland, Mich.
Rev. Jesse W. Brooks, Chicago, Ill.

Reformed Church in the U. S.

Rev. Rufus W. Miller, Philadelphia, Pa.
Rev. Charles E. Schaeffer, Philadelphia, Pa.

Alternates:

Rev. H. J. Christman, Dayton, Ohio.
Rev. W. S. Cramer, Lancaster, Pa.

Reformed Episcopal Church

Bishop Samuel Fallows, Chicago, Ill.
Bishop Robert L. Rudolph, Philadelphia, Pa.

Alternates:

Rev. William D. Stevens, New York City.
Rev. Samuel M. Gibson, Chicago, Ill.

Reformed Presbyterian Church, General Synod
Members and alternates not yet named.

Seventh Day Baptist Church

Rev. Arthur E. Main, Alfred, N. Y.
William C. Hubbard, Plainfield, N. J.

Alternates:

Rev. A. J. C. Bond, Salem, W. Va.
President B. C. Davis, Alfred, N. Y.

United Brethren Church

Bishop G. M. Mathews, Dayton, Ohio.
L. O. Miller, Dayton, Ohio.

Alternates:

Bishop C. J. Kephart, Kansas City, Mo.
W. R. Funk, Dayton, Ohio.

United Evangelical Church

Bishop U. F. Swengel, Harrisburg, Pa.
J. J. Nungesser, Harrisburg, Pa.

Alternates:

Rev. W. M. Stanford, Harrisburg, Pa.
Professor H. H. Rassweiler, Naperville, Ill.

United Presbyterian

Rev. R. A. Hutchison, Pittsburgh, Pa.
M. Clyde Kelly, Washington, D. C.

Alternates:

A. H. Baldinger, Pittsburgh, Pa.
Fred McMillan, Des Moines, Iowa.

Welsh Presbyterian

Rev. John C. Jones, Chicago, Ill.
Dr. E. J. Jones, Oak Hill, Ohio.

Alternates:

Rev. R. E. Williams, Philadelphia, Pa.
Rev. John Hammond, Scranton, Pa.

ADMINISTRATIVE COMMITTEE

Rev. Albert G. Lawson, Chairman

Rev. George U. Wenner, Vice-Chairman

Rev. Alfred Wms. Anthony	Rev. Frederick Lynch
Bishop L. J. Coppin	Rev. Rufus W. Miller
John M. Glenn	Rev. Henry C. Minton
Rev. Howard B. Grose	Rev. Frank Mason North
Dr. A. W. Harris	George A. Plimpton
Rev. William I. Haven	Rev. William H. Roberts
Rev. Finis S. Idleman	Fred B. Smith
Orrin R. Judd	Rev. Ezra S. Tipple
Alfred R. Kimball	Bishop Luther B. Wilson
	James Yereance

ADVISORY COMMITTEE AT WASHINGTON, D. C.

Rt. Rev. Alfred Harding, Chairman

Rev. George A. Miller, Recording-Secretary

Rev. John Lee Allison	Bishop W. F. McDowell
Chaplain G. Livingston Bayard	Rev. Forrest J. Prettyman
Bishop Earl Cranston	Rev. Wallace Radcliffe
Rev. Samuel H. Greene	Rev. Charles F. Steck
John B. Larner	Rev. Clarence A. Vincent

G. W. F. Swartzell

THE NATIONAL OFFICE STAFF

Rev. Charles S. Macfarland, General Secretary

Rev. Charles Stelzle, Field Secretary for Special Service

Rev. Worth M. Tippy, Associate Secretary

Rev. Sidney L. Gulick, Secretary of Commission on International Justice and Good-will

Rev. E. W. Rankin, Assistant Secretary

Miss Caroline W. Chase, Office Director and Private Secretary

Miss Grace M. Turton, Chief Stenographer

Miss Anna M. Anderson, Assistant to the Treasurer

Miss Ruth Taylor, Private Secretary to Mr. Stelzle

Miss Helen M. Roberts, Private Secretary to Dr. Guild

Miss Margaret Renton, Private Secretary to Mr. Rankin

Stanley T. Anderson, Director of the Printing and Publication Department

OTHER EXECUTIVES

Rev. Roy B. Guild, Executive Secretary of the Commission on Interchurch Federations (State and Local)

Rev. Charles O. Gill, Secretary of the Commission on the

Church and Country Life, 104 North Third Street, Columbus, O.

The following denominational secretaries are Associate Secretaries of the Commission on the Church and Social Service:

Rev. Henry A. Atkinson, 14 Beacon Street, Boston, Mass.

Rev. Samuel Z. Batten, 1701 Chestnut Street, Philadelphia, Pa.

Rev. Frank M. Crouch, 281 Fourth Avenue, New York City.

Rev. Harry F. Ward, 72 Mount Vernon Street, Boston, Mass.

J. E. McAfee, 156 Fifth Avenue, New York City.

CONSTITUTION OF THE FEDERAL COUNCIL

Plan of Federation Recommended by The Interchurch Conference of 1905, Adopted by the National Assemblies of Constituent Bodies, 1906-1908, Ratified by the Council at Philadelphia, December 2-8, 1908, Amended December 4-9, 1912, and December 6-11, 1916.

PREAMBLE

Whereas, In the providence of God, the time has come when it seems fitting more fully to manifest the essential oneness of the Christian Churches of America, in Jesus Christ as their Divine Lord and Savior, and to promote the spirit of fellowship, service, and cooperation among them, the delegates to the Interchurch Conference on Federation, assembled in New York City, do hereby recommend the following Plan of Federation to the Christian bodies represented in this Conference for their approval:

PLAN OF FEDERATION

1. For the prosecution of work that can be better done in union than in separation a Council is hereby established whose name shall be the Federal Council of the Churches of Christ in America.

2. The following Christian bodies shall be entitled to representation in this Federal Council on their approval of the purpose and plan of the organization:

The Baptist Churches of the United States
The General Conference of Free Baptists
The National Baptist Convention (African)*
The Christians (The Christian Connection)
The Congregational Churches
The Congregational Methodist Churches*

---

*These bodies were received into the fellowship of the Council under provisions stated in section seven of the Constitution.

The Disciples of Christ
The Evangelical Association
The Evangelical Synod of North America
The Friends
The Evangelical Lutheran Church, General Synod
The Methodist Episcopal Church
The Methodist Episcopal Church, South
The Primitive Methodist Church
The Colored Methodist Episcopal Church in America
The Methodist Protestant Church
The African Methodist Episcopal Church
The African Methodist Episcopal Zion Church
The General Conference of the Mennonite Church of North
America
The Moravian Church
The Presbyterian Church in the U. S. A.
The Presbyterian Church in the U. S.*
The Welsh Calvinistic Methodist or Presbyterian Church
The Reformed Presbyterian Church
The United Presbyterian Church
The Protestant Episcopal Church
The Reformed Church in America
The Reformed Church in the U. S.
The Reformed Episcopal Church
The Seventh Day Baptist Churches
The Swedish Lutheran Augustana Synod*
The United Brethren in Christ
The United Evangelical Church.

3. The object of this Federal Council shall be—

I. To express the fellowship and catholic unity of the Christian Church.

II. To bring the Christian bodies of America into united service for Christ and the world.

III. To encourage devotional fellowship and mutual

*These bodies were received into fellowship of the Council under provisions stated in section seven of the Constitution.

counsel concerning the spiritual life and religious activities of the churches.

IV. To secure a larger combined influence for the churches of Christ in all matters affecting the moral and social condition of the people, so as to promote the application of the law of Christ in every relation of human life.

V. To assist in the organization of local branches of the Federal Council to promote its aims in their communities.

4. This Federal Council shall have no authority over the constituent bodies adhering to it; but its province shall be limited to the expression of its counsel and the recommending of a course of action in matters of common interest to the churches, local councils, and individual Christians.

It has no authority to draw up a common creed or form of government or of worship, or in any way to limit the full autonomy of the Christian bodies adhering to it.

5. Members of this Federal Council shall be appointed as follows:

Each of the Christian bodies adhering to this Federal Council shall be entitled to four members, and shall be further entitled to one member for every 50,000 of its communicants or major fraction thereof. Alternates may be chosen and certified to the Council in the same manner and to the same number as members to fill vacancies caused by the death, resignation, or permanent disqualification of members. Such alternates may also attend sessions of the Council in the absence of members and exercise all powers of members as temporary substitutes during such absence.

6. Any action to be taken by this Federal Council shall be by the general vote of its members. But in case one third of the members present and voting request it, the vote shall be by the bodies represented, the representatives of each body voting separately; and action shall require the vote, not only of a majority of the members voting, but also of the bodies represented.

7. Other Christian bodies may be admitted into membership of this Federal Council on their request if approved by a vote of two thirds of the members voting at a session of this council, and of two thirds of the bodies represented, the representatives of each body voting separately.

8. The Federal Council shall meet once in every four years and the term of service of the members or their alternates shall be four years or until their successors shall be appointed. Special meetings may be called by the Executive Committee.

9. Section a. The officers of this Federal Council shall be a President, one Vice-President from each of its constituent bodies, a Recording Secretary, a Treasurer, and an Executive Committee, who shall perform the duties usually assigned to such officers. Vacancies among the Vice-Presidents or in the Executive Committee may be filled by the Executive Committee on nomination by the representatives on the Executive Committee of the constituent body in which the vacancy may occur.

Section b. The General Secretary and other secretaries of the Council except the Recording Secretary shall be chosen by the Executive Committee, which shall have authority to fix their duties and their salaries, and they shall aid in organizing and assisting local Councils and shall represent the Federal Council in its work under the direction of the Executive Committee.

Section c. The Executive Committee shall consist of two representatives from each of the constituent bodies, preferably one minister and one layman, and one additional representative for every 500,000 of its communicants or major fraction thereof, who may be either a minister or layman, together with the President, all ex-Presidents, the Recording Secretary, and the Treasurer. The Executive Committee shall have authority to attend to all business of the Federal Council in the intervals of its meetings and to fill all vacancies, except that it shall not have power to make any amendments to the Constitution or to the By-Laws. It shall meet for organization at the call of the President of the Council immediately upon the adjournment of the Federal Council, and shall have power to elect its own officers.

Section d. All officers shall be chosen at the quadrennial meetings of the Council and shall hold their offices until their successors take office.

Section e. The President, the Recording Secretary, and the Treasurer shall be elected by the Federal Council on nomination by the Executive Committee, but nominations may be made from the floor of the Council by any member at the time of the election.

Section f. The Vice-Presidents and members of the Executive Committee and their alternates shall be elected by the Council upon nomination by the representatives in attendance of each of their respective constituent bodies.

10. The expenses of the Federal Council shall be provided for by the several constituent bodies.

11. This Plan of Federation may be altered or amended by a majority vote of the members, followed by a majority vote of the representatives of the several constituent bodies, each voting separately. Amendments to this plan shall be reported officially to the several constituent churches.

(The following paragraphs were recommended by Interchurch Conference of 1905, adopted by National Assemblies of Constituent Bodies 1906-1908.)

[*This Plan of Federation shall become operative when it shall have been approved by two thirds of the above bodies to which it shall be presented.*

[*It shall be the duty of each delegation to this Conference to present this Plan of Federation to its national body, and ask its consideration and proper action.*

[*In case this Plan of Federation is approved by two thirds of the proposed constituent bodies the Executive Committee of the National Federation of Churches and Christian Workers, which has called this Conference, is requested to call the Federal Council to meet at a fitting place in December, 1908.*]

BY-LAWS OF THE FEDERAL COUNCIL AS AMENDED

1. The Council shall meet quadrennially on the first Wednesday of December, at such place and hour as the Executive Committee shall from time to time determine. The place and time of special meetings shall be determined by the Executive Committee.

2. The President of the Council, or in case of his absence, the last President present shall open the meetings with an

address and devotional exercises, and preside until a new President is chosen.

3. The Recording Secretary and the Secretary, or Secretaries, to whom this duty may be assigned by the Executive Committee, shall make up the roll of the members in the Council from the certificates of the proper officers of the Constituent Bodies composing the Council, and no one not thus certified shall be enrolled. The Council shall determine any question arising as to the validity of certificates.

4. No President or Vice-President shall be eligible to immediate reelection.

5. A quorum of the Council shall consist of two or more members from a majority of the churches entitled to representation. A quorum of the Executive Committee shall be fifteen persons, and at least five denominations shall be represented.

6. The Council shall appoint a Business Committee to which shall be referred all matters connected with the proceedings of the Council while in session, and all such papers and documents as to the Council may seem proper. It shall consist of two members from each church having twenty or more representatives in the Council, and one from each of the churches having a less number of representatives. The Council may also appoint such other special committees as to it may seem proper.

7. The business expenses of the Council, the expenses of its committees subject to the discretion of the Executive Committee, and the salaries of its officers, shall be paid out of the funds contributed by the churches, but the expenses of the representatives of the churches in the Council shall not be a charge against the funds of the Council.

8. (1) The following Commissions, subject to the Executive Committee, shall be appointed to further the general purposes of the Federal Council as stated in its Constitution within the fields indicated by their respective names.

    a. A Commission on Evangelism.

    b. A Commission on the Church and Social Service.

    c. A Commission on the Church and Country Life.

    d. A Commission on Christian Education.

    e. A Commission on Temperance.

f. A Commission on International Justice and Good-will.

g. A Commission on Interchurch Federations (State and Local).

h. A Commission on Relations with the Orient.

(2) Each Commission shall consist of twenty-five or more members appointed from the Christian bodies appointing members to the Council, by the President of the Council, and confirmed by the Executive Committee.

(3) The members of these Commissions shall serve four years or until their successors are appointed. The Commissions shall report annually to the Executive Committee, and oftener should the Executive Committee require, and quadrennially through the Executive Committee to the Federal Council.

(4) The President of the Council shall appoint the Chairmen of these Commissions, which shall have power to choose such other officers for the conduct of their affairs as may be authorized by the Federal Council or the Executive Committee.

(5) These Commissions shall not commit the Federal Council to any policy or expense until such policy or expense is approved by the Executive Committee of the Federal Council.

(6) The Commissions shall submit their proposed budgets to the Executive Committee, and upon the Committee's authorization of such budgets, may solicit contributions for their work under the direction of the Executive Committee and the Treasurer of the Federal Council.

9. The Secretaries chosen by the Executive Committee shall conduct the correspondence of the Council and of the Executive Committee. The Executive Committee shall have full power to appoint, when necessary, such Secretaries as it may deem advisable and to designate their respective relations and duties.

10. The Recording Secretary shall keep the Minutes of the Council, and shall perform such other duties as may be assigned to him by the Executive Committee. The Executive Committee may appoint such assistant secretaries as may be necessary for the transaction of business, both for the Council and for the Committee.

11. The Treasurer of the Council shall be the custodian of all the funds of the Council and the Committees, and shall perform the duties usually assigned to the office, shall give bond in such sum as the Executive Committee shall determine, and his account shall be annually audited under the direction of the Executive Committee. -

12. The Executive Committee shall have authority to consider during the sessions of the Council or in the intervals between its meetings any business referred to it by the Council. It shall also prepare the docket of the Council, shall have charge of the preparations for the meetings of the Council, and shall exercise general supervision of all its affairs, and shall have authority to adopt its own rules for governing its own business. The Executive Committee shall meet at the call of the Chairman, or in his absence or disability, the call of three of the members representing three of the constituent bodies, and ten days' notice of meeting shall be given. Public meetings under the direction of the Executive Committee may be held annually in various sections of the country. The President shall also appoint the following Standing Committees to work under the direction of the Executive Committee:

> (1) A committee on Foreign Missions to number not more than fifteen members.
>
> (2) A committee on Home Missions to number not more than fifteen members.

(3) A committee on Family Life and Religious Rest Day.

The Executive Committee shall have power to establish Commissions or Committees *ad interim,* which may become permanent by the approval of the Federal Council.

13. The Minutes of the Council shall be published regularly, under the editorship of the Secretary or Secretaries to whom this duty may be assigned by the Executive Committee.

14. These By-laws may be amended at any regular meeting of the Council by a two-thirds vote of the members present.

THE COMMISSIONS OF THE FEDERAL COUNCIL

(The titles of Commissions and Committees as given here conform to the action of the Federal Council at St. Louis. The new Commissions and Committees are just being made up as the Year-Book goes to press. Their officers, in so far as appointed, are given. The commissions for the past quadrennium are printed in full in the 1915 Report of the Council.)

COMMISSION ON EVANGELISM

Organized for the promotion of the spirit of evangelism and evangelistic work in this country.

Chairman, Rev. Charles L. Goodell

COMMISSION ON THE CHURCH AND SOCIAL SERVICE

Created to cooperate with similar church organizations in the study and improvement of social conditions and in securing a more natural relationship between working men and the church, and in enlarging the activities of the churches.

Secretary, Rev. Worth M. Tippy
Field Secretary, Rev. Charles Stelzle

Secretarial Council

Rev. Henry A. Atkinson (Congregational), 14 Beacon Street, Boston, Mass.

Rev. Samuel Z. Batten (Baptist), 1701 Chestnut Street, Philadelphia, Pa.

Rev. Frank M. Crouch (Protestant Episcopal), 281 Fourth Avenue, New York City.

Rev. Charles O. Gill, Secretary of the Commission on the Church and Country Life, Columbus, Ohio.

J. E. McAfee (Presbyterian in U. S. A.), 156 Fifth Avenue, New York City.

Rev. Harry F. Ward (Methodist Episcopal), 72 Mount Vernon Street, Boston, Mass.

Directory of Church Social Service Organizations

I. CONNECTED WITH THE FEDERAL COUNCIL OF THE CHURCHES OF CHRIST IN AMERICA

A. *With Executive or Field Secretaries*

Commission on the Church and Social Service representing constituent bodies of the FEDERAL COUNCIL; Rev. Worth M. Tippy, Secretary, 612 United Charities Building, 105 East 22d Street, New York City.

BAPTIST—Department of Social Service and Brotherhood, Rev. Samuel Z. Batten, Secretary, 1701 Chestnut Street, Philadelphia, Pa.

CONGREGATIONAL—Social Service Commission, Rev. Henry A. Atkinson, Executive Secretary, 14 Beacon Street, Boston, Mass.

METHODIST EPISCOPAL—Federation for Social Service, Rev. Harry F. Ward, Secretary, 72 Mount Vernon Street, Boston, Mass.

PRESBYTERIAN—Department of Social Service and Immigration, J. E. McAfee, Secretary, 156 Fifth Avenue, New York City; Country Church Work, Warren H. Wilson, Secretary, 156 Fifth Avenue, New York City.

PROTESTANT EPISCOPAL—Joint Commission on Christian Unity and Social Service, Rev. Frank M. Crouch, Executive Secretary, The Church Missions House, 281 Fourth Avenue, New York City.

B. *Organized Agencies without Field Secretaries*

CHRISTIAN—Commission on Social Service of the American Christian Convention, Rev. O. W. Powers, Secretary, Dayton, Ohio.

DISCIPLES OF CHRIST—Commission on Social Service and the Country Church, Prof. Alva W. Taylor, Secretary, Bible College, Columbia, Mo.

FRIENDS—Social Service Commission, Prof. Rufus M. Jones, Chairman, Haverford College, Haverford, Pa.

GERMAN EVANGELICAL—General Synod, Commission on Social Service, Rev. J. Stilli, 633 East Market Street, Louisville, Ky.

LUTHERAN, EVANGELICAL—General Synod, The Inner Mission, F. H. Knubel, President, 48 Hamilton Terrace, New York City.

METHODIST EPISCOPAL, SOUTH—Rev. John M. Moore, 810 Broadway, Nashville, Tenn.

REFORMED, IN U. S.—Rev. Charles E. Schaeffer, 15th and Race Streets, Philadelphia, Pa.

UNITED PRESBYTERIAN—Committee on Social and Industrial Conditions. Rev. H. H. Marlin, Secretary, 5151 Penn Avenue, Pittsburgh, Pa.

C. *No Organized Agencies, but for information the following Correspondents may be addressed*

BAPTIST, FREE—Rev. Alfred W. Anthony, Lewiston, Maine.

BAPTIST, NATIONAL CONVENTION—Prof. R. B. Hudson, Selma, Ala.

BAPTIST, SEVENTH DAY—Pres. Boothe C. Davis, Alfred University, Alfred, N. Y.

EVANGELICAL ASSOCIATION—Bishop S. C. Breyfogel, 836 Center Avenue, Reading, Pa.

MENNONITE—Rev. S. K. Mosiman, Bluffton, Ohio.

METHODIST EPISCOPAL, AFRICAN—Bishop Cornelius Shaffer, 3742 Forest Avenue, Chicago, Ill.

METHODIST EPISCOPAL ZION, AFRICAN—Bishop George W. Clinton, 415 N. Myers Street, Charlotte, N. C.

METHODIST EPISCOPAL, IN AMERICA, COLORED—Bishop N. C. Cleaves, Columbia, S. C.

METHODIST PROTESTANT—Pres. H. L. Elderdice, Westminster Theological Seminary, Westminster, Md.

MORAVIAN—Rev. Edward S. Wolle, 601 N. 18th Street, Philadelphia, Pa.

PRESBYTERIAN, IN THE U. S. (SOUTHERN)—Prof. James R. Howerton, Lexington, Va.

REFORMED, IN AMERICA—William T. Demarest, 25 East 22d Street, New York City.

REFORMED EPISCOPAL—Rt. Rev. Samuel Fallows, 2344 Monroe Street, Chicago, Ill.

REFORMED PRESBYTERIAN—General Synod, Rev. J. L. Chesnut, Cedarville, Ohio.

UNITED BRETHREN—Rev. C. Whitney, United Brethren Building, Dayton, Ohio.

UNITED EVANGELICAL—Bishop U. F. Swengel, Harrisburg, Pa.

WELSH PRESBYTERIAN—Rev. Robert E. Roberts, 223 Twin Street, Rome, N. Y.

II. Not Connected with the Federal Council of the Churches of Christ in America

UNITARIAN—Department of Social Service and Public Service, American Unitarian Association, Rev. Elmer S. Forbes, Secretary, 25 Beacon Street, Boston, Mass.

UNIVERSALIST—Social Service Committee of the Universalist Church, Rev. Clarence R. Skinner, Secretary, Universalist Publishing House, 359 Boylston Street, Boston, Mass.

ROMAN CATHOLIC—Social Service Commission of the American Federation of Catholic Societies, Rev. Peter E. Dietz, Secretary, American Academy of Christian Democracy, Hot Springs, N. C.

JEWISH—Central Conference of American Rabbis, Rabbi Solomon Foster, Committee on Synagogue and Industrial Relations, 90 Treacy Avenue, Newark, N. J.

III. SOCIAL SERVICE ORGANIZATIONS IN CANADA AND ENGLAND

Canada:

SOCIAL SERVICE COUNCIL OF CANADA—Joint Secretaries, Rev. J. G. Shearer, Confederation Life Building, Toronto, Ont., and Rev. T. Albert Moore, Wesley Buildings, Toronto, Ont.

BAPTIST—Department of Social Service, no General Secretary at present time.

CHURCH OF ENGLAND—Committee on Moral and Social Reform, Secretary, Rev. R. L. Bridges, St. James Parish House, Toronto, Ont.

METHODIST—Department of Social Service and Evangelism, General Secretary, Rev. T. Albert Moore, Wesley Buildings, Toronto, Ont.

PRESBYTERIAN—Board of Social Service and Evangelism, General Secretary, Rev. J. G. Shearer, Confederation Life Building, Toronto, Ont.

England:

INTERDENOMINATIONAL CONFERENCE OF SOCIAL SERVICE UNIONS—Miss Lucy Gardner, 92 St. George's Square, London, S. W.

BAPTIST UNION—Social Service Section, Edward E. Hayward, Hon. Secretary, Baptist Church House, Southampton Row, London, W. C.

CATHOLIC SOCIAL GUILD—Mrs. V. M. Crawford, Secretary, 105 Marylebone Road, London.

CHRISTIAN SOCIAL UNION—L. V. Lester-Garland, 26 Norfolk Square, London, W.

CONGREGATIONAL UNION SOCIAL SERVICE COMMITTEE—Rev. William Reason, Secretary, Memorial Hall, Farringdon Street, London, E. C.

FRIENDS SOCIAL UNION—J. St. G. Heath, Secretary, Woodbrooke Settlement, Selly Oak, Birmingham.

NATIONAL CONFERENCE UNION FOR SOCIAL SERVICE—Rev. H. H. Johnson, The Orchardcroft Road, Evesham.

PRESBYTERIAN SOCIAL SERVICE UNION—Rev. J. A. Wilson, Secretary, 21 Rowlandson Terrace, Sunderland.

PRIMITIVE METHODIST UNION FOR SOCIAL SERVICE—Rev. E. B. Storr, Secretary, 49 Oakwood Road, Blackhill, Co. Durham.

UNITED METHODIST CHURCH SOCIAL SERVICE UNION—Rev. W. G. Peck, Secretary, 18 Wellington Street, Blackburn.

WESLEYAN METHODIST UNION FOR SOCIAL SERVICE—Rev. Henry Carter, Central Buildings, Westminster, S. W., and W. H. Armstrong.

HISTORY AND ORGANIZATION OF COMMISSION ON THE CHURCH AND SOCIAL SERVICE

The Federal Council, including thirty evangelical denominations and communions as constituent bodies, operates in the interest of Social Service through the Commission on the Church and Social Service, appointed at the organization of the Council in Philadelphia, 1908. At Philadelphia the previous Committee on the Church and Modern Industry gave utterance to a message which was unanimously adopted by the Council, has become historic, has since been reaffirmed by practically all the leading church assemblies and received with gladness by social leaders and workers in all spheres of service.

The Commission on the Church and Social Service was thoroughly organized, and in the spring of 1911, Rev. Charles S. Macfarland was elected as its Secretary, its offices being in association with those of the Federal Council.

Dr. Tippy, now the Associate Secretary of the Federal Council, also serves as the Secretary of the Commission, in association with the denominational social service secretaries, all of whom are associate secretaries of the Federal Council Commission, forming what is known as the Secretarial Council, and Rev. Charles Stelzle acts as Field Secretary.

The offices of the Commission contain a large Social Service Library, which adds all the latest books, has on file about two hundred social and industrial magazines and papers, and contains the literature pertaining to social work issued by all the movements, both religious and general.

Its most important work is that of correlating and coordinating the various denominational commissions and movements; and it has already gone a long way in bringing the denominational work into unity.

CONFERENCES

Its first interdenominational conference was held at Boston in June, 1911, and consisted of representatives of the evangelical denominations which were definitely organized in the interest of social service. This preliminary conference requested that Secretaries Macfarland, Atkinson, Crouch, Stelzle, and Ward arrange for an interdenominational conference to which all the constituent bodies of the Federal Council should be invited to send delegates. In accordance with this action, at an interdenominational conference held at Chicago, November, 1911, seventeen denominations were represented by delegates elected or appointed by denominational action, and the agreement was that the various denominational committees and departments should cooperate through the Federal Council Commission.

A third conference, with a large attendance representing nearly all the constituent denominations of the Federal Council, was held at Chicago in December, 1912.

SECRETARIAL FORCES

A secretarial council was recommended, to consist of the denominational secretaries of those Commissions having such executives, with the understanding that the secretary of the Federal Council Commission on Social Service should represent in the council all the other denominations which did not have executive secretaries.

The Commission has voted that these secretaries be made associate secretaries of the Federal Council Commission, subject to the acceptance of the arrangement by the denominational organizations. These associate secretaries are as follows: Rev. Henry A. Atkinson, Secretary of the Congregational Commission on Social Service; Rev. Samuel Z. Batten, Secretary of the Baptist Department of Social Service and the Brotherhood; Rev. Frank M. Crouch, Executive Secretary of the Protestant Episcopal Joint Commission; Rev. Harry F. Ward, Secretary of the Methodist Federation for Social Service; J. E. McAfee, of the Board of Home Missions of the Presbyterian Church; Rev. Charles O. Gill, Secretary of the Federal Council Commission on the Church and Country Life, and Rev. Charles Stelzle. Through this Council the denominational agencies are working together, issuing their literature in common, dividing the work and cooperating at every possible point, both nationally and locally, and each secretary, so far as it does not interfere with his denominational interests, is making his work interdenominational.

GENERAL PLAN OF WORK

The work of the Commission is proceeding in this way, conceiving its function to be mainly that of bringing the denominational forces to work together and stimulating their activities rather than considering itself as an independent body. Its "Plan of Work" has been approved and adopted by the Executive Committee of the Federal Council, the Interdenominational Social Service Conference at Chicago, the various denominational Commissions or Committees, and was also approved by the Federal Council in its sessions at Chicago, December, 1912, and at St. Louis, December, 1916.

The Commission is made up of about 125 of the leading social workers of the nation, who represent distinctively the view-point of the churches, and some of the important items in its current program are as follows:

Close relationship is being established with the theological seminaries, the schools for training social workers, and other institutions of learning, in the particular interest of training men and women for a social service which will have the distinctively spiritual point of view.

The commission has placed itself at the disposal of such appropriate organizations as the National Conference of Charities and Correction, the Southern Sociological Congress, the National Child Labor Committee, the American Public Health Association, the American Institute of Criminal Law and Criminology, the Playground and Recreation Association of America, the Child Welfare Congress, the National Municipal League, and National Purity Congress, the National Civic Federation, the Consumers' League, the American Association for Labor Legislation, the National Association for the Prevention of Tuberculosis, the American Social Hygiene Association, the National Prison Committee, the Russell Sage Foundation Department of Surveys and Exhibits, the American Sociological Society, the Academy of Political and Social Science, the various schools of civics, philanthropy, and social work, and other similar organizations, and has sent fraternal visitors to their annual meetings.

Plans are arranged to cooperate with the Industrial and Social Service Departments of the International Committee of the Young Men's Christian Associations, and the Industrial Department of the Young Women's Christian Association, and the Young People's Society of Christian Endeavor and kindred societies, so that the work of these important agencies may be fully available for the use of the churches.

One of its most important movements is its nation-wide campaign for one-day-in-seven for industrial workers, which has been unanimously approved by the constituent bodies and also officially by the American Federation of Labor. Labor Sunday was appointed by the Federal Council at the suggestion of the American Federation of Labor. The secretaries of the Commission are received as fraternal delegates at the annual sessions of the American Federation of Labor and also of the Women's Trade Union League. Rev. Charles Stelzle is directing movements for the conservation of human life and temperance among working men.

The various secretaries of the Council are developing social evangelism and civic revivals, and they are available for the services of church federations and other organizations in local communities for this purpose.

Several important investigations have been made, particularly of the industrial conditions in the steel industry at South Bethlehem, Pennsylvania, and the industrial warfare at Muscatine, Iowa. Secretary Henry A. Atkinson also prepared a report on the industrial situation in Michigan and Colorado, and a committee of the Massachusetts Federation of Churches prepared for the Commission a report on the situation at Lawrence, Massachusetts, and a committee has been making an inquiry in the anthracite region in Pennsylvania. A committee has also been instructed to report on prison conditions.

The literature of the Commission is assuming large proportions, and includes the reports of these investigations, study courses and bibliographies, social service catechisms, and similar material for the guidance and instruction of pastors and church classes, covering social questions and presenting them from the point of view of the obligation and opportunity of the churches. Arrangements are being made to secure the publication of books jointly with other organizations issuing common publications, especially those issuing home mission, industrial, and social service handbooks, like the Missionary Education Movement, and the Association Press. The secretaries themselves contribute to the literature on social service, new books having recently appeared, by Secretaries Ward, Batten, Macfarland, Gill, Atkinson, and Stelzle.

The churches are also working increasingly together in local communities. Most of the federations of churches are formed with community problems and social uplift as their objectives.

In some cities, social service secretaries have been engaged to give their whole time to the work of the federated churches.

The Commission on the Church and Social Service has the cooperation of other commissions and departments of the Federal Council of the Churches of Christ in America, including the Commission on the Church and Country Life, the Commission on Interchurch Federations (State and

Local), the Commission on International Justice and Goodwill, the Commission on Temperance, and the Commission on Christian Education, which has assisted in preparing social service material for study courses.

The Commission on the Church and Social Service also works in sympathetic relation with the Federal Council Commission on Evangelism, both of these commissions realizing that their work is a common one.

During the Panama-Pacific Exposition an exhibit was maintained by the Commission, and its work was also set forth by daily illustrated lectures in a hall connected with the exhibit under the direction of Mr. G. B. St. John.

Literature describing the work of the churches in association with the Federal Council may be obtained on application to the Rev. Worth M. Tippy, Secretary, 612 United Charities Building, 105 East 22d Street, New York City.

The *Year Book of the Church and Social Service* gives in full the information here referred to.

COMMISSION ON INTERNATIONAL JUSTICE AND GOOD-WILL

Created to promote peace and international arbitration on a basis of justice and good-will. The Commission cooperates with the American Council of the World Alliance for Promoting International Friendship through the Churches and invites every denomination to establish a Peacemakers' Commission and every congregation to form a Peacemakers' Committee to secure wide study of international problems with the hope of ultimately Christianizing America's international relations, and of helping to bring in a Christian world order.

Secretaries, Rev. Charles S. Macfarland, Rev. Sidney L. Gulick

COMMISSION ON CHRISTIAN EDUCATION

This Commission considers and reports upon matters of moral and religious education. The Commission has adopted a plan for promoting religious instruction among the pupils of the public schools and has had prepared an outline of twelve lessons on international peace for the guidance of denominational committees and editors in the preparation of a course of study for adult Bible classes, young people's societies, missionary and fraternal societies, etc.

COMMISSION ON TEMPERANCE AND NATIONAL TEMPERANCE SOCIETY

The Commission and the National Temperance Society have been merged.

The aim of the Commission is to cooperate as much as possible with the denominational temperance commissions of the constituent churches and to aid in organizing such commissions where they do not now exist.

The purposes are to compile the information, through a research department, of the results of experience obtained in industrial plants, on railroads, and in the army and navy since the principle of temperance has been applied.

To cooperate with and furnish temperance information and exhibits to the welfare, health, safety, and efficiency departments of municipalities, railroads, industrial plants, and business corporations.

To hold educational and welfare expositions throughout the United States, in cooperation with other temperance organizations and civic agencies, showing the underlying causes of poverty, crime, and domestic unhappiness, and the beneficial economic results secured through temperance.

To secure the active cooperation of the moving picture film companies, theater owners and their trade publications, in presenting temperance information through special slides and photoplays.

To urge the universal observance of the annual "World's Temperance Sunday."

To emphasize the importance of temperance as an economic issue in connection with civic celebrations on the Fourth of July, and

To stress voluntary personal abstinence—a practical solution of the problem.

Chairman, Hon. Carl E. Milliken
Acting Secretary, Rev. Charles S. Macfarland
Field Secretary, Rev. Charles Stelzle
105 East 22d Street
New York City

COMMISSION ON THE CHURCH AND COUNTRY LIFE

To investigate and report upon conditions of country life as affecting the churches. An elaborate survey is being made of country districts in Ohio, by the secretary, the Rev. Charles O. Gill.

Chairman, Gifford Pinchot
Secretary, Rev. Charles O. Gill
104 North Third Street, Columbus, O.

Until 1915 this work was operated as a department of the Commission on the Church and Social Service.

The Rev. Charles O. Gill has been engaged as field investigator in this department, and the first results of this work appear in *The Country Church,* an important volume published by authority of the Federal Council. Mr. Gill has also investigated rural church conditions in Europe, as a commissioner of the Federal Council, and his report was published in part in the annual report to the Executive Committee, in 1914.

In December, 1915, the Commission held a Conference on the Church and Country Life at Columbus, Ohio, the attendance at which 600 delegates from 31 states were registered. In recognition of the significance of the country church movement in the life of the nation, the President of the United States made a special journey from Washington to Columbus to attend and address this convention. Important reports on subjects relating to church and country life have been issued by the subcommittees of the Commission.

COMMISSION ON INTERCHURCH FEDERATIONS
(State and Local)

Purpose: Christian conquests through interchurch activities in every community, county, and state.

Plan: Community, County, and State Organization and comprehensive progress by which these forces may unitedly perform the Christian task common to all.

Chairman, Fred B. Smith
Treasurer, Alfred R. Kimball
Executive Secretary, Rev. Roy B. Guild
105 East Twenty-second Street, New York City

Committee of Direction

Frank L. Brown, New York City
Rev. Henry Sloane Coffin, New York City
Harry Wade Hicks, New York City
Alfred R. Kimball, New York City
Landreth H. King, New York City
William B. Millar, New York City
John R. Mott, New York City
James H. Post, New York City
Gifford Pinchot, Milford, Pa.
Edwin L. Shuey, Dayton, Ohio
Fred B. Smith, New York City

Commission on Relations with the Orient

This Commission was established on the authority of the Executive Committee in May, 1914, in response to memorials from missionaries in Japan.

Chairman, Rev. William I. Haven
Secretary, Rev. Charles S. Macfarland
Representative, Rev. Sidney L. Gulick
105 East Twenty-second Street, New York City

Committee on Family Life and Religious Rest Day

(The Committees on Family Life and a Religious Rest Day are to be consolidated.)

This committee is created to consider and report upon matters relating to marriage and divorce and the development of family life, and to consider and report upon matters relating to a better observance of the Lord's Day.

Chairman, Rev. Finis S. Idleman
Secretary, Rev. Charles S. Macfarland

Committee on Ministerial Relief (not yet appointed).

Committee on Foreign Missions

This commitee is to number when organized not more than fifteen members with instructions to confer with the Conference of Foreign Mission Boards, through its Committee on Reference and Counsel for the purpose of establishing such relationship with that Conference as may serve the largest interests involved.

Chairman, Rev. James I. Vance

Committee on Home Missions

This committee is to consist of not more than fifteen members, and to have power when organized to confer with the Home Missions Council on the question of so developing the administration of the Home Missions Council and so strengthening the cooperative relationship between the two bodies as to meet more fully the needs of the churches in the home mission field.

Chairman, Rev. John M. Moore

The Home Missions Council
(Cooperating Body)
Chairman, Rev. Charles L. Thompson

Executive Committee

Rev. Charles H. Beck	Rt. Rev. A. S. Lloyd
Rev. D. D. Forsyth	Rev. R. D. Lord
William T. Demarest	Rev. John M. Moore
Rev. Charles E. Burton.	Rev. H. L. Moorehouse
Rev. R. A. Hutchison	Rev. S. L. Morris
Rev. J. C. Kunzmann	Rev. C. E. Schaeffer
Rev. Grant K. Lewis	Rev. Charles Whitney

Rev. Charles L. Thompson

LOCAL FEDERATIONS OF CHURCHES

The most noteworthy progress toward Christian unity in the last five years has come through the cooperation of the Churches in efforts to correct community conditions which militate against the influence of the churches. During this period the Commission of the Federal Council on State and Local Federations has been cultivating this spirit of fellowship. The literature prepared by the secretary, Professor Alfred Williams Anthony, has not only helped to create public opinion, but to indicate lines of cooperation.

The Men and Religion Forward Movement gave a great impetus to this work. In several cities the conservation of the messages and methods of this movement resulted in the forming of permanent interchurch organizations. In each case there has been a gradual evolution of these organizations. Through varied experiences they have come to be very similar. There was formed a year ago an association of the executive secretaries of these bodies. Each was a pioneer, each was working without precedents, yet when these men came together for the first time, there was remarkable agreement between them as to principles, scope of work, and methods.

Two years ago the Commission on Federated Movements was formed with Mr. Fred B. Smith Chairman, Rev. Roy B. Guild, Executive Secretary, and Mr. James A. Whitmore, Field Secretary. This Commission has made a careful study of the status of interchurch work, has brought into closest fellowship may interdenominational and non-denominational organizations. Recently it has been engaged in more aggressive work in forming state and local federations.

At the last meeting of the Federal Council the two Commissions named above were merged into the "Commission on Interchurch Federation (State and Local)." Mr. Fred B. Smith is the Chairman of this newly formed Commission, Rev. Roy B. Guild is the Executive Secretary. The offices of the Commission are at 105 East 22d Street.

For the sake of those who wish to secure information about existing federations, the following list is given of those states and cities which have employed executive secretaries.

NOTE.—Where the secretary is employed for part time, it is indicated by a single star (*). Where the secretary is an office secretary, it is indicated by a double star (**)

State Federations

Root, Rev. E. T., 53 Mt. Vernon St., Boston Mass.

Talbott, Rev. E. Guy, Wright & Callender Bldg., Los Angeles, Cal.

City Federations

Ames, Rev. Clair E., 919 Federal Reserve Bank Bldg., St. Louis, Mo.

*Boyce, Rev. Lester S., 130 Richmond Ave., Dayton, Ohio.

A. H. Briggs, San Francisco, Cal.

*Eldredge, Hermon, Y. M. C. A. Bldg., Erie, Pa.

Fagley, Rev. Fred'k L., 616 Union Central Bldg. Cincinnati, Ohio.

**Homer, Miss Clara B., 1101 Wright & Callender Bldg., Los Angeles, Cal.

Laidlaw, Rev. Walter, 200 Fifth Ave., New York City.

*Mayer, Rev. F. S., 277 Walnut St., Fall River, Mass.

McConoughey, Rev. E. M., 208 Y. M. C. A. Bldg., Sacramento, Cal.

Meddis, C. J., 1116 Inter-Southern Bldg., Louisville, Ky.

Millard, Rev. W. B., 19 So. La Salle St., Chicago, Ill.

Montague, J. Y., 622 Nasby Bldg., Toledo, Ohio.

Morton, James, 211 Y. M. C. A. Bldg., Atlanta, Ga.

Pearson, Rev. Morton C., Y. M. C. A. Bldg., Indianapolis, Ind.

*Piper, Harry L., Box 1151, Springfield, Mass.

Smith, C. McLeod, Buffalo, N. Y.

Spencer, Nat., 412 Scarritt Arcade, Kansas City, Mo.

**Stevenson, Miss Harriet, Y. M. C. A. Bldg., Portland, Me.

Wright, Rev. E. R., 1223 Scofield Bldg., Cleveland, Ohio.

Zahniser, Rev. Charles R., 245 Fourth Ave., Pittsburgh, Pa.

Besides the above named federations, this Commission by a recent questionnaire learned that there are at least sixty-one other Interchurch Federations or councils including laymen in their membership. One hundred and seventy cities have ministerial alliances or unions. This questionnaire has made clear that continuity of effort in the church's work for the entire community depends upon bringing the laymen into such an organization. "Ministers come and ministers go, but the laymen stay on forever." A Ministers' Union can render no larger service to a community than to develop inter-church organizations, including laymen and ministers. In larger cities no measurable degree of success can be expected except by securing an executive secretary for all or part time.

The literature for forming such organizations and working out a program is now available. ᐧThe Commission when possible will contribute the service of its secretary.

COMMITTEE ON THE CELEBRATION OF THE FOUR HUNDREDTH ANNIVERSARY OF THE PROTESTANT REFORMATION

Ordered by the Federal Council for cooperation with similar Committees of various denominations for the observance of the anniversary in 1917.

Rev. William H. Roberts, 515 Witherspoon Building, Philadelphia, Pa.

Rev. W. C. Bitting, 5109 Waterman Avenue, St. Louis, Mo.

Rev. J. F. Burnett, Lock Box 274, Dayton, Ohio.

Bishop Morris W. Leibert, 112 Lexington Avenue, New York City.

Rev. B. S. Winchester, 263 Willow Street, New Haven, Conn.
Rev. Peter Ainslie, 537 North Fulton Avenue, Baltimore, Md.
Rev. Finis S. Idleman, 375 Central Park, West, New York City.
Bishop S. C. Breyfogel, 836 Center Avenue, Reading, Pa.
Rev. Charles Enders, Chester Street, Baltimore, Md.
Rev. E. Heyl Delk, 630 North Broad Street, Philadelphia, Pa.
Rev. George U. Wenner, 319 East Nineteenth Street, New York City.
Rev. F. J. Prettyman, 1308 Columbia Road, Washington, D. C.
Rev. Edgar Blake, 1024 Wabash Avenue, Chicago, Ill.
Rev. Frank M. Thomas, 526 West St. Catherine Street, Louisville, Ky.
Rev. Lyman E. Davis, 219 Federal Street, Pittsburgh, Pa.
Rev. Elias B. Sanford, Rockfall, Conn.
Rev. R. A. Webb, 109 East Broadway, Louisville, Ky.
Rev. D. S. Schaff, Des Moines, Iowa.
Rev. P. S. Leinbach, 600 West 146th Street, New York City.
Rev. James I. Good, 3260 Chestnut Street, Philadelphia, Pa.
Dr. George W. Richards, Lancaster, Pa.
Prof. M. G. Kyle, 302 East Market Street, Xenia, Ohio.
Rev. B. F. McGill, 224 Ridge Avenue, Ben Avon, Pa.
Rev. H. R. Gold, 925 Chestnut Street, Philadelphia, Pa.
Mr. William H. Scott, 1211 Clover Street, Philadelphia, Pa.

Joint Lutheran Committee

There is a Joint Lutheran Quadri-Centennial Jubilee Committee.

Office: 925 Chestnut Street, Philadelphia, Pa.

Officers: *Chairman,* Rev. S. W. Herman, 212 Pine Street, Harrisburg, Pa.; *Secretary,* Rev. H. R. Gold, 925 Chestnut Street, Philadelphia, Pa.

American War Relief Organizations

Federal Council War Relief Movement

General Secretary, Rev. Charles S. Macfarland; *Assistant Secretary,* Rev. E. W. Rankin; *Treasurer,* Alfred R. Kimball. Address, 105 East Twenty-second Street, New York City. While the Federal Council has not set up a war relief treasury of its own it will receive contributions and apply them as directed or designated, or according to its wisdom.

OTHER RELIEF ORGANIZATIONS WHICH HAVE ASKED THE FEDERAL COUNCIL TO COOPERATE WITH THEM AND SPEAK FOR THEM, AND WHICH RECEIVE CONTRIBUTIONS:

American Committee for Armenian and Syrian Relief. *Treasurer,* Charles R. Crane, 70 Fifth Avenue, New York City.

American Huguenot Committee. *Treasurer,* Edmond E. Robert, 105 East 22d Street, New York City.

American National Red Cross. *Treasurer,* Hon. John Skelton Williams, 1624 H Street, Washington, D. C. (The Red Cross has a Department of Non-Combatant Relief.)

American Relief Committee for Widows and Orphans of the War in Germany. *Treasurer,* John D. Crimmins, 30 East 42d Street, New York City.

B. F. B. Permanent Blind Relief War Fund. *Treasurer,* Frank A. Vanderlip, 590 Fifth Avenue, New York City.

British War Relief Association, Inc. *Treasurer,* Henry Clews, 542 Fifth Avenue, New York City.

Commission for Relief in Belgium. *Treasurer,* Alexander J. Hemphill, 120 Broadway, New York City.

East Prussia Relief Fund. *Treasurer,* Hubert Cillis, 17 Battery Place, New York City.

Fund for Starving Children. *Treasurer,* Frederick Lynch, 70 Fifth Avenue, New York City.

German General Relief Committee for War Sufferers in Germany and Austria-Hungary. *Treasurer,* Charles Froeb, 531 Broadway, Brooklyn, N. Y.

Joint Distribution Committee, consisting of American Jewish Relief Committee, Central Relief Committee and People's Relief Committee. *Treasurer,* Felix M. Warburg, 174 Second Avenue, New York City.

Polish Victims' Relief Fund. *Treasurer,* Frank A. Vanderlip, Aeolian Building, New York City.

Serbian Relief Committee of America. *Treasurer,* Murray H. Coggeshall, 70 Fifth Avenue, New York City.

Union Nationale des Eglises Reformees Evangeliques de France, Emergency Relief Fund. *Treasurer,* Alfred R. Kimball, 105 East 22d Street, New York City.

At the end of April, 1916, according to information gathered by the Carnegie Endowment for Peace, Washington, D. C., 49 different relief committees had raised $28,896,277 for European war sufferers. At the end of 1916 the amount was estimated at about $50,000,000.

DIRECTORY OF CONSTITUENT BODIES OF THE FEDERAL COUNCIL OF THE CHURCHES OF CHRIST IN AMERICA

Baptists

The Baptist World Alliance is a general organization including Baptists throughout the world. Its last session was held in Philadelphia, Pa., in 1911. *President,* Rev. R. S. MacArthur, New York City.

General Convention of Baptists of North America, including Northern, Southern and Canadian Baptists. *President,* A. L. McCrimmon; *Recording Secretary,* Prof. W. O. Carver, Louisville, Ky.; *Corresponding Secretary,* Rev. Spenser B. Meeser, Chester, Pa.; *Treasurer,* Joshua Levering, Baltimore, Md.

NORTHERN BAPTIST CONVENTION

(For other Baptist bodies, not constituent members of the Federal Council, see Directory of other Religious Bodies, pages 112-116.)

The Northern Baptist Convention, annual, holds its next meeting at Cleveland, O., May 16-26, 1917.

There are state conventions and numerous associations.

Officers: *President,* Rev. C. A. Barbour, Rochester, N. Y.; *Corresponding Secretary,* Rev. William C. Bitting, St. Louis, Mo.; *Recording Secretary,* Rev. Maurice A. Levy, New York City; *Treasurer,* Frank L. Miner, Des Moines, Ia.

American Baptist Foreign Mission Society, Ford Building, Boston, Mass. *President,* Rev. Emory W. Hunt, Newton Center, Mass.; *Recording Secretary,* George B. Huntington; *Home Secretaries,* Rev. J. Y. Aitchison, Rev. W. R. Lipphard; *Foreign Secretaries,* Rev. James H. Franklin, Rev. J. C. Robbins; *Treasurer,* Ernest S. Butler.

American Baptist Publication Society, Roger Williams Building, Philadelphia, Pa. *President,* Rev. J. Whitcomb Brougher,

Los Angeles, Cal.; *Secretary,* Rev. G. C. Lamson; *Recording Secretary,* Rev. B. D. Stelle, Upland, Pa.; *Treasurer,* H. S. Hopper; *Missionary and Bible Secretary,* Rev. G. C. Lamson; *Business Manager,* Harry V. Meyer; *Book Editor,* Rev. D. G. Stevens; *Editor of Periodicals,* Rev. C. R. Blackall; *Associate Editor of Periodicals,* Rev. George T. Webb; *Educational Secretary,* Rev. W. E. Chalmers; *General Director of Elementary Work,* Miss Mame Brockway; *Secretary of Social Service and Brotherhood,* Rev. Samuel Z. Batten; *Director of Vacation Bible Schools,* Rev. W. E. Raffety.

American Baptist Home Mission Society, 23 East Twenty-sixth Street, New York City. *President,* Frank C. Nickels, Minneapolis, Minn.; *Corresponding Secretary,* Rev. H. L. Morehouse; *Associate Corresponding Secretary,* Rev. Charles L. White; *Field Secretary,* Rev. L. C. Barnes; *Recording Secretary,* Rev. Ambrose M. Bailey, St. Paul, Minn.; *Treasurer,* Frank T. Moulton, Mountain Lakes, N. J.

Woman's American Baptist Foreign Mission Society, Ford Building, Boston, Mass. *President,* Mrs. W. A. Montgomery, Rochester, N. Y.; *Recording Secretary,* Mrs. T. E. Adams, Cleveland, O.; *Treasurer,* Miss Alice E. Stedman; *Foreign Secretaries,* Mrs. H. G. Safford, Miss Nellie G. Prescott; *Home Secretary,* Miss Eleanor Mare, Chicago, Ill.; *Field Secretary,* Miss Ella D. MacLaurin, Chicago, Ill.; *Young Woman's Secretary,* Miss Alma J. Noble, Buffalo, N. Y.

Woman's American Baptist Home Mission Society, 2969 Vernon Avenue, Chicago, Ill. *President,* Mrs. S. T. Ford; *Corresponding Secretary,* Mrs. Katherine S. Westfall; *Recording Secretary,* Mrs. Charles N. Wilkinson, Canon City, Colo.; *Treasurer,* Mrs. John Nuveen.

Board of Education, Ford Building, Boston, Mass. *Chairman,* Prof. Ernest D. Burton, Chicago, Ill.; *Secretary,* Rev. Frank W. Padelford.

Baptist Brotherhood, 1701 Chestnut Street, Philadelphia, Pa. *President,* W. G. Grimson; *Executive Secretary,* Rev. S. Z. Batten; *Executive Committee:* R. S. Bouslog, Allen Hoben, C. L. Major, E. W. Parker, S. G. Young and the officers.

The brotherhood organization in any church represents the definite work in that church by men or with men. It is an organization for combining and federating all existing agencies of men's work and making them most efficient.

Baptist Young People's Union of America, Chicago, Ill. *President,* Rev. Frank L. Anderson; *General Secretary,* J. A. White; *Treasurer,* A. D. Henderson.

Colleges and Universities

Institution	Location	President or Dean
Arkansas Baptist College†	Little Rock, Ark	Joseph A. Booker.
Bacone College†	Bacone, Okla	J. Harvey Randall.
Bates College‡	Lewiston, Me	George C. Chase.
Benedict College†	Columbia, S. C	B. W. Valentine.
Brown University	Providence, R. I	W. H. P. Faunce.
Bucknell University	Lewisburg, Pa	J. H. Harris.
Colby College	Waterville, Me	Arthur J. Roberts.
Colgate University	Hamilton, N. Y	E. B. Bryan.
Colorado Woman's College	Montclair, Colo	J. P. Treat.
Denison University	Granville, Ohio	C. W. Chamberlain.
Franklin College	Franklin, Ind	E. A. Hanley.
Grand Island College	Grand Island, Neb	G. W. Taft.
Hartshorn Memorial College†	Richmond, Va	G. W. Regler.
Hillsdale College‡	Hillsdale, Mich	Joseph W. Mauck.
Kalamazoo College	Kalamazoo, Mich	H. L. Stetson.
Keuka College†	Keuka Park, N. Y	Joseph A. Serena.
La Grange College	La Grange, Mo	D. J. Scott.
McMinnville College	McMinnville, Ore	Leonard W. Riley.
Morehouse College†	Atlanta, Ga.	
Ottawa University	Ottawa, Kan	S. E. Price.
Rio Grande College‡	Rio Grande, Ohio	Simeon H. Bing.
Roger Williams University†	Nashville, Tenn	R. M. Townsend.
Shaw University†	Raleigh, N. C	Charles F. Meserve.
Shurtleff College	Alton, Ill	George M. Potter.
Sioux Falls College	Sioux Falls, S. D	Rolvix Harlan.
Stephens Women's College	Columbia, Mo	J. M. Wood.
Storer College†‡	Harpers Ferry, W. Va	Henry T. McDonald.
Temple University	Philadelphia, Pa	R. H. Conwell.
Union College	Des Moines, Ia	John A. Earl.
University of Chicago*	Chicago, Ill	Harry Pratt Judson.
University of Redlands	Redlands, Cal	V. L. Duke.
University of Rochester*	Rochester, N. Y	Rush Rhees.
Vassar College*	Poughkeepsie, N. Y	Henry Noble MacCracken
William Jewell College	Liberty, Mo	John P. Greene.

* Founded by Baptists. Not now under denominational control.
† Home Mission School.
‡ Free Baptist. Not now under denominational control.

Theological Seminaries

Institution	Location	President or Dean
Berkeley Baptist Divinity School	Berkeley, Cal	C. M. Hill.
Colgate Theological Seminary	Hamilton, N. Y	J. H. Vichert.
Crozer Theological Seminary	Upland, Pa	Milton G. Evans.
Danish Baptist Theological Seminary	Des Moines, Ia	N. S. Lawdahl.
Divinity School, University of Chicago	Chicago, Ill	Sballer Mathews.
Hungarian Theological Seminary	Cleveland, Ohio	Stephen Orosz.
Kansas City Baptist Theological Seminary	Kansas City, Kan	Philip W. Crannell.
Negro Theological Seminary	Memphis, Tenn.	
Newton Theological Institution	Newton Center, Mass	George E. Horr.
Northern Baptist Theological Seminary	Chicago, Ill	John Marvin Dean.
Rochester Theological Seminary	Rochester, N. Y	C. A. Barbour.
Rochester Theological Sem., German Dept	Rochester, N. Y	C. A. Barbour.
Swedish Baptist Theological Seminary	St. Paul, Minn	C. Arvid Hagstrom

For list of ministers with addresses of the Northern Baptist Convention, the Southern Baptist Convention and the National Baptist Convention see American Baptist Year Book published by the American Baptist Publication Society, Philadelphia, Pa.

Baptist Charitable Institutions

Baptist Home for Aged Women, Cambridgeport, Mass.; *Baptist Home for City Missionaries,* New York City; *Baptist Home of Brooklyn,* Brooklyn, N. Y.; *Baptist Home of New York,* New York City; *Baptist Home of Northern Ohio,* Cleveland, Ohio; *Baptist Home of Philadelphia,* Philadelphia, Pa.; *Baptist Home of Washington,* Washington, D. C.; *Baptist Home Society of New Jersey,* Newark, N. J.; *Baptist Hospital,* Chicago, Ill.; *Baptist Ministers' Aid Society,* Fenton, Mich.; *Baptist Ministers' Home Society,* Mount Vernon, N. Y.; *Baptist Orphanage and Home,* Pittsburgh, Pa.; *Baptist Orphanage, Pennsylvania,* Angora, Philadelphia, Pa.; *Central Baptist Children's Home,* Maywood, Ill.; *Choctaw Orphans' Home,* Atoka, Okla.; *Crawford Baptist Industrial School,* Zionsville, Ind.; *Deitz Memorial Home,* New York City; *Faith Home for Aged Widows,* New Orleans, La.; *German Baptist Home for the Aged,* Chicago, Ill.; *German Baptist Home for the Aged,* Philadelphia, Pa.; *George Nugent Home,* Philadelphia, Pa.; *Hudelson Orphanage,* Irvington, Ill.; *Jennie Clarkson Home,* Katonah, N. Y.; *Kodiak Baptist Orphanage,* Kodiak, Wood Island, Alaska; *Mounds Park Sanitarium,* St. Paul, Minn.; *Murrow Indian Orphans' Home,* Bacone, Okla.; *New Britain Children's Home,* New Britain, Conn.; *New England Baptist Hospital,* Boston, Mass.; *Samaritan Hospital,* Philadelphia, Pa.; *Sunset Home* (Swedish), Clay Center, Kansas; *Swedish Baptist Home for the Aged,* Morgan Park, Ill.; *Wisler Memorial Home,* Chalfont, Pa.

Periodicals

New Jersey Baptist Bulletin (monthly), Newark N. J., Editor, Rev. D. Dewolf; *Baptist Commonwealth* (weekly), Philadelphia, Pa., Editor, Rev. R. M. Hunsicker; *Baptist Observer* (weekly), Seymour, Ind., Editor, T. C. Smith; *Baptist Record,* Pella, Ia., Editor, Rev. R. R. Sadler; *Christian Banner* (weekly), Philadelphia, Pa., Editor, Rev. J. C. Jackson; *Chrestinal (Rumanian)* (monthly), Cleveland, O., Editor, Rev. L. A. Gredys; *Jugend-Herold (German)* (monthly), Cleveland, O., Editor, Rev. F. W. C. Meyer; *Muntere Säeman* (monthly), Cleveland, O., Editor, Rev. Gottlob Fetzer; *Sendbote* (weekly), Cleveland, O., Editor, Rev. Gottlob Fetzer; *Wegweiser* (monthly), Cleveland, O., Editor, Rev. Gottlob Fetzer; *Evangelista (Spanish)* (monthly), Ponce, P. R., Editor, J. R. Cepero; *Församlingen och Hemmet (Swedish)* (monthly), Chicago, Ill., Editor, Thorsten Clafford; *Cristiano (Italian)* (weekly), Philadelphia, Pa., Editor, Rev. A. di Domenica; *Journal and Messenger* (weekly), Cincinnati, O., Editor, Rev. G. W. Lasher; *Missions* (monthly), Boston, Mass., Editor, Rev. H. R. Grose; *Nya Vecko-Posten* (*Swedish*) (weekly), Chicago, Ill., Editor, Rev. E. Wingren; *Pacific Baptist* (weekly), McMinnville, Ore., Editor, Rev. J. A. Clarke; *Standard* (weekly), Chicago, Ill., Editor, Rev. Clifton D. Gray; *Svenska Standaret* (weekly), Chicago, Ill., Editor, Rev. E. Sjöstrand; *Vaegteren* (*Danish-Norwegian*) (weekly), Harlan, Ia., Editor, Rev. R. J. Petersen; *Watchman-Examiner* (weekly), New York, N. Y., Editor, Rev. Curtis Lee Laws; *Wawr* (*Welsh*) (monthly), Utica, N. Y., Editor, G. Griffith; *Zion's Advocate* (weekly), Portland, Me., Editor, Rev. William Abbot Smith.

FREE BAPTISTS

The Free Baptists are in process of merging with the Northern Baptist Convention. Their benevolent societies have already been consolidated with those of the Northern Baptist Convention, and it is estimated that the majority of the Free Baptist ministers, churches, and communicants are now included in the Baptist enumerations.

General Conference, quadrennial. The next meeting will be held at Ocean Park, Me., in July, 1917. *Secretary,* Prof. A. W. Anthony, Lewiston, Maine.

For list of Free Baptist colleges see under "Colleges and Universities" of the Northern Baptist Convention.

NATIONAL BAPTIST CONVENTION

National Baptist Convention, annual; held its last meeting at Savannah, Ga., in September, 1916.

This body was divided in Chicago, September, 1915, and there are now two National Baptist Conventions—the National Baptist Convention (Incorporated) and the National Baptist Convention (Unincorporated). The former, which was represented at the quadrennial session of the Federal Council at St. Louis, Mo., in December, 1916, held its annual session at Savannah, Ga., in September, 1916. For officers of the other Convention, see Directory of other Religious Bodies, page 115.

Officers of the National Baptist Convention (Incorporated) : *President,* Rev. E. C. Morris, Helena, Ark.; *Secretary,* Prof. R. B. Hudson, Selma, Ala.; *Treasurer,* Rev. A. J. Stokes, Montgomery, Ala.

Foreign Mission Board, Philadelphia, Pa., *Secretary,* Rev. L. G. Jordan.

Home Mission Board, Little Rock, Ark., *Secretary,* Rev. J. A. Booker.

Publishing Board, Nashville, Tenn., *Secretary,* Prof. S. P. Harris.

Educational Board, Memphis, Tenn., *Secretary,* Rev. S. E. Griggs.

Baptist Young People's Board, Nashville, Tenn., *Secretary,* Rev. E. W. D. Isaac.

National Baptist Benefit Board, Helena, Ark., *Secretary,* Rev. J. M. Washington.

Woman's Auxiliary Board, Washington, D. C., *Secretary,* Miss N. H. Burroughs.

There are no colleges, benevolent, and charitable institutions under the direct control of the National Baptist Convention.

Periodical. *National Baptist Voice* (official organ), Nashville, Tenn., *Editor,* Rev. J. D. Crenshaw.

SEVENTH-DAY BAPTISTS

General Conference, annual, held its last session at Salem, W. Va., August, 1916.

Officers: *President,* Rev. George B. Shaw, Ashaway, R. I.; *Recording Secretary,* Rev. Earl P. Saunders, Alfred, N. Y.; *Corresponding Secretary,* Rev. Henry N. Jordan, Milton Junction, Wis.; *Treasurer,* Rev. William C. Whitford, Alfred, N. Y.

Seventh-Day Baptist Missionary Society. *President,* William L. Clarke, Ashaway, R. I.; *Corresponding Secretary,* Rev. Edwin Shaw, Plainfield, N. J.; *Treasurer,* Samuel H. Davis, Westerly, R. I.

Seventh-Day Baptist Education Society. *President,* Rev. William C. Whitford, Alfred, N. Y.; *Corresponding Secretary,* Rev. Arthur E. Main, Alfred, N. Y.; *Treasurer,* Prof. Paul E. Titsworth, Alfred, N. Y.

Sabbath School Board. *President,* Prof. Alfred E. Whitford, Milton, Wis.; *Secretary,* A. L. Burdick, Milton, Wis.; *Treasurer,* W. H. Greenman, Milton Junction, Wis.

Woman's Executive Board. *President,* Mrs. Allen B. West, Milton Junction, Wis.; *Corresponding Secretary,* Mrs. J. H. Babcock, Milton, Wis.; *Treasurer,* Mrs. Alfred E. Whitford, Milton, Wis.

Young People's Board of Christian Endeavor. *President,*

Rev. Henry N. Jordan, Milton Junction, Wis.; *Corresponding Secretary*, Miss Minnie Godfrey, Walworth, Wis.; *Treasurer*, Prof. Leman H. Stringer, Milton, Wis.

Board of Pulpit Supply and Ministerial Employment. *President*, Ira B. Crandall, Westerly, R. I.; *Corresponding Secretary*, Rev. Edwin Shaw, Plainfield, N. J.

American Sabbath Tract Society. *President*, Corliss F. Randolph, Newark, N. J.; *Corresponding Secretary*, Rev. Edwin Shaw, Plainfield, N. J.; *Treasurer*, Frank J. Hubbard, Plainfield, N. J.

Board of Finance. *President*, Rev. George W. Port, Chicago, Ill.; *Secretary*, Allen B. West, Milton Junction, Wis.

Colleges and Universities

Institution	Location	President
Alfred University	Alfred, N. Y	Boothe Colwell Davis.
Milton College	Milton, Wis	William C. Daland.
Salem College	Salem, W. Va	Charles B. Clark.

Theological Seminary. Theological Seminary, Alfred, New York. *Dean*, Rev. Arthur E. Main.

For list of ministers with addresses see Seventh-Day Baptist Year Book published by the American Sabbath Tract Society, Plainfield, N. J.

Periodical. *Sabbath Recorder*, Plainfield, N. J., Editor, Rev. Theodore L. Gardiner.

CHRISTIAN CHURCH

The American Christian Convention, quadrennial, met last in 1914. There are annual conferences and group conventions, as New England, Southern, Western, etc.

American Christian Convention. *President*, Rev. Frank G. Coffin, Albany, N. Y.; *Secretary*, Rev. John Franklin Burnett, Dayton, Ohio.

The Executive Board of the American Christian Convention is composed of the officers of the Convention and the secretaries of the seven departments. It transacts all business which would come before the Convention itself if it were in session. Its members also constitute the Board of Trustees of the Convention. It meets biennially for a survey of the work of the Church at large. It may meet at any time at the call of the president, or any three members of the Board.

Home Mission Board, Dayton, Ohio. *Secretary,* Rev. Omer S. Thomas, Dayton, Ohio.

Foreign Mission Board, Dayton, Ohio. *Secretary,* Rev. Milo T. Morrill.

Finance Secretary, Prof. Samuel Oscar Albaugh, Dayton, Ohio.

Board of Education, Dayton, Ohio. *Secretary,* Rev. William G. Sargent, Providence, R. I.

Sunday School Board, Dayton, Ohio. *Secretary,* Rev. Walton C. Wicker, Elon College, N. C.

Christian Endeavor Board, Dayton, Ohio. *Secretary,* William A. Harper, Elon College, N. C.

Secretary for Publishing, Hon. Orlando W. Whitelock, Huntington, Ind.

Woman's Board for Home Missions, Dayton, Ohio. *President,* Rev. Emily K. Bishop; *Corresponding Secretary,* Mrs. Alice M. Burnett.

Woman's Board for Foreign Missions, Dayton, Ohio. *President,* Mrs. Alice V. Morrill; *Corresponding Secretary,* Mrs. Lulu Craig Helfenstein.

The Christian Publishing Association, Fifth and Ludlow Streets, Dayton, Ohio. *Manager,* Netum Rathbun.

Sunday School Department. *Secretary,* Rev. W. C. Wicker, Elon College, N. C.; *Editor Sunday School Literature.* Rev. S. Q. Helfenstein; *Superintendent of the Adult Department,* Rev. McD. Howsare; *Editor of the Teachers' and Officers' Journal,* Herman Eldredge; *Superintendent of the Elementary Department,* Mrs. F. Bullock; *Superintendent of Teacher Training,* Rev. A. B. Kendall; *Superintendent of the Secretary Department,* Rev. H. G. Rowe.

Peacemakers' Commission. Rev. H. G. Rowe, Farmer City, Ill.; Rev. F. H. Peters, New Bedford, Mass.; Rev. J. F. Burnett, Dayton, Ohio; Prof. W. A. Harper, Elon College, N. C.; Rev. L. E. Smith, Huntington, Ind.

Colleges

Institution	Location	President
Defiance College	Defiance, O.	P. W. McReynolds.
Elon College	Elon College, N. C.	W. A. Harper.
Franklinton Christian College	Franklinton, N. C.	(Acting) H. E. Long.
Jireh College	Jireh, Wyo.	D. B. Atkinson.
Palmer College	Albany, Mo.	E. A. Watkins.
Union Christian College	Merom, Ind.	D. A. Long.

For list of ministers with addresses see Christian Annual published by the Christian Publishing Association, Dayton, O.

Charitable Institution. *The Christian Orphanage,* Elon College, N. C.

Periodicals

Herald of Gospel Liberty (weekly), Dayton, O., Editor, Rev. J. Pressley Barrett; *Christian Missionary* (monthly), Dayton, O., Editors, Rev. Milo T. Morrill, Rev. Omer S. Thomas.

CONGREGATIONAL CHURCHES

The National Council of the Congregational Churches of the United States, biennial; next session at Los Angeles, Cal., June 6-July 3, 1917.

Moderator, Mr. H. M. Beardsley; *Secretary,* Rev. Hubert C. Herring, Boston, Mass.; *Treasurer,* Rev. John J. Walker, 14 Beacon Street, Boston, Mass.

Congregational Education Society, 14 Beacon Street, Boston, Mass. *President,* Rev. Clarence F. Swift; *Secretaries,* Rev. F. M. Sheldon, Rev. Edward S. Tead; *Treasurer,* S. F. Wilkins.

American Congregational Association, Library, Congregational House, Boston, Mass. *President,* Arthur S. Johnson, Boston; *Corresponding and Recording Secretary,* Thomas Todd, Jr., Concord, Mass.; *Treasurer,* Augustus S. Lovett, Brookline, Mass.; *Librarian,* Rev. William H. Cobb.

American Board of Commissioners for Foreign Missions, 14 Beacon Street, Boston, Mass. *President,* Rev. Edward C. Moore; *Corresponding Secretaries,* Rev. James L. Barton, Rev. Cornelius H. Patton, Rev. Edward Lincoln Smith; *Treasurer,* Frank H. Wiggin.

Congregational Home Missionary Society, 287 Fourth Avenue, New York City. *President,* Rev. Rockwell H. Potter; *General Secretary,* Rev. Charles E. Burton; *Secretary of Woman's Department,* Miss Miriam L. Woodberry; *Treasurer,* Charles H. Baker.

American Missionary Association, 287 Fourth Avenue, New York City. *President,* Rev. Henry C. King; *Corresponding Secretaries,* Rev. Charles J. Ryder, Rev. H. Paul Douglass; *Secretary of Bureau of Woman's Work,* Mrs. F. W. Wilcox; *Treasurer,* Irving C. Gaylord.

Congregational Church Building Society, 287 Fourth Avenue, New York City. *President,* Lucien C. Warner; *Secretary,* Rev. Charles H. Richards; *Treasurer,* Charles H. Baker.

Congregational Board of Ministerial Relief, 287 Fourth Avenue, New York City. *President,* Rev. Henry A. Stimson; *Recording Secretary,* Rev. L. F. Berry; *Secretary,* Rev. William A. Rice; *Treasurer,* B. H. Fancher.

Annuity Fund for Congregational Ministers, 287 Fourth

Avenue, New York City.   *Secretary,* Rev. William A. Rice; *Treasurer,* B. H. Fancher.

Congregational Sunday School and Publishing Society, 14 Beacon Street, Boston, Mass., and 19 West Jackson Street, Chicago, Ill.   *President,* Rev. Clarence F. Swift, Fall River, Mass.; *Treasurer,* S. F. Wilkins; *Recording Secretary,* Thomas Weston, Jr.; *Missionary and Extension Secretary,* Rev. William Ewing.

Woman's Home Missionary Federation.   *President,* Mrs. H. H. Hart, 7 Colden Avenue, White Plains, N. Y.; *Corresponding Secretary,* Mrs. William G. Frost, 56 Park Street, Montclair, N. J.; *Editorial Secretary,* Mrs. Edward H. Scott, 287 Fourth Avenue, New York City; *Treasurer,* Mrs. H. A. Flint, 604 Willis Avenue, Syracuse, N. Y.   Monthly publication, *American Missionary.*

Woman's Board of Missions, 14 Beacon Street, Boston, Mass. *President,* Mrs. C. H. Daniels; *Foreign Secretary,* Miss Kate G. Lamson; *Home Secretary,* Miss Helen B. Calder; *Editorial Secretary,* Miss Alice M. Kyle; *Secretary of Young People's Work,* Miss Mary Preston; *Treasurer,* Miss Sarah Louise Day.

The territory of this Board includes New England and the states east of Ohio.   It supports 126 missionaries and assistants and 15 retired missionaries; also 34 boarding schools, about 300 day-schools, in whole or in part, and 225 Bible women.   Monthly publication, *Life and Light.*

Woman's Board of Missions of the Interior, 19 South La Salle Street, Chicago, Ill.   *President,* Mrs. George M. Clark; *Secretary,* Mrs. Lucius O. Lee; *Treasurer,* Mrs. S. E. Hurlbut.

Its territory includes the states from Ohio to Wyoming and Montana inclusive.   It supports 86 missionaries, 100 Bible women, 260 native teachers, 3 colleges, 24 boarding schools, 2 kindergarten training schools, 3 Bible training schools, 2 hospitals, besides kindergartens, village and day-schools.   Monthly publication, *Mission Studies.*

Woman's Board of Missions for the Pacific, 417 Market Street, San Francisco, Cal.   *President,* Mrs. R. B. Cherington, *Home Secretary,* Mrs. H. M. Tenney, 311 East Lake Avenue, Watsonville, Cal.; *Foreign Secretary,* Mrs. E. R. Wagner, 355 Reed Street, San Jose, Cal.; *Treasurer,* Mrs. W. W. Ferrier, 2716 Hillegass Avenue, Berkeley, Cal.

The territory of this Board includes California, Oregon, Washington, Idaho, Utah, Nevada, and Arizona.   It supports 8 missionaries, 15 native helpers and teachers, 1 hospital, 2 boarding schools, 2 kindergartens; contributes towards several schools and kindergartens, and assists in medical work in India.   Quarterly publication, *Our Work.*

Congregational Board of Pastoral Supply, 14 Beacon Street,

Boston, Mass. *Chairman of the Board of Directors,* Appleton P. Williams; *Secretary,* Rev. Arthur J. Covell.

Boston Seaman's Friend Society, 14 Beacon Street, Boston, Mass. *Vice-President,* Samuel Usher; *Secretary and Treasurer,* Charles F. Stratton; *Corresponding Secretary,* Rev. Merritt A. Farren.

Colleges and Universities*

Institution	Location	President or Dean
American International College	Springfield, Mass	C. S. McGown.
Amherst College	Amherst, Mass	Alexander Meiklejohn.
Atlanta University	Atlanta, Ga.	E. T. Ware.
Beloit College	Beloit, Wis	E. D. Eaton.
Bowdoin College	Brunswick, Me	W. D. Hyde.
Carleton College	Northfield, Minn	D. J. Cowling.
Colorado College	Colorado Springs, Colo	W. F. Slocum.
Dartmouth College	Hanover, N. H	E. F. Nichols.
Doane College	Crete, Neb	W. G. Allen.
Drury College	Springfield, Mo	James G. McMurtry.
Fairmount College	Wichita, Kan	W. H. Rollins.
Fargo College	Fargo, N. D	John W. Hansel.
Fisk University	Nashville, Tenn	F. A. MacKenzie.
Grinnell College	Grinnell, Ia	J. H. T. Main.
Illinois College	Jacksonville, Ill	C. H. Rammelkamp.
Kingfisher College	Kingfisher, Okla	G. B. Hatfield.
Marietta College	Marietta, O.	George W. Hinman.
Middlebury College	Middlebury, Vt	J. M. Thomas.
Mount Holyoke College	South Hadley, Mass	Mary E. Woolley.
Northland College	Ashland, Wis	J. D. Brownell.
Oberlin College	Oberlin, O.	H. C. King.
Olivet College	Olivet, Mich	Thomas W. Nadel.
Pacific University	Forest Grove, Ore	C. J. Bushnell.
Piedmont College	Demorest, Ga	F. E. Jenkins.
Pomona College	Claremont, Cal	J. A. Blaisdell.
Redfield College	Redfield, S. D	E. A. Fath.
Ripon College	Ripon, Wis	Silas Evans.
Rollins College	Winter Park, Fla	A. D. Enyart.
Smith College	Northampton, Mass	M. L. Burton.
Straight University	New Orleans, La	E. M. Stevens.
Tabor College	Tabor, Ia	Nelson W. Wehrhan.
Talladega College	Talladega, Ala	J. M. P. Metcalf.
Tillotson College	Austin, Tex	Isaac M. Agard.
Tougaloo College	Tougaloo, Miss	F. G. Woodworth.
Washburn College	Topeka, Kan	Parley P. Womer.
Wellesley College	Wellesley, Mass	Ellen F. Pendleton.
Wheaton College	Wheaton, Ill	C. A. Blanchard.
Whitman College	Walla Walla, Wash	S. B. L. Penrose.
Williams College	Williamstown, Mass	H. A. Garfield.
Yale University	New Haven, Conn	A. T. Hadley.
Yankton College	Yankton, S. D	H. K. Warren.

Theological Seminaries

Institutio	Location	President or Dean
Andover Theological Seminary	Cambridge, Mass	A. P. Fitch.
Atlanta Theological Seminary	Atlanta, Ga	E. L. Hood.
Bangor Theological Seminary	Bangor, Me	D. N. Beach.
Chicago Theological Seminary	Chicago, Ill	O. S. Davis.
Hartford Theological Seminary	Hartford, Conn	W. D. Mackenzie.
Oberlin Theological Seminary	Oberlin, O.	E. I. Bosworth.
Pacific Theological Seminary	Berkeley, Cal	C. S. Nash.
Talladega College Theological Department	Talladega, Ala	J. M. P. Metcalf.
Yale University Divinity School	New Haven, Conn	Charles R. Brown.

* Including those which in one way or another have had historical connection with Congregationalism.

For list of ministers with addresses see Congregational Year Book, published at 14 Beacon Street, Boston, Mass.

Periodicals

Congregationalist (weekly), Boston, Mass., Editor, Rev. Howard A. Bridgman; *Advance* (weekly), Chicago, Ill., Editor, Rev. William E. Barton.

DISCIPLES OF CHRIST

A general Convention, consisting of delegates from the churches, meets annually in October. Its object is to promote unity, economy, and efficiency among the benevolent organizations of the Churches of Christ, promote equitable representation and secure closer cooperation. Its powers are advisory. There are also annual conventions in the various states. *President,* Judge J. N. Haymaker, Wichita, Kansas; *Secretary,* Rev. Robert Graham Frank, Liberty, Mo.

American Christian Missionary Society, Carew Building, Cincinnati, O. It operates in all North America and has departmental work for church sustenance, Sunday Schools, Social Service, Rural Church, Immigrants, and Foreign Relations. *President,* Rev. F. W. Burnham; *Secretary* Rev. Grant K. Lewis; *Bible School Secretary,* Rev. Robert M. Hopkins.

Christian Woman's Board of Missions, College of Missions Buildings, Indianapolis, Ind. *President,* Mrs. Anna R. Atwater; *Secretaries,* Mrs. Effie L. Cunningham, Mrs. J. McDaniel Stearns, and Mrs. Ellie K. Payne; *Treasurer,* Mrs. W. S. Moffett.

Foreign Christian Missionary Society, Cincinnati, O. *President,* Rev. A. McLean; *Secretaries,* Rev. F. M. Rains, Rev. Stephen J. Corey, R. A. Doan.

Board of Church Extension, New England Building, Kansas City, Mo. *President,* Rev. Fletcher Cowherd; *Secretaries,* Rev. G. W. Muckley, and Rev. John H. Booth.

National Benevolent Association, St. Louis, Mo. *President,* J. W. Perry, Kansas City, Mo.; *General Secretary,* Rev. James H. Mohorter; *Treasurer and General Counsel,* Lee W. Grant.

Board of Ministerial Relief, 120 East Market Street, Indianapolis, Ind. *President,* A. L. Orcutt; *Secretary,* Rev. W. R. Warren; *Treasurer,* Samuel Ashby.

American Temperance Board, Indianapolis, Ind. *President,* Rev. David H. Shields, Kokomo, Ind.; *Secretary,* Rev. L. E. Sellers, Box 501, Indianapolis, Ind.

Commission on Christian Union. *President,* Rev. Peter Ainslie, Baltimore, Md.

Board of Education, Indianapolis, Ind. *President,* R. H. Crossfield, Lexington, Ky.; *Secretary,* Prof. Charles E. Underwood, 70 Layman Avenue, Indianapolis, Ind.

National Board of Christian Endeavor. *President,* Rev. Austin Hunter, 2431 Flournay Street, Chicago, Ill.; *Treasurer,* Henry B. Brown; *Secretary, and National Superintendent,* Rev. Claude E. Hill, Chattanooga, Tenn.

Colleges, Universities, and Schools

Institution	Location	President, Dean, or Principa
Atlantic Christian College	Wilson, N. C.	Raymond A. Smith.
Beckley Institute	Beckley, W. Va.	W. R. Howell.
Bethany College	Bethany, W. Va.	Thomas E. Cramblet.
The Bible College of Missouri (adjacent to and affiliated with the University of Missouri)	Columbia, Mo.	Granville D. Edwards.
Bible School of Drury College	Springfield, Mo.	W. J. Lhamon.
Butler College	Indianapolis, Ind.	Thomas Carr Howe.
Carr-Carlton College	Sherman, Tex.	C. T. Carlton.
Central Christian Institute	Near Hopkinsville, Ky.	W. H. Dickerson.
Christian College	Auburn, Ga.	John H. Wood.
Christian College	Columbia, Mo.	Mrs. L. W. St. Clair-Moss.
Christian University	Canton, Mo.	Earle Marion Todd.
College of Missions	Indianapolis, Ind.	Charles T. Paul.
Cotner University	Bethany, Neb.	J. H. Bicknell, Sec'y.
Disciples' Divinity House of the University of Chicago	Chicago, Ill.	Herbert L. Willett.
Drake University	Des Moines, Ia.	Hill M. Bell.
Eugene Bible University	Eugene, Ore.	Eugene C. Sanderson.
Eureka College	Eureka, Ill.	H. O. Pritchard.
Hiram College	Hiram, O.	Miner Lee Bates.
Johnson Bible College	Kimberlin Heights, Tenn.	Ashley Sidney Johnson.
Midland College	Midland, Tex.	Frank G. Jones.
Milligan College	Milligan College, Tenn.	Josephus Hopwood.
Missouri Christian College	Camden Point, Mo.	R. L. Thorp.
Morehead Normal School	Morehead, Rowan Co., Ky.	J. Wesley Hatcher.
Phillips University	Enid, Okla.	I. N. McCash.
Southern Christian College	West Point, Miss.	H. B. Abernethy.
Spokane University	Spokane, Wash.	A. M. Meldrum.
Texas Bible Chair	Austin, Tex.	Frank L. Jewett.
Texas Christian University	Fort Worth, Tex.	E. M. Waits.
Transylvania College	Lexington, Ky.	R. H. Crossfield.
The College of the Bible	Lexington, Ky.	R. H. Crossfield.
Hamilton Junior College for Women of Transylvania	Lexington, Ky.	R. H. Crossfield.
Virginia Christian College	Lynchburg, Va.	J. T. T. Hundley.
William Woods College	Fulton, Mo.	Joseph A. Serena.

For list of ministers with addresses see Year Book of the Disciples of Christ, published by the American Christian Missionary Society, Carew Building, Cincinnati, O.

Charitable Institutions of the National Benevolent Association

Hospitals: *Christian Hospital,* Valparaiso, Ind.; *Kansas City Christian Hospital,* Kansas City, Mo.

Homes for the Aged: *Christian Old People's Home,* Jacksonville, Ill.; *Havens Home for the Aged,* East Aurora, N. Y.; *The Northwestern Christian Home for the Aged,* Walla Walla, Wash.; *Sarah A. Harwood Hall, Home for the Aged,* Dallas, Tex.

Homes and Institutions for Children: *Christian Orphans' Home,* 2951 North Euclid Avenue, St. Louis, Mo.; *The Cleveland Christian Orphans' Home,* Lorain and Bosworth Road, Cleveland, O.; *The Juliette Fowler Christian Home,* Dallas, Tex.; *The Southern Christian Home,* 299 Lee Street, Atlanta, Ga.; *The Colorado Christian Home,* Twenty-ninth and Tennyson Avenues, Denver, Colorado; *The Child Saving Institute,* Forty-second and Jackson Streets, Omaha, Neb.

Periodicals

Christian Century, Chicago, Ill., Editor, C. C. Morrison; *Conquest,* Chicago, Ill., Editor, T. C. Clark; *Missionary Tidings,* Indianapolis, Ind., Editor, Mrs. Effie L. Cunningham; *Christian News,* Des Moines, Ia., Editor, Charles Blanchard; *Christian Worker,* Des Moines, Ia., Editor, W. A. Shullenberger; *Christian Union Quarterly,* Baltimore, Md., Editor, Peter Ainslie; *Gospel Plea,* Edwards, Miss., Editor, J. B. Lehman; *Christian Evangelist,* St. Louis, Mo., Editor, F. D. Kershner; *Christian Philanthropist,* St. Louis, Mo., Editor, J. H. Mohorter; *Business in Christianity,* Kansas City, Mo., Editors, G. W. Muckley and John H. Booth; *Front Rank,* St. Louis, Mo., Editor, Richard Heilbron; *Christian Standard,* Cincinnati, O., Editor, G. A. Rutledge; *Missionary Intelligencer,* Cincinnati, O., Editor, F. M. Rains; *American Home Missionary,* Cincinnati, O., Editors, F. W. Burnham, G. K. Lewis and R. M. Hopkins; *Lookout,* Cincinnati, O., Editor, E. J. Meacham; *Christian Courier,* Dallas, Tex., Editor, A. E. Ewell.

EVANGELICAL ASSOCIATION

There is a General Conference, quadrennial; 25 annual conferences, 21 in America. The next session of the General Conference will be held in 1919.

Bishops

S. C. Breyfogel, 836 Center Avenue, Reading, Pa.

Samuel P. Spreng, 106 Columbia Avenue, Naperville, Ill.

G. Heinmiller, 2184 East 82nd Street, Cleveland, O.

L. H. Seager, 104 Sleight Street, Naperville, Ill.

William Horn (retired), 1504 East 107th Street, Cleveland, O.

Thomas Bowman (retired), 734 Turner Street, Allentown, Pa.

Secretary of the General Conference, Rev. T. C. Meckel, 1903 Woodland Avenue, Cleveland, O.

Board of Publication and Church Extension, 1903 Woodland Avenue, South East, Cleveland, O. *President,* Bishop S. C. Breyfogel; *Secretary,* Bishop William Horn.

Missionary Society, 1903 Woodland Avenue, South East, Cleveland, O. *President,* Rev. T. C. Meckel; *Treasurer,* Geo. Johnson; *Field Secretary,* B. R. Wiener.

Woman's Missionary Society, 9502 Wamelink Avenue, Cleveland, O. *President,* Mrs. E. M. Spreng, Cleveland, O.; *Corresponding Secretary,* Mrs. J. S. Miller, Hutchinson, Kan.; *Treasurer,* Miss Ella Horn, Cleveland, O.; *Secretary Young Woman's Work,* Mrs. L. H. Seager, Naperville, Ill.; *Secretary Message Bearers,* Mrs. H. J. Niebaum, Pittsburgh, Pa.; *Secretary Little Heralds,* Mrs. W. H. Hammer, Cleveland, O.

Board of Administration of the Superannuation Fund. *President,* Hon. Wm. Grote, Elgin, Ill.; *Corresponding Secretary,* Bishop S. C. Breyfogel, Reading, Pa.; *Recording Secretary,* Bishop G. Heinmiller, Cleveland, O.; *Treasurer,* Rev. George Johnson, Cleveland, O.

Young People's Alliance. *President,* Rev. H. A. Kramer, 1903 Woodland Avenue, South East, Cleveland, O.; *General Secretary,* Rev. F. C. Berger; *Treasurer,* L. D. Zachman, Marion, O.; *Missionary Secretary,* Rev. W. C. Hallwachs, Cleveland, O.; *Junior Superintendent,* Miss Lois F. Kramer, Cleveland, O.

Board of Sunday Schools, 1903 Woodland Avenue, South East, Cleveland, O. *President,* Rev. Chr. Staebler, Cleveland, O.; *Vice-Presidents,* Bishops S. C. Breyfogel and Samuel P. Spreng; *Secretary,* A. L. Breithaupt, Berlin, Ont.; *Treasurer,* John Etjen, Cleveland, O.

Sunday School and Tract Union, 1903 Woodland Avenue, South East, Cleveland, O. Officers same as those of Board of Sunday Schools.

Colleges and Theological Seminaries

Institution	Location	President, Principal, or Director
Correspondence College	Reading, Pa	S. C. Breyfogel.
Evangelical Theological Seminary	Naperville, Ill	S. J. Gamertsfelder.
Northwestern College	Naperville, Ill	E. E. Rall.
Preachers' Seminary	Reutlingen, Germany	J. Schempp.
Schuylkill Seminary	Reading, Pa	W. F. Teel.

For list of ministers with addresses see minutes of the several annual conferences.

Benevolent Institutions

Ebenezer Orphans' Home, Flat Rock, O., *Superintendent,* Rev. W. H. Messerschmidt; *Ebenezer Old People's Home,* Ebenezer, N. Y.; *Superintendent,* Rev. H. P. Merle; *Western Old People's Home,* Cedar Falls, Ia., *Superintendent,* Rev. A. L. Hauser; *Deaconess Home and Training School,* 408 Wisconsin Street, Chicago, Ill., *Superintendent,* Rev. J. H. Bauernfeind.

Periodicals

Evangelical Messenger (weekly), Cleveland, O., Editor, W. H. Bucks; *Evangelical Herald* (weekly), Cleveland, O., Editor, H. A. Kramer; *Missionary Messenger* (monthly), Naperville, Ill., Editor, Mrs. S. J. Gamertsfelder; *Evangelical Sunday School Teacher* (monthly), Editor, H. A. Kramer.

Christliche Botschafter (weekly), Editor, T. C. Meckel; *Evangelische Missionsbote* (monthly), Editor, T. C. Meckel; *Evangelische Magazin* (monthly), Editor, Chr. Staebler.

C. Hauser, *Publishing Agent,* 1903 Woodland Avenue, South East, Cleveland, O.

G. W. Bader, *Publishing Agent for Germany and Switzerland,* Stuttgart, Germany.

UNITED EVANGELICAL CHURCH

General Conference, quadrennial; next session, 1918, at York, Pa. There are ten annual conferences.

Bishops

U. F. Swengel, 75 North Eighteenth Street, Harrisburg, Pa.
W. H. Fouke, 105 North Street, Naperville, Ill.

Publishing House, 201 North Second Street, Harrisburg, Pa. *Publisher,* J. J. Nungesser; *President,* Rev. J. W. Thompson, York, Pa.

Board of Church Extension. *President,* Rev. W. M. Stamford, 201 North Second Street, Harrisburg, Pa.; *Secretary,* Rev. B. H. Niebel, Penbrook, Pa.; *Treasurer,* A. P. Schnader, Lancaster, Pa.

Board of Education. *President,* Rev. H. Franklin Schlegel, Lancaster, Pa.; *Secretary,* Prof. A. E. Gobble, Myerstown, Pa.

Board of Missions. *President,* Rev. H. B. Hartzler, Harrisburg, Pa.; *Corresponding Secretary,* Rev. B. H. Niebel, Penbrook, Pa.; Treasurer, Jeremiah G. Mohn, 1028 Penn Street, Reading, Pa.

Sunday School and Keystone League of Christian En-

deavor. *President,* Rev. J. L. A. Curry, Johnstown, Pa.; *General Secretary,* Rev. W. E. Peffley, 201 North Second Street, Harrisburg, Pa.; *Treasurer,* Robert G. Munday, 106 North La Salle Street, Chicago, Ill.

General Statistical Secretary, Rev. A. A. Couser, 510 East Thirteenth Street, Des Moines, Ia.

Woman's Home and Foreign Missionary Society. *President,* Mrs. W. J. Gruhler, 219 High Street, Germantown, Pa.; *Secretary,* Mrs. Emma Divan, Ottawa, Ill.; *Treasurer,* Mrs. W. E. Detwiler, Marysville, Pa.

Charitable Society. *President,* D. S. Stauffer, Oley, Pa.; *Treasurer,* W. W. Fetter, Reading, Pa.

Deaconess Home, 842 Harlem Avenue, Baltimore, Md.

United Evangelical Home, Lewisburg, Pa., Superintendent, Rev. A. A. Winter.

Colleges

Institution	Location	President
Albright College	Myerstown, Pa	L. Clarence Hunt.
Oregon Bible Training School	Corvallis, Ore.	C. C. Poling.
Western Union College	LeMars, Ia	C. A. Mock.

For list of ministers with addresses see Year Book of the United Evangelical Church, published at 201 North Second Street, Harrisburg, Pa.

Periodicals

Evangelical, Harrisburg, Pa., Editor, Rev. H. B. Hartzler; *Evangelische Zeitschrift,* Harrisburg, Pa., Editor, Rev. G. Ott; *Evangelical Endeavor and Sunday School Literature,* Harrisburg, Pa., Editor, Rev. W. M. Stamford; *Missionary Tidings and Missionary Gem,* Hanover, Pa., Editor, Miss Emma D. Messinger. *Evangelical Men,* Editor, Rev. J. W. Hoover, Reading, Pa.

SOCIETY OF FRIENDS (ORTHODOX)

(For other bodies of Friends, not constituent members of the Federal Council, see Directory of Other Religious Bodies, page 124.)

Five Years' Meeting, quinquennial, composed of delegates from twelve of the fourteen yearly meetings in the United States and one in Canada. The next meeting of the Five Years' Meeting will be held in Richmond, Ind., beginning on the third Tuesday in October, 1917.

Clerk, or Presiding Officer, Joseph John Mills, 525 South

Catalina Avenue, Pasadena, Cal.; *First Assistant, or Secretary,* Emma Spencer Townsend, Martinsville, Ohio; *Treasurer,* Francis A. Wright, Jr., 520 American Bank Building, Kansas City, Mo.

General Secretary, Walter C. Woodward, to assume office January 1, 1917; address, 207 College Avenue, Richmond, Ind.

The Executive Committee of the Five Years' Meeting, chairman, Allen D. Hole, Earlham College, Richmond, Ind.

Finance Board. *Secretary,* John H. Johnson, Richmond, Ind.

American Friends Board of Foreign Missions, Richmond, Ind. *General Secretary,* Charles E. Tebbetts.

Evangelistic and Church Extension Board. *Secretary,* Esther Cook, New Castle, Ind.

Board on Education, Richmond, Ind. *Chairman,* Robert L. Kelly.

Board on Legislation and Temperance, Richmond, Ind. *Chairman,* S. E. Nicholson.

Bible School Board, Richmond, Ind. *Chairman,* Richard Haworth, Earlham, Iowa.

Young People's Board, Richmond, Ind. *Chairman,* W. O. Trueblood, 313 East Thirteenth Street, Indianapolis, Ind.

Social Service Board. *Chairman,* Rufus M. Jones, Haverford, Pa.

Peace Board, Richmond, Ind. *Chairman,* Allen D. Hole.

Board on Condition of Negroes. *Secretary and Treasurer,* John C. Thomas, 1063 Calvert Building, Baltimore, Md.

Committee on Indian Affairs. *Chairman,* Edward M. Wistar, Provident Building, Philadelphia, Pa.

Colleges

Institution	Location	President
Central College	Central City, Neb	Eli Parisho.
Earlham College	Richmond, Ind	Robert L. Kelly.
Friends College	Wichita, Kan	Edmund Stanley.
Guilford College	Guilford College, N. C	Thomas Newlin.
Haverford College	Haverford, Pa	Isaac Sharpless.
Pacific College	Newberg, Ore	Levi T. Pennington.
Penn College	Oskaloosa, Ia	David M. Edwards.
Whittier College	Whittier, Cal	A. Rosenberger.
Wilmington College	Wilmington, O	J. Edwin Jay.

For list of ministers with addresses see minutes of various yearly meetings.

Periodicals. *American Friend* (weekly), Richmond, Ind., Editor, S. E. Nicholson. *Messenger of Peace* (monthly), Richmond, Ind., Editor, Allen D. Hole. *Friends' Missionary Advocate* (monthly), Bloomingdale, Ind., Editor, Lenora Newlin Hobbs; *Bible School Quarterlies,* Roxbury, Boston, Mass., Editor, Wilbur K. Thomas.

EVANGELICAL LUTHERAN CHURCH, GENERAL SYNOD

(For other Lutheran bodies, not constituent members of the Federal Council, see Directory of other Religious Bodies, pages 126-139.)

General Synod, biennial; holds its next meeting at Chicago, Ill., in 1917.

There are 24 district synods.

President, Rev. J. A. Singmaster, Gettysburg, Pa.; *Secretary,* Rev. F. P. Manhart, Selinsgrove, Pa.; *Treasurer,* George H. Knollenberg, 132 South Fourth Street, Richmond, Ind.

Board of Foreign Missions, 21 West Saratoga Street, Baltimore, Md. *Secretary and Treasurer,* Rev. L. B. Wolf.

Board of Home Missions and Church Extension, Security Building, York, Pa. *Secretary and Treasurer,* Rev. J. H. Weber.

Board of Publication, Ninth and Sansom Streets, Philadelphia, Pa. *Superintendent,* Rev. T. L. Sigmund; *Corresponding Secretary,* Rev. F. P. Manhart, Selinsgrove, Pa.

Board of Education, 1200 Farragut Street, Pittsburgh, Pa. *Secretary,* Rev. C. S. Bauslin, Harrisburg, Pa.; *Treasurer,* William Pore.

Deaconess Board, Baltimore, Md. *Secretary,* Rev. Charles E. Hay.

Woman's Home and Foreign Missionary Society. *Secretary,* Mary H. Morris, Lutherville, Md.

Pastors' Fund Society. *Secretary,* Rev. G. M. Diffenderfer, Carlisle, Pa.; *Treasurer,* Mr. J. B. Downing, 1404 North Bouvier Street, Philadelphia, Pa.

Parent Educational Society, Gettysburg, Pa. *Secretary,* Rev. P. M. Bikle; *Treasurer,* Rev. J. A. Singmaster.

Inner Mission Board. *Secretary,* Rev. William Freas, 162 Mercer Street, Jersey City, N. J.

Colleges and University

Institution	Location	President
Carthage College	Carthage, Ill	H. D. Hoover.
Midland College	Atchison, Kan	R. M. Perry.
Pennsylvania College	Gettysburg, Pa	William A. Granville
Susquehanna University	Selinsgrove, Pa	Charles T. Aikens.
Wittenberg College	Springfield, O	C. G. Heckert.

Theological Seminaries

Institution	Location	President or Dean
Hamma Divinity School	Springfield, O.	D. H. Bauslin.
Hartwick Seminary	Hartwick Seminary, N. Y.	J. G. Traver.
Martin Luther Seminary	Lincoln, Neb.	F. Wapper.
Theological Seminary	Gettysburg, Pa.	J. A. Singmaster.
Theological Dept., Susquehanna Univ.	Selinsgrove, Pa.	F. P. Manhart.
Theological Seminary	Guntur, India.	J. Aberly.
Western Seminary	Atchison, Kan.	H. Dysinger.

For list of ministers of all Lutheran bodies in the United States see Lutheran Almanac and Year Book, Philadelphia, Pa.

Charitable Institutions

Deaconess Motherhouse, 2500 West North Avenue, Baltimore, Md. *Pastor,* Rev. Chas. E. Hay.

Hospitals: *Chirala,* Chirala, India, *Superintendent,* Dr. Mary Baer; *Tabitha,* 452 Randolph Street, Lincoln, Neb., *Superintendent,* E. Walter.

Homes for the Aged: *Feghtly,* Tippecanoe City, O., *Superintendent,* B. W. Zregler; *National Lutheran,* Washington, D. C., Station K., *Superintendent,* Sister F. Ohler.

Orphans' Homes: *Nachusa,* Nachusa, Ill., *Superintendent,* Sister Alberta Harris; *Oesterlen,* North Lagonda Avenue, Springfield, O., *Superintendent,* W. M. Habey; *Tabitha,* Forty-fifth and Randolph Streets, Lincoln, Neb., *Superintendent,* E. Walter; *Tressler,* Loysville, Pa., *Superintendent,* Mr. C. A. Widle; *Loats,* Frederick, Md., *Superintendent,* Z. H. Zimmerman.

Periodicals

Lutheran Church Work and Observer (weekly), official organ, York, Pa., Editor, Rev. F. G. Gotwald; *Lutheran Quarterly Review,* Gettysburg, Pa., Editor, Rev. J. A. Singmaster.

GERMAN EVANGELICAL SYNOD OF NORTH AMERICA

The German Evangelical Synod meets quadrennially. The next session will be held in 1917.

There are 17 district conferences and 5 mission districts.

Officers: *President General,* John Baltzer, 2506 Benton Street, St. Louis, Mo.; *Vice-President,* Rev. D. Irion, Elmhurst, Ill.; *General Secretary,* Rev. Gustave Fischer, 671

Madison Street, Milwaukee, Wis.; *General Treasurer,* Rev. Henry Bode, 1740 North Euclid Avenue, St. Louis, Mo.

Board of Foreign Missions, 1337 Main Street, Buffalo, N. Y. *Secretary,* Rev. C. W. Locher, Baltimore, Md.; *Treasurer,* Rev. T. Lehmann, Columbus, O.; *General Secretary,* Rev. E. Schmidt.

Central Board for Home Missions, 841 Fourth Street, Milwaukee, Wis. *Chairman,* Rev. F. G. Ludwig; *Treasurer,* Rev. J. Nuesch, Keokuk, Ia.

Sunday School Board. *Secretary,* Rev. Alfred E. Meyer, 1718 Chouteau Avenue, St. Louis, Mo. *Chairman,* Rev. Paul Pfeiffer, 505 Jefferson Avenue, Evansville, Ind.; *Secretary,* Rev. W. F. Simon, 1115 Victor Street, St. Louis, Mo.; *Treasurer,* Rev. C. L. Langerhans, Addieville, Ill.

Evangelical League. *President,* Rev. W. N. Dresel, 31 Lower Third Street, Evansville, Ind.; *Corresponding Secretary,* Miss Anna Rahe, 548 East Drive, Woodruff Place, Indianapolis, Ind.; *Treasurer,* Mr. Reinhold J. Tietze, 2622 Indiana Avenue, St. Louis, Mo.

Evangelical Brotherhood. *President,* Rev. E. A. R. Torsch, 714 Starks Building, Louisville, Ky.; *Secretary,* Mr. John C. Fischer, 819 Blackford Avenue, Evansville, Ind.; *Treasurer,* Mr. W. C. Hazelbeck, 819 Gallia Street, Portsmouth, O.

Immigrant Mission. *Secretary,* Rev. F. H. Klemme, 421 West Henrietta Street, Baltimore, Md.; *Treasurer,* Rev. W. H. Aufderhaar, 1319 Myrtle Avenue, Baltimore, Md.

Church Extension. *Secretary,* Rev. F. J. Bushmann, R. R. No. 6, Edwardsville, Ill.; *Treasurer,* F. H. Krafft, Red Bud and Rosalie Avenues, St. Louis, Mo.

Commission on the Common Welfare. *Secretary,* Rev. John Goebel, 1353 State Street, Chicago, Ill.; *Treasurer,* Rev. F. Weber, Chicago, Ill.

Board of Publications, Eden Publishing House, 1716 Chouteau Avenue, St. Louis, Mo. *Chairman English Literary Committee,* Prof. S. D. Press, Eden Seminary, St. Louis, Mo.; *Chairman German Literary Committee,* Rev. A. Muecke, Garretson, S. D.

Seminaries and College

Institution	Location	Director
Eden Seminary	St. Louis, Mo	W. Becker.
Elmhurst College	Elmhurst, Ill	D. Irion.
Fort Collins Seminary	Fort Collins, Colo	J. Jans.

For list of ministers with addresses see Evangelical Year Book, published at the Eden Publishing House, St. Louis, Mo.

Charitable Institutions

Deaconess Homes: St. Louis, Mo., *Superintendent,* F. P. Jens, 4117 West Belle Place; Evansville, Ind., *Superintendent,* J. U. Schneider, 116 Lower Sixth Street; Lincoln, Ill., *Superintendent,* C. Hoffman, 112 Fifth Street; Faribault, Minn., *Superintendent,* Wm. Meyer, 718 Fifth Avenue; Chicago, Ill., *Superintendent,* F. Weber, Fifty-fourth Place and Morgan; Louisville, Ky., *Superintendent,* W. F. Mehl, 219 East Broadway; Milwaukee, Wis., *Superintendent,* Rev. J. L. Haack, 1807 Grand Avenue; Cincinnati, O., *Superintendent,* A. G. Lohmann, Clifton Heights; Buffalo, N. Y., *Superintendent,* C. G. Haas, 562 Ellicott Street; Marshalltown, Ia., *Superintendent,* K. Rest, 204 South Fourth Avenue.

Emmaus Homes for Epileptics and Feeble-Minded: St. Charles, Mo., *Superintendent,* J. W. Frankenfeld; Near Marthasville, Mo., *Superintendent,* C. F. Sturm.

Orphans' Homes: St. Charles Rock Road, St. Louis, Mo., *Superintendent,* F. W. Helmkamp, R. R. 29, Wellston, Mo.; Hoyleton, Ill., *Superintendent,* J. H. Koenig; Detroit, Mich., *Superintendent,* J. B. Meister, 1852 West Grand Boulevard; Bensenville, Ill.

Homes for the Aged: St. Louis, Mo., *Superintendent,* Mrs. E. S. Lewis, Dayton Street and Jefferson Avenue; Detroit, Mich., *Superintendent,* J. B. Meister, 1852 West Grand Boulevard; Bensenville, Ill.; San Antonio, Tex., *Superintendent,* C. Saenger, R. R. I., Box 153.

Pastors' Home: Near Blue Springs, Mo., *Superintendent,* J. Sauer, 5018 Euclid Avenue, Kansas City, Mo.

Periodicals

Evangelical Herald (weekly), St. Louis, Mo., Editor, Rev. J. H. Horstmann; *Evangelical Tidings* (weekly), St. Louis, Mo., Editor, Rev. H. Katterjohn; *Evangelical Companion,* St. Louis, Mo., Editor, Rev. H. Katterjohn; *Friedensbote,* St. Louis, Mo., Editor, Rev. W. T. Jungk; *Magazine fuer Theologie und Kirche,* Spokane Bridge, Wash., Editor, Rev. L. J. Haas, R. R. I.; *Jugendfreund,* Chelsea, Mich., Editor, Rev. G. Eisen; *Christliche Kinderzeitung,* St. Louis, Mo., Editor, Rev. K. Kissling.

MENNONITE CHURCH, GENERAL CONFERENCE

(For other Mennonite bodies, not constituent members of the Federal Council, see Directory of other Religious Bodies, pages 140-142.)

General Conference: 6 district conferences, including 1 in Canada.

Officers: *President*, Rev. H. D. Penner, Newton, Kan.; *Secretary*, H. A. Bachman, Freeman, S. Dak.; *Treasurer*, F. C. Claassen, Newton, Kan.

Board of Foreign Missions *President*, Rev. J. W. Kliewer, Newton, Kan.; *Secretary*, Rev. P. H. Richert, Goessel, Kan.; *Treasurer*, Rev. Gustav Harder, Whitewater, Kan.

Board of Home Missions. *President*, Rev. W. S. Gottshall, Bluffton, O.; *Secretary*, Rev. H. P. Krehbiel, Newton, Kan.; *Treasurer*, Prof. G. A. Haury, Newton, Kan.

Board of Publication. *President*, Rev. N. B. Grubb, Philadelphia, Pa.; *Secretary*, Rev. W. J. Ewert, Hillsboro, Kan.; *Business Manager*, J. F. Lehman, Berne, Ind.

Board of Education. *President*, Rev. H. H. Ewert, Gretna, Manitoba; *Secretary*, Rev. J. H. Langenwalter, Bluffton, O.; *Treasurer*, D. H. Rickert, Newton, Kan.

Emergency Relief Committee. *President*, Rev. J. C. Goering, Moundridge, Kan.; *Secretary*, Rev. John Lichti, Deer Creek, Okla.; *Treasurer*, P. P. Hilty, Donnellson, Iowa.

Colleges and Theological Seminary

Institution	Location	President
Bethel College	Newton, Kan	J. W. Kliewer.
Bluffton College and Mennonite Theological Seminary	Bluffton, O.	S. K. Mosiman.
Freeman College	Freeman, S. Dak.	Eddison Mosiman.

For list of ministers of various branches with addresses see Bundesbote Kalendar, published at the Mennonite Book Concern, Berne, Ind.

Charitable Institutions

Bethel Deaconess Home and Hospital, Newton, Kan.; *Deaconess Hospital*, Mt. Lake, Minn.; *Mennonite Deaconess Home and Hospital*, Beatrice, Neb.; *Mennonite Sanitarium*, Upland, Cal.; *Mennonite Home for the Aged*, Frederick, Pa.

Periodicals

Mennonite (weekly), Berne, Ind., Editor, Rev. S. M. Grubb; *Christlicher Bundesbote* (weekly), Berne, Ind., Editor, Rev. C. H. Van der Smissen; *Bethesda Herold* (monthly), Newton, Kan., Editor, Rev. Henry Banman.

Methodists

Methodist branches in all parts of the world are represented in an Ecumenical Methodist Conference, which meets once every ten years. The fourth Conference of the series was held in Toronto, Canada, in October, 1911. There is an Ecumenical Methodist Commission, in two sections, Eastern and Western, which represents the Conference *ad interim*.

Ecumenical Methodist Commission, Western Section. *President,* Bishop E. E. Hoss; *Secretary,* Rev. H. K. Carroll, 1114 Woodward Building, Washington, D. C.; *Chairman of the Executive Committee,* Bishop John W. Hamilton; *Secretary,* Rev. H. K. Carroll.

METHODIST EPISCOPAL CHURCH

(For other Methodist bodies, not constituent members of the Federal Council, see Directory of other Religious Bodies, pages 142-145.)

General Conference, quadrennial; next session in May, 1920.

Annual Conferences and Missions at home and abroad, 158.

Secretary of the General Conference, Rev. Edwin Locke, Topeka, Kan.

Treasurer of the General Conference, Oscar P. Miller, Rock Rapids, Ia.

Bishops

John H. Vincent (retired), 5700 Blackstone Avenue, Chicago, Ill.

Earl Cranston (retired), 1811 Irving Street, Washington, D. C.

John W. Hamilton (retired), American University, Washington, D. C.

Joseph F. Berry, 1701 Arch Street, Philadelphia, Pa.

Wm. F. McDowell, 1509 Sixteenth Street, Washington, D. C.

James W. Bashford, Methodist Mission, Peking, China.

William Burt, 455 Franklin Street, Buffalo, N. Y.

Luther B. Wilson, 150 Fifth Avenue, New York City.

Thomas B. Neely (retired), 4513 Chester Avenue, Philadelphia, Pa.

William F. Anderson, 420 Plum Street, Cincinnati, O.

John L. Nuelsen, Zurich, Switzerland.

William A. Quayle, St. Louis, Mo.

Wilson S. Lewis, Foochow, China.

Edwin H. Hughes, 235 Sumner Street, Malden, Mass.

Frank M. Bristol, Chattanooga, Tenn.

Homer C. Stuntz, Omaha, Neb.

Theodore S. Henderson, Detroit, Mich.
William O. Shepard, Wichita, Kan.
Francis J. McConnell, 963 Logan Street, Denver, Colo.
Frederick D. Leete, 621 Rhodes Building, Atlanta, Ga.
Richard J. Cooke, Helena, Mont.
Wilbur P. Thirkield, Hotel De Soto, New Orleans, La.
Herbert Welch, Seoul, Korea.
Thomas Nicholson, 740 Rush Street, Chicago, Ill.
Adna W. Leonard, 435 Buchanan Street, San Francisco, Cal.
Matthew S. Hughes, Portland, Ore.
William F. Oldham, Buenos Ayres, Argentina, South America.
Charles B. Mitchell, Saint Paul, Minn.
Franklin Hamilton, 524 Penn Avenue, Pittsburgh, Pa.

Missionary Bishops

James M. Thoburn (retired), Meadville, Pa.
Joseph C. Hartzell (retired), Blue Ash, O.
Frank W. Warne, Lucknow, India.
Isaiah B. Scott (retired), 125 Fourteenth Avenue North, Nashville, Tenn.
John E. Robinson, Bangalore, India.
Merriman C. Harris (retired), Tokyo, Japan.
John W. Robinson, Bombay, India.
Alexander P. Camphor, Monrovia, Liberia.
Eben S. Johnson, Umtali, Rhodesia, South Africa.

Methodist Book Concern: 150 Fifth Avenue, New York City; 420 Plum Street, Cincinnati, O.; 740 Rush Street, Chicago, Ill.

General Agent, Henry C. Jennings, 740 Rush Street, Chicago, Ill.; *Agent at New York,* Edwin R. Graham, 150 Fifth Avenue, New York City; *Agent at Cincinnati,* John H. Race, 420 Plum Street, Cincinnati, O.; *Agent Emeritus,* George P. Mains, 150 Fifth Avenue, New York City; *Book Editor,* David G. Downey, 150 Fifth Avenue, New York City; 420 Plum Street, Cincinnati, O.

Board of Foreign Missions, 150 Fifth Avenue, New York City. *President,* Bishop Luther B. Wilson; *Corresponding Secretaries,* Mr. S. Earl Taylor, Rev. Frank Mason North; *Treasurer,* Rev. George M. Fowles.

Board of Home Missions and Church Extension, Arch and Seventeenth Streets, Philadelphia, Pa. *President,* Bishop Joseph F. Berry; *Corresponding Secretary,* Rev. D. D. Forsyth; *Treasurer,* Samuel Shaw; *Superintendent,* Church Extension, Rev. W. L. McDowell; *Superintendent,* Cities, Rev. Melvin P. Burns; *Superintendent,* Rural Work, Paul L. Voght; *Superin-*

tendent, Frontier, Rev. Edward L. Mills; *Superintendent,* Evangelism, Rev. George B. Dean.

Freedmen's Aid Society, 420 Plum Street, Cincinnati, O. *President,* Bishop William F. Anderson; *Corresponding Secretaries,* Rev. P. J. Maveety and I. Garland Penn; *Treasurer,* Rev. John H. Race.

Board of Education, 150 Fifth Avenue, New York City. *President,* Bishop William F. McDowell; *Corresponding Secretary,* Abram W. Harris.

Board of Sunday Schools, 58 East Washington Street, Chicago, Ill. *President,* Bishop Thomas Nicholson; *Corresponding Secretary,* Rev. Edgar Blake; *Editor Sunday School Publications,* Rev. Henry H. Meyer.

(The Methodist Brotherhood transferred to control of Board of Sunday Schools.)

Board of Conference Claimants, 820 Garland Building, Chicago, Ill. *Corresponding Secretary,* Rev. J. B. Hingeley.

General Deaconess Board, 483 Ellicott Square, Buffalo, N. Y. *President,* Bishop William Burt; *Corresponding Secretary,* Rev. D. W. Howell.

Epworth League Board of Control. *General Secretary,* Rev. Wilbur F. Sheridan, 740 Rush Street, Chicago, Ill.

See Epworth League under Directory of Interchurch Organizations, page 169.)

Board of Temperance, Prohibition, and Public Morals, Washington, D. C. *General Secretary,* Rev. Clarence True Wilson.

Commission on Finance. *General Secretary,* Rev. Joseph W. Van Cleve, Chicago, Ill.

Methodist Federation for Social Service. *President,* Bishop F. J. McConnell, Denver, Colo.; *Secretary,* Rev. Harry F. Ward, 72 Mount Vernon Street, Boston, Mass.

Woman's Foreign Missionary Society. *President,* Mrs. W. F. McDowell, 1509 Sixteenth Street, Washington, D. C.; *Secretary,* Mrs. C. W. Barnes, 511 Greenup Street, Covington, Ky.; *Treasurer,* Miss Florence Hooper, 10 South Street, Baltimore, Md.

Woman's Home Missionary Society, 222 West Fourth Street, Cincinnati, O. *President,* Mrs. Wilbur P. Thirkield, The De Soto, New Orleans, La.; *Corresponding Secretary,* Mrs. May Leonard Woodruff, Allendale, N. J.; *Recording Secretary,* Mrs. D. D. Thompson, 1629 Hinman Avenue, Evanston, Ill.; *Treasurer,* Mrs. H. C. Jennings, 3638 Zumstein Avenue, Cincinnati, O.

Colleges and Universities

Institution	Location	President or Chancellor
Albion College	Albion, Mich	Samuel Dickie.
Allegheny College	Meadville, Pa	W. H. Crawford.
Baker University	Baldwin, Kan	Wilbur N. Mason.
Baldwin-Wallace College	Berea, O	Arthur L. Breslich.
Boston University	Boston, Mass	Lemuel H. Murlin.
Central Wesleyan College	Warrenton, Mo	Otto E. Kriege.
College of Puget Sound	Tacoma, Wash	E. H. Todd.
College of the Pacific	San Jose, Cal	John L. Seaton.
Cornell College	Mount Vernon, Ia	Charles W. Flint.
Dakota Wesleyan University	Mitchell, S. D	C. V. Gilliland.
De Pauw University	Greencastle, Ind	George Richmond Grose.
Dickinson College	Carlisle, Pa	J. H. Morgan.
Goucher College (for Women)	Baltimore, Md	W. W. Guth.
Hamline University	St. Paul, Minn	S. F. Kerfoot.
Hedding College	Abingdon, Ill	W. D. Agnew.
Illinois Wesleyan University	Bloomington, Ill	Theodore Kemp.
Illinois Woman's College	Jacksonville, Ill	J. R. Harker.
Iowa Wesleyan College	Mount Pleasant, Ia	Edwin A. Schell.
Kansas Wesleyan University	Salina, Kan	J. F. Harmon.
Lawrence College	Appleton, Wis	Samuel Plantz.
McKendree College	Lebanon, Ill	Huber William Hurt.
Missouri Wesleyan College	Cameron, Mo	H. R. DeBra.
Morningside College	Sioux City, Ia	Alfred E. Craig.
Mount Union College	Alliance, O	W. H. McMaster.
Nebraska Wesleyan University	University Place, Neb	C. A. Fulmer.
Northwestern University	Evanston & Chicago, Ill	T. F. Holgate.
Ohio Wesleyan University	Delaware, O	J. W. Hoffman.
Simpson College	Indianola, Ia	J. W. Campbell.
Syracuse University	Syracuse, N. Y	James Roscoe Day
University of Chattanooga	Chattanooga and Athens, Tenn	Fred W. Hixson
University of Denver	Denver, Colo	H. A. Buchtel.
University of Southern California	Los Angeles, Cal	G. F. Bovard.
Upper Iowa University	Fayette, Ia	C. P. Colgrove.
Wesley College (affiliated with State Univ.)	University, N. D	E. P. Robertson.
Wesleyan University (for Men)	Middletown, Conn	William Arnold Shanklin.
West Virginia Female College	Buckhannon, W. V	W. B. Fleming.
Willamette University	Salem, Ore	Carl G. Doney.

Colleges and Universities

(Institutions which fail to meet the requirements of the University Senate)

Institution	Location	President or Chancellor
Beaver College	Beaver, Pa	Le Roy Weller.
Methodist University of Oklahoma	Guthrie, Okla	Edward Hislop.
Moores Hill College	Moores Hill, Ind	A. J. Bigney (acting).
Ohio Northern University	Ada. O	Albert Edwin Smith.
Southwestern College	Winfield, Kan	Frank E. Mossman.

Schools for Negroes

(Institutions which fail to meet the requirements of the University Senate)

Institution	Location	President
Claflin College	Orangeburg, S. C	L. M. Dunton.
Clark University	Atlanta, Ga	Harry Andrews King.
Morgan College	Baltimore, Md	J. O. Spencer.
New Orleans College	New Orleans, La	C. M. Melden.
Philander Smith College	Little Rock, Ark	J. M. Cox.
Rust College	Holly Springs, Miss	George Evans.
Walden College	Nashville, Tenn	G. F. Durgin.
Wiley College	Marshall, Tex	M. W. Dogan.

Theological Seminaries

Institution	Location	President or Dean
Boston University School of Theology	Boston, Mass	Lauress J. Birney.
Central Wesleyan & German Theol. Sem.	Warrenton, Mo	Frederick Munz.
Drew Theological Seminary	Madison, N. J	Ezra Squier Tipple.
Garrett Biblical Institute	Evanston, Ill	Charles M. Stuart.
Iliff School of Theology	Denver, Colo	J. A. Beebe.
Kimball College of Theology	Salem, Ore	H. J. Talbott.
Maclay College of Theology	Los Angeles, Cal	Ezra A. Healy.
Nast Theological Seminary	Berea, O	A. L. Breslich.
Norwegian-Danish Theological Seminary	Evanston, Ill	N. E. Simonsen.
Swedish Theological Seminary	Evanston, Ill	Carl G. Wallenius.

Professional Schools for Negroes

Institution	Location	President or Dean
Gammon Theological Seminary	South Atlanta, Ga	Philip M. Watters.
Meharry Medical College	Nashville, Tenn	George W. Hubbard.
Walden University School of Law	Nashville, Tenn.	

For list of ministers with addresses see Minutes of the Annual Conferences of the Methodist Episcopal Church in two volumes, Spring Minutes and Fall Minutes, published by The Methodist Book Concern.

Hospitals

Methodist Episcopal Hospital, Brooklyn, N. Y., *Superintendent,* Rev. James E. Holmes; *Bethany Hospital,* Brooklyn, N. Y., *Superintendent,* Rev. G. F. Hausser; *Deaconess Hospital,* Boston, Mass., *Superintendent,* Miss Adeliza A. Betts; *Deaconess Hospital,* Concord, Mass., *Superintendent,* Miss Edith F. Bennett; *Wesley Memorial Hospital,* Chicago, Ill., *Superintendent,* E. S. Gilmore; *The Christ Hospital,* Cincinnati, O., *Superintendent,* Miss Alice Thatcher; *Saint Luke's Hospital of the Methodist Episcopal Church,* Cleveland, O., *Superintendent,* C. B. Hildreth; *Bethel Hospital,* Colorado Springs, Colo., *Superintendent,* Walter Merritt; *Iowa Methodist Hospital,* Des Moines, Ia., *President,* E. D. Sampson; *The Methodist Episcopal Hospital of Indiana,* Indianapolis, Ind.; *Bethany Methodist Hospital,* Kansas City, Kan., *Superintendent,* J. A. Motter; *Memorial Methodist Hospital and Training School for Nurses,* Mattoon, Ill., *Superintendent,* Delphine Pearson; *Asbury Hospital,* Minneapolis, Minn., *Superintendent,* Mrs. S. H. Knight; *Nebraska Methodist Episcopal Hospital,* Omaha, Neb., *Superintendent,* Allie P. McLaughlin; *Oklahoma Methodist Episcopal Hospital and Training School,* Guthrie, Okla.; *Methodist Episcopal Hospital,* Philadelphia, Pa., *Corresponding Secretary,* Rev. J. D. Martin; *Sibley Memorial Hospital,* Washington, D. C., *Acting Superintendent,* Miss Frances W. Moore; *National Methodist Sanatorium for Tuberculosis,* Silver City, New Mexico, *Manager,* Rev. M. O. Stockland; *Meth-*

odist State Hospital of Southern California, 2826 South Hope Street, Los Angeles, Cal., *Superintendent,* Charlotte Armstrong; *Hospital of the Good Shepherd,* Syracuse, N. Y.

Homes for the Aged

Home for the Aged of the Methodist Episcopal Church, Baltimore, Md., *Corresponding Secretary,* Mrs. William M. Winks; *The Blocher Homes,* Williamsville, N. Y., *Secretary,* Mr. Percival M. White; *The Methodist Home for the Aged,* Brooklyn, N. Y., *Corresponding Secretary,* Mrs. Franklin Bennett; *The Home for the Aged and Infirm,* Camden, N. J., *Corresponding Secretary,* Mrs. Ida B. Cooper; *Methodist Episcopal Old People's Home,* Chicago, Ill., *Superintendent,* Mr. W. A. Philips; *The Methodist Home for the Aged,* College Hill, Cincinnati, O., *Superintendent,* Mrs. Florence P. Good; *Crowell Memorial Home,* Blair, Neb., *Superintendent,* William Esplin; *The Old Ladies' Home,* Elyria, O., *Superintendent,* R. M. Yoder; *The Methodist Episcopal Home for the Aged,* 63 Clark Avenue, Ocean Grove, N. J., *President,* Mrs. John H. Parker; *Methodist Episcopal Home for the Aged,* Philadelphia, Pa., *Corresponding Secretary,* Mrs. W. H. Hickman; *Old People's Home,* Saint Louis German Conference, Quincy, Ill., *Superintendent,* W. C. Schultz; *The Methodist Episcopal Church Home in the City of New York,* Corresponding *Secretary,* Mrs. Alexander Carmichel; *Methodist Episcopal Memorial Home for the Aged,* Warren, Ind., *Corresponding Secretary and Superintendent,* Rev. E. L. Jones; *The Methodist Home for the Aged,* Washington, D. C., *Corresponding Secretary,* Mrs. Howell Bartle; *Methodist Episcopal Home for the Aged,* Topeka, Kan., *Matron,* Miss Dona E. Cooley; *Methodist Home,* Chelsea, Mich., *Corresponding Secretary,* Rev. J. E. Jacklin; *Frances Campbell Hamilton Memorial Methodist Episcopal Church Home for Aged,* Dravosburg, Pa., *Superintendent,* Delbert L. Johnson; *Home for Aged Methodist Women,* Concord, Mass., *Superintendent,* Nettie B. Hathorn; *Swedish Bethany Home for the Aged,* Chicago, Ill., *President,* Alfred Anderson.

Children's Institutions

Methodist Children's Home Association of Ohio, Worthington, O., *Secretary,* Rev. F. I. Johnson, Conneaut, O.; *Kelso Home,* Baltimore, Md., *Secretary,* W. A. Leitch; *The Elizabeth A. Bradley Children's Home,* Hulton, Pa., *Superintendent,* Mrs. George Eyster; *Orphans and Children's Home, Southern Illinois Conference,* Creal Springs, Williamson Co., Ill., *Superintendent,* Dan. W. Hopkins; *The Watts de Peyster Home and School for*

Girls, Tivoli, N. Y., *Superintendent,* Miss F. C. Boddington; *Central Wesleyan Orphan Asylum,* Warrenton, Mo., *Superintendent,* Rev. F. H. Wippermann; *Fred Finch Orphanage,* Oakland, Cal.; *McKinley Orphanage,* San Francisco, Cal., *Matron,* Mrs. L. R. Courneen; *Saint Christopher's Home,* Dobbs Ferry, N. Y., *Superintendent,* Burdette B. Brown; *German Methodist Orphan Asylum,* Berea, O., *Superintendent,* Geo. Kaletsch; *Methodist Deaconess Orphanage,* Lake Bluff, Ill., *Superintendent,* Lucy J. Judson; *Five Points Mission,* New York City, *Superintendent,* Rev. F. J. Belcher, 129 Worth Street, New York City.

Children's Homes. Methodist Institutions for Homeless and Destitute Children; Number of Institutions, 33; as reported by Burdette B. Brown, Secretary of the Methodist Child's Welfare Society and Superintendent of Saint Christopher's Home. *The Methodist Child Welfare Society,* General Secretary, Burdette B. Brown.

Official Periodicals

Methodist Review (bi-monthly), New York City, Editor, Rev. W. V. Kelley.

English (weekly)

California Christian Advocate, San Francisco, Cal., Editor, Rev. F. M. Larkin; *Central Christian Advocate,* Kansas City, Mo., Editor, Rev. C. B. Spencer; *Christian Advocate,* New York City, Editor, James R. Joy; *Epworth Herald,* Chicago, Ill., Editor, Dan. B. Brummitt; *Methodist Advocate-Journal,* Athens, Tenn., Editor, J. M. Melear; *Northwestern Christian Advocate,* Chicago, Ill., Editor, Rev. E. Robb Zaring; *Pacific Christian Advocate,* Portland, Ore., Editor, Robert H. Hughes; *Pittsburgh Christian Advocate,* Pittsburgh, Pa., Editor, Rev. J. J. Wallace; *Southwestern Christian Advocate,* New Orleans, La., Editor, Rev. Robert E. Jones; *Western Christian Advocate,* Cincinnati, O., Editor, Rev. Ernest C. Wareing.

German

Christliche Apologete (weekly), Cincinnati, O., Editor, Rev. A. J. Nast; *Haus und Herd* (monthly), Cincinnati, O., Editor, Rev. A. J. Bucher; *Glocke* (semi-monthly), Cincinnati, O., Editor, Rev. A. J. Bucher.

Semiofficial and Unofficial (weekly)

Kristelige Talsmand, (Norwegian), Chicago, Ill., Editor, Rev. C. A. Anderson; *Christian Standard and Guide to Holiness,* Upland, Ind., Editor, Rev. E. S. Dunham; *Christian Witness and Advocate of Bible Holiness,* Chicago, Ill.; *Hyrde-Stemmen,*

Chicago, Ill., Editor, Rev. C. A. Anderson; *La Fiaccola,* New York City, Editor, Rev. F. M. Petacci; *Michigan Christian Advocate,* Detroit, Mich., Editor, Rev. J. H. Potts; *Sandebudet* (Swedish), Chicago, Ill., Editor, J. M. Hillberg; *Methodist,* Baltimore, Md. (under the auspices of the Baltimore and Wilmington Annual Conferences); *Vestra Sandebudet* (Swedish), San Francisco, Cal., Editor, A. E. Lind; *Vidnesbyrdet,* Seattle, Wash., Editor, O. O. Twede; *Zion's Herald,* Boston, Mass., Editor, Rev. Charles Parkhurst; *Wisconsin Christian Advocate,* Milwaukee, Wis., Editor, A. J. Benjamin.

METHODIST EPISCOPAL CHURCH, SOUTH

General Conference, quadrennial; next session in 1918. There are 39 Annual Conferences.

Bishops

Eugene Russell Hendrix, Kansas City, Mo.
Joseph Staunton Key (retired), Sherman, Tex.
Henry Clay Morrison, Leesburg, Fla.
Warren Akin Candler, Atlanta, Ga.
Elijah Embree Hoss, Nashville, Tenn.
James Atkins, Waynesville, N. C.
Collins Denny, Richmond, Va.
John Carlisle Kilgo, Charlotte, N. C.
Walter Russell Lambuth, Nashville, Tenn.
William Belton Murrah, Memphis, Tenn.
Richard Green Waterhouse, Los Angeles, Cal.
James Henry McCoy, Birmingham, Ala.
Edwin DuBose Mouzon, Dallas, Tex.

Board of Missions, 810 Broadway, Nashville, Tenn. *Secretary,* Rev. W. W. Pinson; *Secretary Foreign Department,* Rev. Ed F. Cook; *Secretary Foreign Department* (for women), Miss Mabel Head; *Secretary Home Department,* Rev. John M. Moore; *Secretary Home Department (for women),* Mrs. R. W. Mac-Donnell; *Educational Secretary,* Rev. E. H. Rawlings; *Educational Secretary* (for women), Mrs. Hume R. Steele; *Home Base Secretary,* Mrs. B. W. Lipscomb; *Treasurers,* J. D. Hamilton and Mrs. F. H. Ross.

Board of Church Extension, Louisville, Ky. *Secretary,* Rev. W. F. McMurry.

Board of Education, Nashville, Tenn. *Secretary,* Rev. Stonewall Anderson.

Epworth League, Nashville, Tenn. *Secretary,* Rev. F. S. Parker.

Sunday School Board, Nashville, Tenn. *Corresponding Secretary,* Rev. C. D. Bulla.

Laymen's Missionary Movement, Nashville, Tenn. *Secretaries,* Rev. E. H. Rawlings, and Mr. A. C. Tippens.

Department of Ministerial Supply and Training, Atlanta, Ga. *Secretary,* Rev. R. H. Bennett.

Superannuate Fund, *Agent,* Rev. John R. Stewart, Nashville, Tenn.

Publishing House, Nashville, Tenn. *Publishing Agents,* D. M. Smith and Rev. A. J. Lamar.

Sunday School Board, Nashville, Tenn. *Sunday School Editor,* Rev. E. B. Chappell. *Superintendent Sunday School Training Work,* Rev. J. W. Shackford; *Primary Assistant,* Miss Minnie Kennedy; *Superintendent Southern Methodist Assembly,* Rev. James Cannon, Waynesville, N. C.

Colleges

Institution	Location	President
Athens College	Athens, Ala	B. B. Glasgow.
Birmingham College	Birmingham, Ala	T. Haynes.
Carolina College	Maxton, N. C	S. E. Mercer.
Centenary College of Louisiana	Shreveport, La	R. H. Wynn.
Centenary Female College	Cleveland, Tenn	Barney Thompson.
Central College	Fayette, Mo	P. H. Linn.
Columbia College	Columbia, S. C	G. T. Pugh.
Emory College	Oxford, Ga	James E. Dickey.
Emory and Henry College	Emory, Va	C. C. Weaver.
Emory University	Atlanta, Ga	W. A. Candler.
Galloway College	Searcy, Ark	J. M. Williams.
Greensboro College for Women	Greensboro, N. C	S. B. Turrentine.
Grenada College	Grenada, Miss	J. R. Countiss.
Henderson-Brown College	Arkadelphia, Ark	J. M. Workman.
Hendrix College	Conway, Ark	John H. Reynolds.
Kentucky Wesleyan College	Winchester, Ky	J. L. Clark.
Lagrange College	Lagrange, Ga	Miss Daisy Davies.
Lander College	Greenwood, S. C	John O. Willson.
Martha Washington College	Abingdon, Va	S. D. Long.
Millsaps College	Jackson, Miss	A. F. Watkins.
Port Gibson Female College	Port Gibson, Miss	T. J. O'Neil.
Randolph-Macon College	Ashland, Va	R. E. Blackwell.
Randolph-Macon Woman's College	Lynchburg, Va	William A. Webb.
Southern College	Sutherland, Fla	R. H. Alderman.
Southern Methodist University	Dallas, Tex	R. S. Hyer.
Southern University	Greensboro, Ala	C. A. Rush.
Southwestern University	Georgetown, Tex	C. M. Bishop.
Texas Woman's College	Fort Worth, Tex	H. A. Boaz.
Trinity College	Durham, N. C	W. P. Few.
Wesleyan College	Macon, Ga	C. R. Jenkins.
Whitworth College	Brookhaven, Miss	I. W. Cooper.
Wofford College	Spartanburg, S. C	H. N. Snyder.
Woman's College of Alabama	Montgomery, Ala	M. W. Swartz.

For list of ministers with addresses see Minutes of the

Annual Conferences, published at the Southern Methodist Publishing House, Nashville, Tenn.

Hospitals

Barnes Hospital, St. Louis, Mo.; *Galloway Memorial Hospital,* Nashville, Tenn.; *Wesley Memorial Hospital,* Atlanta, Ga.; *Methodist Hospital,* Memphis, Tenn.

Orphanages

Alabama Methodist Orphanage, Selma, Ala., *Superintendent,* J. C. Craig; *Arkansas Methodist Orphanage,* Little Rock, Ark., *Matron,* Mrs. M. L. Donner; *Holston Industrial School and Home,* Greenville, Tenn.; *Louisiana Methodist Orphans' Home,* Ruston, La., *Superintendent,* Robert W. Vaughan; *Methodist Orphanage,* Jackson, Miss., *Manager,* M. L. Burton; *Methodist Orphanage,* Waco, Tex., *Superintendent,* R. A. Burroughs; *North Georgia Conference Orphans' Home,* Decatur, Ga., *Agent and Superintendent,* J. M. Hawkins; *South Georgia Conference Orphans' Home,* Macon, Ga., *Agent,* J. A. Smith; *Methodist Orphanage,* Raleigh, N. C., *Superintendent,* John N. Cole; *Virginia Conference Orphanage,* Richmond, Va., *President,* W. H. Vincent, Capron, Va.; *Epworth Orphanage,* Columbia, S. C., *Superintendent,* W. B. Wharton; *Children's Home,* Winston-Salem, N. C., *Superintendent,* Walter Thompson; *President of Board of Trustees,* T. F. Marr, Charlotte, N. C.; *Methodist Orphans' Home Association,* St. Louis, Mo., *President,* Mrs. J. J. O'Fallon.

Periodicals

Christian Advocate, Nashville, Tenn., Editor, Rev. Thomas N. Ivey; *Methodist Quarterly Review,* Nashville, Tenn., Editor, Rev. H. M. DuBose; *Epworth Era,* Nashville, Tenn., Editor, Rev. F. S. Parker; *Missionary Voice,* Nashville, Tenn., Managing Editor, R. B. Eleazer; *Alabama Christian Advocate,* Birmingham, Ala., Editor, Rev. L. C. Branscomb; *Baltimore-Richmond Christian Advocate,* Richmond, Va., Editor, Rev. James Cannon, Jr.; *Baltimore Southern Methodist,* Baltimore, Md., Editor, Rev. Carlton D. Harris; *Central Methodist,* Lexington, Ky., Editor, Rev. W. A. Swift; *Missions Freund,* San Antonio, Tex., Editor, Rev. John A. G. Rabe; *Florida Christian Advocate,* Lakeland, Fla., Editor, Rev. J. Edgar Wilson; *Methodist Advocate,* Sutton, W. Va., Editors, John A. Grose and Rev. W. I. Canter; *Midland Methodist,* Nashville, Tenn., Editor, Rev. J. A. Burrow; *New Orleans Christian Advocate,* New Orleans, La., Editor, Rev. R. A. Meek; *North Carolina Christian Advocate,* Greensboro, N.

C., Editor, Rev. Hugh M. Blair; *Pacific Methodist Advocate,* San Francisco, Cal., Editor, Rev. W. E. Vaughan; *Raleigh Christian Advocate,* Raleigh, N. C., Editor, Rev. L. S. Massey; *St. Louis Christian Advocate,* St. Louis, Mo., Editor, Rev. C. C. Woods; *Southern Christian Advocate,* Greenville, S. C., Editor, Rev. W. C. Kirkland; *Texas Christian Advocate,* Dallas, Tex., Editor, Rev. W. D. Bradfield; *Wesleyan Christian Advocate,* Atlanta, Ga., Editor, Rev. W. C. Lovett; *Western Methodist,* Little Rock, Ark., Editor, Rev. A. C. Miller.

AFRICAN METHODIST EPISCOPAL CHURCH

General Conference, quadrennial; next session meets in May, 1920 (place not yet selected).

Bishops

Benjamin Tucker Tanner (retired), 2908 Diamond Street, Philadelphia, Pa.

Benjamin Franklin Lee, Wilberforce, O.

Evans Tyree, 15 North Hill Street, Nashville, Tenn.

Charles Spencer Smith, 35 East Alexandrine Avenue, Detroit, Mich.

Cornelius Thaddeus Shaffer, 3742 Forest Avenue, Chicago, Ill.

Levi Jenkins Coppin, 1913 Bainbridge Street, Philadelphia, Pa.

Henry Blanton Parks, 3312 Calumet Street, Chicago, Ill.

Joseph Simeon Flipper, 401 Houston Street, Atlanta, Ga.

J. Albert Johnson, 1412 North Eighteenth Street, Philadelphia, Pa.

William Henry Heard, 1426 Rockland Street, Philadelphia, Pa.

John Hurst, 1808 McCulloh Street, Baltimore, Md.

William D. Chappelle, 1208 Harden Street, Columbia, S. C.

Joshua H. Jones, Wilberforce, O.

James M. Connor, 1519 Pulaski Street, Little Rock, Ark.

William W. Beckett, 2 Hanover Street, Cape Town, South Africa. American address, 378 Cumberland Street, Brooklyn, N. Y.

Isaac N. Ross, Sierra Leone, West Africa; American address, 1413 Seventeenth Street, N. W., Washington, D. C.

Board of Missions, 61 Bible House, New York City. *Secretary,* J. W. Rankin.

Board of Education, Waco, Tex. *Secretary,* A. S. Jackson.

Society of Church Extension, 1535 Fourteenth Street, N. W., Washington, D. C. *Secretary,* B. F. Watson.

Sunday School Union, Cor. Eighth and Lea Avenues, Nashville, Tenn. *Secretary,* Ira T. Bryant.

Allen Christian Endeavor League, Sunday School Union Building, Nashville, Tenn. *Secretary,* J. C. Caldwell.

Board of Finance, 1541 Fourteenth Street, N. W., Washington, D. C. *Secretary,* J. R. Hawkins.

Publication Board, African Methodist Episcopal Book Concern, 631 Pine Street, Philadelphia, Pa. *General Business Manager,* R. R. Wright, Jr.

Women's Parent Mite Missionary Society, Philadelphia, Pa. *President,* Mrs. Mary F. Handy, 1341 North Carey Street, Baltimore, Md.

Women's Home and Foreign Missionary Society, Charleston, S. C. *President,* Mrs. S. G. Simmons.

Colleges and Universities

Institution	Location	President
Allen University	Columbia, S. C.	R. W. Mounce
Campbell College	Jackson, Miss.	
Edward Waters College	Jacksonville, Fla.	J. A. Gregg
Kittrul College	Kittrul, N. C.	C. G. O'Kely.
Morris Brown College	Atlanta, Ga.	W. A. Fountain.
Payne University	Selma, Ala.	H. E. Archer
Paul Quinn College	Waco, Tex.	J. K. Williams.
Shorter College	Argenta, Ark.	William Byrd.
Turner College	Nashville, Tenn.	J. A. Jones.
Western University	Quindaro, Kan.	H. T. Kealing.
Wilberforce University	Wilberforce, O.	W. S. Scarborough

For list of ministers with addresses see the Minutes of the several Annual Conferences.

Periodicals

Christian Recorder (weekly), Philadelphia, Pa., Editor, R. R. Wright, Jr.; *African Methodist Episcopal Review,* Philadelphia, Pa., Editor, R. C. Ranson; *Southern Christian Recorder,* Columbus, Ga., Editor, G. W. Allen; *Western Christian Recorder,* Kansas City, Mo., Editor, J. Frank McDonald; *Voice of Missions,* New York City, Editor, J. W. Rankin; *The Allenite,* Nashville, Tenn., Editor, J. C. Caldwell; *Woman's Christian Recorder,* Columbia, S. C., Editress, Mrs. R. C. Chapel.

AFRICAN METHODIST EPISCOPAL ZION CHURCH

General Conference, quadrennial; next session in May, 1920.

Bishops

J. W. Hood (retired), 445 Ramsey Street, Fayetteville, N. C.
C. R. Harris (retired), 302 Monroe Street, Salisbury, N. C.
G. W. Clinton, 415 North Myers Street, Charlotte, N. C.
J. W. Alstork, 231 Cleveland Avenue, Montgomery, Ala.
J. S. Caldwell, 420 South Eleventh Street, Philadelphia, Pa.
G. L. Blackwell, 420 South Eleventh Street, Philadelphia, Pa.
A. J. Warner, 220 East Boundary Street, Charlotte, N. C.
L. W. Kyles, 4301 West Bell Place, St. Louis, Mo.
R. B. Bruce, 203 South Brevard Street, Charlotte, N. C.
W. L. Lee, 338 Bridge Street, Brooklyn, N. Y.
G. C. Clement, 1425 West Walnut Street, Louisville, Ky.

Church Extension, 420 South Eleventh Street, Philadelphia, Pa. *President,* Bishop W. L. Lee; *Corresponding Secretary,* J. C. Dancy.

Education, 613 North Garrison Avenue, St. Louis, Mo. *President,* Bishop G. L. Blackwell; *Corresponding Secretary,* J. W. Martin.

Finance, 420 South Eleventh Street, Philadelphia, Pa. *President,* Bishop J. S. Caldwell; *Financial Secretary,* Rev. W. H. Goler.

Foreign Missions, 1046 Traub Avenue, Indianapolis, Ind. *President,* Bishop A. Walters;* *Corresponding Secretary,* J. W. Wood.

Women's Home and Foreign Missionary Society, 624 South Sixteenth Street, Philadelphia, Pa. *President,* Mrs. Florence Randolph; *Corresponding Secretary,* Mrs. A. W. Blackwell.

Publication, Charlotte, N. C. *President,* Bishop G. W. Clinton; *Manager,* J. W. Crockett.

Superannuated Ministers, Widows, and Orphans, 420 South Eleventh Street, Philadelphia, Pa. *President,* Bishop A. J. Warner; *Corresponding Secretary,* Rev. C. S. Whitted.

Sunday School Union, Charlotte, N. C. *President,* Bishop R. B. Bruce; *Corresponding Secretary,* J. W. Eichelberger, Jr.

Ministerial Brotherhood, New Haven, Conn. *President,* Bishop L. W. Kyles; *Corresponding Secretary,* Rev. C. S. Whitted.

Evangelism, Louisville, Ky. *President,* Bishop G. C. Clement; *Secretary,* Dr. E. L. Watkins.

Varick Christian Endeavor Union, Pensacola, Fla. *President,* Rev. J. W. Brown; *Corresponding Secretary,* Aaron Brown.

Legion of Financiers. *President,* Rev. W. D. Clinton; *Secretary,* Rev. J. J. Smyer.

*Deceased.

Schools and Colleges

Institution	Location	President
Atkinson College	Madisonville, Ky	J. W. Muir.
Clinton College	Rock Hill, S. C	R. J. Boulware.
Dinwiddie A and I School	Dinwiddie, Va	W. E. Woodyard.
Eastern North Carolina High School	Newbern, N. C	W. M. Sutton.
Edenton Normal and Industrial School	Edenton, N. C	W. F. Gaines.
Greenville College	Greenville, Tenn	E. P. Mayo.
Lancaster High School	Lancaster, S. C	M. D. Lee.
Livingstone College	Salisbury, N. C	W. H. Goler.
Lomax-Hannon High School	Greenville, Ala	J. W. Wingfield.
Macon Industrial School	Macon, Ga	B. J. Bridges.

For list of ministers with addresses see the Minutes of the several Annual Conferences.

Institution. *Harriet Tubman Home,* Auburn, N. Y. *President,* Bishop G. L. Blackwell; *Superintendent,* Rev. P. K. Fonvielle.

Periodicals

Star of Zion (weekly), Charlotte, N. C., Editor, Rev. J. Harvey Anderson; *Western Star of Zion* (weekly), East St. Louis, Ill., Editor, Rev. T. W. Wallace; *Quarterly Review,* Charlotte, N. C., Editor, Rev. C. C. Alleyne; *Missionary Seer* (monthly), Indianapolis, Ind., Editor, Rev. J. W. Wood.

COLORED METHODIST EPISCOPAL CHURCH

General Conference, quadrennial; next session in May, 1918.

Secretary of the General Conference, Bishop N. C. Cleaves, 633 South Lauderdale Street, Memphis, Tenn.

There are a number of Annual Conferences.

Bishops

L. H. Holsey, 335 Auburn Avenue, Atlanta, Ga.

Isaac Lane, 422 Laconte Street, Jackson, Tenn.

R. S. Williams, 912 Fifteenth Street, Augusta, Ga.

E. Cottrell, Holly Springs, Miss.

C. H. Phillips, 123 Fourteenth Avenue, Nashville, Tenn.

M. F. Jamison, Leigh, Tex.

R. A. Carter, 37 Howell Street, Atlanta, Ga.

N. C. Cleaves, 633 South Lauderdale Street, Memphis, Tenn.

Board of Missions. *Secretary,* Rev. J. H. Moore, Holly Springs, Miss.

Board of Education. *Secretary,* Rev. J. A. Bray, Birmingham, Ala.

Board of Church Extension. *Secretary,* Rev. R. R. Stout, Pine Bluff, Ark.

Epworth League. *General Secretary,* Rev. A. R. Calhoun, Pine Bluff, Ark.

Board of Publication. *Agent,* Rev. J. C. Martin, 109 Shannon Street, Jackson, Tenn.

Superintendent of African Missions, Rev. J. W. Gilbert, Augusta, Ga.

Colleges

Institution	Location	President
Arkansas Industrial College	Pine Bluff, Ark	C. C. Neal.
Homer College	Homer, La	A. M. D. Langrum.
Lane College	Jackson, Tenn	J. F. Lane.
Miles Memorial College	Birmingham, Ala	G. A. Payne.
Mississippi Industrial College	Holly Springs, Miss	F. H. Rodgers.
Paine College	Augusta, Ga.	
Texas College	Tyler, Tex	——— Banks.

For list of ministers with addresses see Minutes of the several Annual Conferences.

Periodicals

Christian Index (weekly), Jackson, Tenn., Editor, J. A. Hamlett; *Western Index* (weekly), Fort Worth, Tex., Editor, J. R. Starks; *North Carolina Index* (weekly), Pittsboro, N. C., Editor, J. C. Stanton.

METHODIST PROTESTANT CHURCH

General Conference, quadrennial; next meeting in May, 1920.

There are 29 Annual Conferences and 11 Mission Conferences.

Officers: *President,* Rev. Lyman E. Davis, 219 Federal Street, Pittsburgh, Pa.; *Secretary,* Rev. Charles H. Beck, West Lafayette, O.

Board of Foreign Missions, Baltimore, Md. *President,* Rev. Lyman E. Davis, Pittsburgh, Pa.; *Secretary,* Rev. F. C. Klein, Baltimore, Md.

Board of Home Missions, Pittsburgh, Pa. *President,* Rev. Lyman E. Davis; *Secretary,* Rev. Charles H. Beck, West Lafayette, O.

Board of Ministerial Education, Pittsburgh, Pa. *Secretary-Treasurer,* Rev. George R. Brown, Westminster, Md.

Board of Publication. *Agents,* Charles Reiner, Jr., 316 North

Charles Street, Baltimore, Md., and F. W. Pierpont, 219 Sixth Street, Pittsburgh, Pa.

Board of Young People's Work, Pittsburgh, Pa. *President,* Rev. J. W. Haddaway, 2504 Garrison Avenue, Baltimore, Md.; *Secretary,* Rev. H. L. Feeman, Westminster, Md.

Woman's Board of Foreign Missions, Kansas City, Kan. *Corresponding Secretary,* Mrs. D. S. Stevens, Kansas City, Kan.

Colleges and Theological Seminary

Institution	Location	President
Adrian College	Adrian, Mich	A. F. Hess.
Kansas City University	Kansas City, Kan	J. H. Lucas.
West Lafayette College	West Lafayette, O	A. G. Steel.
Western Maryland College	Westminster, Md	T. H. Lewis.
Westminster College	Tehuacana, Tex	J. C. Williams.
Westminster Theological Seminary	Westminster, Md	H. L. Elderdice.

For list of ministers see Minutes of the various Annual Conferences.

Charitable Institutions

Orphans' Home, High Point, N. C., *Manager,* H. A. Garrett; *Aged People's Home,* Westminster, Md., *President,* Mr. O. E. Grimes; *Secretary,* Rev. F. T. Tagg.

Periodicals

Methodist Protestant, Baltimore, Md., Editor, Rev. Frank T. Benson; *Methodist Recorder,* Pittsburgh, Pa., Editor, Rev. Lyman E. Davis.

MORAVIAN CHURCH

There are two coordinate Provinces of the Unity in America: the Northern, with a Provincial Synod meeting every five years; the Southern, with a Provincial Synod meeting every three years.

Bishops

Rt. Rev. Clement Hoyler, 9857 Eighty-fourth Avenue, Edmonton, Alberta, Can.

Rt. Rev. Morris W. Leibert, 112 Lexington Avenue, New York City.

Rt. Rev. Charles L. Moench, Bethlehem, Pa.

Rt. Rev. Karl A. Mueller, Watertown, Wis.

Rt. Rev. Edmund Oerter (retired), Canal Dover, O.

Rt. Rev. Clement L. Reinke (retired), Gnadenhutten, O.

Rt. Rev. Edward Rondthaler, Winston-Salem, N. C.

The Provincial Elders' Conference (Executive Board) of the

Northern Province, 20 Church Street, Bethlehem, Pa. *President,* Bishop C. L. Moench; *Secretary,* John S. Romig; *Treasurer,* Rev. Paul de Schweinitz.

The Provincial Elders' Conference (Executive Board) of the Southern Province, Winston-Salem, N. C. *President,* Bishop Edward Rondthaler; *Secretary,* James E. Hall; *Treasurer,* E. H. Stockton.

Board of Church Extension, 20 Church Street, Bethlehem, Pa. *President,* Rev. Paul de Schweinitz; *Secretary,* Bishop C. L. Moench; *Treasurer,* Emil J. Bishop.

Society of the United Brethren for Propagating the Gospel among the Heathen, 20 Church Street, Bethlehem, Pa. *President,* Bishop C. L. Moench; *Secretary,* John S. Romig; *Vice-President and Treasurer,* Rev. Paul de Schweinitz.

Colleges and Seminaries

Institution	Location	President
Moravian College and Theological Seminary	Bethlehem, Pa	Augustus Schultze.
Moravian Seminary and College for Women	Bethlehem, Pa	J. H. Clewell.
Salem Academy and College for Women	Winston-Salem, N. C	H. E. Rondthaler.

For list of ministers with addresses see Appendix of the annual devotional manual called Daily Texts. The Moravian Book Store, 146 South Main Street, Bethlehem, Pa.

Charitable Institutions

Ephrata Missionary Home (Home for Retired Missionaries), Nazareth, Pa., *Curator,* F. H. Martin; *Widows' House* (Home for the Widows and Daughters of Ministers and Missionaries), *Superintendent,* F. E. Lennox, Bethlehem, Pa.; *Moravian Home for Aged Women,* Lititz, Pa.

Periodicals

The Moravian, Nazareth, Pa., Editor, C. D. Kreider; *The Little Missionary,* West New Brighton, Staten Island, N. Y., Editor, F. R. Nitzschke; *Der Brueder-Botschafter and Der Missionsfreund,* Watertown, Wis., Editor, Bishop Karl A. Mueller.

Presbyterians

Alliance of the Reformed Churches throughout the World holding the Presbyterian System.

Organized in London in 1875.

Churches connected with the Alliance number 106; members and adherents estimated at 30,000,000. Next meeting of the Alliance will be held in Pittsburgh, Pa., in September, 1917.

President, Rev. William Park, Belfast, Ireland; *General Secretary,* Rev. Robert Dykes Shaw; *American Secretary,* Rev. W. H. Roberts, Witherspoon Building, Philadelphia, Pa.

COUNCIL OF THE REFORMED CHURCHES IN AMERICA HOLDING THE PRESBYTERIAN SYSTEM

Embracing seven Churches, viz.: Presbyterian Church in the United States of America, Presbyterian Church in the United States, United Presbyterian Church, Cumberland Presbyterian Church, Associate Reformed Presbyterian Synod, Reformed Church in America, Reformed Church in the United States.

Last session of the Council was held in March, 1916.

President, Rev. George Alexander, New York City; *Stated Clerk,* Rev. W. H. Roberts, Witherspoon Building, Philadelphia, Pa.; *Treasurer,* Rev. D. F. McGill, 224 Ridge Avenue, Ben Avon, Pa.

PRESBYTERIAN CHURCH IN THE UNITED STATES OF AMERICA

(For other Presbyterian Bodies, not constituent members of the Federal Council, see Directory of other Religious Bodies, pages 146-149.)

General Assembly, annual, holds its next meeting in Dallas, Tex., May 17, 1917.

There are 40 synods; 291 presbyteries.

Officers of the General Assembly: *Moderator,* Rev. John A. Marquis, Cedar Rapids, Ia.; *Stated Clerk,* Rev. William Henry Roberts, 515 Witherspoon Building, Philadelphia, Pa.

Trustees of the General Assembly, 1319 Walnut Street, Philadelphia, Pa.; *President,* Mr. George Stevenson; *Corresponding Secretary,* Rev. Joseph W. Cochran; *Recording Secretary,* Mr. Edward R. Sterrett; *Treasurer,* The Philadelphia Trust Company, Philadelphia, Pa.

Board of Home Missions, 156 Fifth Avenue, New York City.

President, Rev. Wilton Merle-Smith; *Secretaries,* Rev. John Dixon, Mr. Joseph Ernest McAfee, Rev. B. P. Fullerton; *Treasurer,* Mr. Harvey C. Olin.

Board of Foreign Missions, 156 Fifth Avenue, New York City. *President,* Rev. George Alexander; *Corresponding Secretaries,* Mr. Robert E. Speer, Rev. Arthur J. Brown, Rev. A. W. Halsey, Rev. Stanley White; *Treasurer,* Mr. Dwight H. Day.

Board of Education, 1319 Walnut Street, Philadelphia, Pa. *President,* Rev. Charles Wadsworth, Jr.; *Secretary,* Rev. Joseph W. Cochran; *Secretary for University Work,* Rev. Richard C. Hughes; *Secretary for Candidates, Enlistment and College Visitation,* Rev. William H. Crothers; *Treasurer and Recording Secretary,* Mr. Edward R. Sterrett.

Board of Publication and Sabbath School Work, Witherspoon Building, 1319 Walnut Street, Philadelphia, Pa. *President,* Mr. William H. Scott; *Secretary,* Rev. Alexander Henry; *Business Superintendent and Treasurer,* Mr. F. M. Braselmann; *Superintendent of Depositories,* Mr. Walter S. Lewis; *Editor,* Rev. John T. Faris; *Secretary of Religious Education,* Rev. R. W. Veach; *Superintendent of Missions,* John M. Somerndike; *Manufacturer,* Mr. Henry F. Scheetz; *Assistant Treasurer,* Marshall S. Collingwood.

Board of Church Erection, 156 Fifth Avenue, New York City. *President,* Rev. Newell W. Wells; *Corresponding Secretary,* Rev. David G. Wylie; *Field Secretary,* Rev. Jesse C. Bruce; *Treasurer,* Rev. George R. Brauer.

Board of Ministerial Relief and Sustentation, 423-429 Witherspoon Building, 1319 Walnut Street, Philadelphia, Pa. *President,* Rev. John R. Davies; *General Secretary,* Rev. William H. Foulkes; *Associate Secretaries,* Rev. John R. Sutherland, Rev. Wm. S. Holt; *Treasurer and Recording Secretary,* Rev. William W. Heberton.

Board of Missions for Freedmen, 515 Bessemer Building, Sixth Street, Pittsburgh, Pa. *President,* Rev. Samuel J. Fisher; *Corresponding Secretary and Treasurer,* Rev. E. P. Cowan; *Associate Secretary,* Rev. John M. Gaston.

College Board, 156 Fifth Avenue, New York City. *President,* Rev. Edwin A. McAlpin, Jr.; *Secretary,* Rev. Robert Mackenzie; *Associate Secretaries,* Rev. J. E. Clarke, Rev. C. H. French; *Treasurer,* Mr. Henry L. Smith.

Board of Temperance, Columbia National Bank Building, Pittsburgh, Pa. *President,* Rev. Thomas Watters; *General Secretary,* Prof. Charles Scanlon; *Treasurer,* Mr. J. R. Park.

Permanent Committee on Vacancy and Supply. *Chairman,*

Rev. George N. Luccock, Oak Park, Ill.; *Secretary,* Rev. Walter H. Houston, Commercial Building, Columbus, O.

Permanent Committee on Evangelism, 612 Witherspoon Building, Philadelphia, Pa. *Chairman,* Mr. Charles L. Huston; *Corresponding Secretary,* Rev. George G. Mahy.

Brotherhood of the Presbyterian Church. *Chairman of the Assembly's Permanent Committee,* Rev. William F. Weir, Wooster, O.

Woman's Board of Home Missions. Organized, 1879; incorporated, 1915. *President,* Mrs. F. S. Bennett; *Secretary,* Miss Edith G. Long; *Treasurer,* Miss Edna R. Voss, 156 Fifth Avenue, New York City.

This organization has charge of the mission school work and medical missions among Alaskans, Indians, Mexicans, Mormons, Mountaineers of the South, Cubans, Porto Ricans.

Woman's Foreign Missionary Society of the Presbyterian Church. *President,* Miss Margaret E. Hodge; *Treasurer,* Miss Sarah W. Cattell, 501 Witherspoon Building, 1319 Walnut Street, Philadelphia, Pa.

Woman's Presbyterian Board of Missions of the Northwest. *President,* Mrs. Oliver R. Williamson; *Treasurer,* Mrs. Thomas E. D. Bradley, 509 South Wabash Avenue, Chicago, Ill.

Women's Board of Foreign Missions of the Presbyterian Church. *President,* Miss Alice M. Davison; *Treasurer,* Mrs. Joshua A. Hatfield, Room 818, 156 Fifth Avenue, New York City.

Woman's Presbyterian Board of Foreign Missions of the Southwest. *President,* Mrs. W. H. Bissland; *Treasurer,* Mrs. William Burg, Room 707, 816 Olive Street, St. Louis, Mo.

Woman's North Pacific Presbyterian Board of Foreign Missions. *President,* Mrs. John W. Goss; *Treasurer,* Mrs. C. M. Barbee, 454 Alder Street, Portland, Ore.

Woman's Occidental Board of Foreign Missions. *President,* Mrs. H. B. Pinney; *Treasurer,* Mrs. E. G. Denniston, 920 Sacramento Street, San Francisco, Cal.

Colleges and Universities

Institution	Location	President or Dean
Albany College	Albany, Ore	Wallace H. Lee.
Albert Lea College	Albert Lea, Minn	Gertrude S. Kingsland.
Alma College	Alma, Mich	H. M. Crooks.
Arkansas Cumberland College	Clarksville, Ark	L. J. Spence.
Bellevue College	Bellevue, Neb	David R. Kerr.
Biddle University	Charlotte, N. C	H. L. McCrorey.
Blackburn College	Carlinville, Ill	William M. Hudson.
Bloomfield Seminary (College Dept.)	Bloomfield, N. J	D. R. Fraser (acting).
Buena Vista College	Storm Lake, Ia	R. D. Echlin.
Carroll College	Waukesha, Wis	Wilbur O. Carrier.

Institution	Location	President or Dean
Central University of Kentucky	Danville, Ky	W. A. Ganfield.
Coe College	Cedar Rapids, Ia	John A. Marquis.
Cumberland University	Lebanon, Tenn	H. A. Hill (acting).
Davis and Elkins College	Elkins, W. Va	James E. Allen.
Dubuque German College and Seminary	Dubuque, Ia	C. M. Steffens.
Elmira College	Elmira, N. Y	J. Balcom Shaw.
Emporia, College of	Emporia, Kan	Henry C. Culbertson.
Geneseo Collegiate Institute	Geneseo, Ill	N. W. Thornton.
Grove City College	Grove City, Pa	Weir C. Ketler.
Hamilton College*	Clinton, N. Y	M. W. Stryker.
Hanover College	Hanover, Ind	William A. Millis.
Hastings College	Hastings, Neb	R. B. Crone.
Henry Kendall College	Tulsa, Okla	Charles Evans.
Highland College	Highland, Kan	W. Gilbert James (acting)
Highland Park College	Des Moines, Ia	George P. Magill.
Huron College	Huron, S. D	H. M. Gage.
Idaho, College of	Caldwell, Ida	W. J. Boone.
Illinois College	Jacksonville, Ill	C. H. Rammelkamp.
James Milliken University	Decatur, Ill	A. R. Taylor, *Emer.*
Jamestown College	Jamestown, N. D	B. H. Kroeze.
Kentucky College for Women	Danville, Ky	M. M. Allen.
Lafayette College	Easton, Pa	John H. MacCracken.
Lake Forest College	Lake Forest, Ia	John S. Nollen.
Lenox College	Hopkinton, Ia	A. S. Mackenzie
Lincoln College	Lincoln, Ill	J. H. McMurray.
Lincoln University	Lincoln University, Pa	John B. Rendall.
Lindenwood College	St. Charles, Mo	John L. Roemer.
Macalester College	St. Paul, Minn	T. M. Hodgman.
Maryville College	Maryville, Tenn	S. T. Wilson.
Missouri Valley College	Marshall, Mo	W. H. Black.
Montana, College of	Deer Lodge, Mont	Harris Pillsbury.
New York University	New York City	Elmer E. Brown.
Oswego College	Oswego, Kan	I. F. Mather.
Occidental College	Los Angeles, Cal	
Park College	Parkville, Mo	F. W. Hawley.
Parsons College	Fairfield, Ia	
Pikeville College	Pikeville, Ky	J. F. Record.
Princeton University*	Princeton, N. J	John G. Hibben.
Stanley McCormick School	Burnsville, N. C	T. U. Cheesebrough.
Texas Fairemont Seminary	Weatherford, Tex	J. L. McKee.
Trinity University	Waxahachie, Tex	Samuel L. Hornbeak.
Tusculum College	Greenville, Tenn	C. O. Gray.
Wabash College	Crawfordsville, Ind	G. L. Mackintosh.
Washington and Jefferson College	Washington, Pa	Frederick W. Hinitt.
Waynesburg College	Waynesburg, Pa	H. P. Houghton.
Western College for Women	Oxford, O	William W. Boyd.
Westminster College	Denver, Colo	W. A. Philips
Westminster College	Fulton, Mo	E. E. Reed.
Westminster College	Salt Lake City, Utah	H. W. Reherd.
Whitworth College	Spokane, Wash	D. D. McKay.
Wilson College for Women	Chambersburg, Pa	E. D. Warfield.
Wooster, College of	Wooster, O	J. Campbell White.

* Has had historical connection with Presbyterianism.

Theological Seminaries

The twelve following Seminaries report a total of 87 professors, with 42 instructors, lecturers, etc. Their students in 1916 numbered 840, of whom 192 graduated. Their libraries contain 324,-709 volumes, their total assets amount to $12,678,538; income, $546,487; disbursements, $698,102, including $120,665 for permanent equipment.

Institution	Location	President
Auburn Theological Seminary	Auburn, N. Y.	George B. Stewart.
Biddle University, Theological Dept.	Charlotte, N. C.	H. L. McCrorey.
Bloomfield Theological Seminary	Bloomfield, N. J.	David R. Fraser.
Dubuque German College and Seminary	Dubuque, Ia.	Cornelius M. Steffens.
Lane Theological Seminary	Walnut Hills, Cincinnati, O.	William McKibbin.
Lincoln University, Theological Dept.	Lincoln University, Pa.	John B. Rendall.
McCormick Theological Seminary	Chicago, Ill.	James G. K. McClure.
Presbyterian Theological Seminary	Omaha, Neb.	A. B. Marshall.
Princeton Theological Seminary	Princeton, N. J.	J. Ross Stevenson.
San Francisco Theological Seminary	San Anselmo, Cal.	Warren H. Landon.
Theological Seminary of Kentucky	Louisville, Ky.	Charles R. Hemphill.
Western Theological Seminary	Pittsburgh, Pa.	James A. Kelso.

A list of ministers and addresses will be found in the Minutes of the General Assembly, published by the Stated Clerk of the General Assembly, Witherspoon Building, 1319 Walnut Street, Philadelphia, Pa.

Hospitals

Presbyterian Hospital, Madison Avenue and Seventieth Street, New York City, *President,* Frederick Sturges; *Presbyterian Hospital,* Thirty-ninth and Filbert Street, Philadelphia, Pa., *President,* Charles H. Mathews; *Presbyterian Hospital,* Congress and Wood Streets, Chicago, Ill., *President,* Albert M. Day; *Presbyterian Hospital,* Montgomery and Sherman Avenues, Pittsburgh, Pa., *President of Association,* F. W. Sneed; *President of the Trustees,* J. J. Mathews; *Presbyterian Hospital,* 13-23 South Ninth Street, Newark, N. J., *President,* Davis W. Lusk.

NOTE.—More than one million patients are annually reached by medical missionaries of the Mission Boards through over one hundred and seventy Hospitals and Dispensaries maintained in Alaska, Porto Rico, Africa, China, India, Chosen (Korea), Persia, the Philippines, Siam, Central America, and Syria.

Periodicals

Assembly Herald (monthly), organ of the Mission Boards, 1329 Chestnut Street, Philadelphia, Pa., Business Manager, Mr. Horace P. Camden; *Presbyterian Advance,* Nashville, Tenn.; *Continent* (weekly), New York City and Chicago, Ill.; *Presbyterian* (weekly), Philadelphia, Pa.; *Presbyterian Banner,* Pittsburgh, Pa.; *Herald and Presbyter* (weekly), Cincinnati, O.

PRESBYTERIAN CHURCH IN THE UNITED STATES (SOUTH)

The General Assembly, annual, will hold its next meeting at Birmingham, Ala., May 17, 1917.

There are 16 synods; 85 presbyteries.

Officers of the General Assembly. *Moderator,* Rev. C. W. Grafton, Union Church, Miss.; *Stated Clerk and Treasurer,* Rev. Thomas H. Law, Spartanburg, S. C.; *Permanent Clerk,* Rev. J. D. Leslie, Cisco, Tex.

Executive Committee of Foreign Missions, 154 Fifth Avenue, North, Nashville, Tenn. *Executive Secretary,* Rev. Egbert W. Smith; *Secretary Foreign Correspondence and Editor,* Rev. S. H. Chester; *Field Secretary,* Rev. H. F. Williams; *Educational Secretary,* Rev. John I. Armstrong; *Treasurer,* Edwin F. Willis.

Executive Committee of Home Missions, 1522 Hurt Building, Atlanta, Ga. *Executive Secretary,* Rev. S. L. Morris; *Secretary Field Work, Literature and Publicity,* Rev. Homer McMillan; *Treasurer,* A. N. Sharp.

Executive Committee of Christian Education and Ministerial Relief, 122 South Fourth Avenue, Louisville, Ky. *Executive Secretary,* Rev. Henry H. Sweets; *Treasurer,* John Stites, Fifth and Market Streets, Louisville, Ky.

Executive Committee of Publication and Sabbath School Work, Publishing House, 6 and 8 North Sixth Street, Richmond, Va. *Executive Secretary and Treasurer,* Mr. R. E. Magill.

Permanent Committee on the Bible Cause. *Chairman,* Rev. M. B. Porter, Richmond, Va.

Permanent Committee on Systematic Beneficence. *Secretary,* Rev. R. E. Vinson, Austin, Tex.

Permanent Committee on the Sabbath and Family Religion. *Chairman,* Rev. Robert Hill, Tyler, Tex.

Superintendent of Evangelism, Rev. W. H. Miley, Atlanta, Ga.

Superintendent Sunday School Young People's Societies, Rev. Gilbert Glass, Richmond, Va.

Campaign Committee on Stewardship. *Secretary,* Rev. R. L. Walkup, Jackson, Miss.

Colleges

Institution	Location	President or Dean
Agnes Scott College	Decatur, Ga	F. H. Gaines.
Alabama Presbyterian College for Men	Anniston, Ala	W. A. White.
Alabama Synodical College for Women	Talladega, Ala	J. R. Thompson.
Arkansas College	Batesville, Ark	E. D. Brown.
Austin College	Sherman, Tex	T. S. Clyce.
Central University of Kentucky	Danville, Ky	
Chicasaw Female College	Pontotoc, Miss	
Chicora College for Women	Columbia, S. C	S. C. Byrd.
Daniel Baker College	Brownwood, Tex	T. P. Junkin.
Davidson College	Davidson, N. C	William J. Martin.
Davis and Elkins College	Elkins, W. Va	James E. Allen.
Flora McDonald College	Red Springs, N. C	C. G. Vardell.
Hampden-Sidney College	Hampden-Sidney, Va	Henry Tucker Graham.
King College	Bristol, Tenn	Tilden Scherer.
Mississippi Synodical College	Holly Springs, Miss	T. W. Raymond.

Institution	Location	President or Dean
Oklahoma Presbyterian College for Girls	Durant, Okla	W. B. Morrison.
Palmer College	De Funiak Springs, Fla.	W. M. Kemper.
Presbyterian College of South Carolina	Clinton, S. C	D. M. Douglas.
Queens College	Charlotte, N. C	J. R. Bridges.
Rogersville Synodical College	Rogersville, Tenn	(Not open this year.)
Sayre College	Lexington, Ky	J. M. Spencer.
Southwestern Presbyterian University	Clarksville, Tenn	
Statesville Female College	Statesville, N. C	
Stonewall Jackson College	Abingdon, Va	
Synodical College	Fulton, Mo	Lawrence I. MacQueen.
Texas Presbyterian College	Milford, Tex	R. C. Somerville.
Westminster College	Fulton, Mo	

Theological Seminaries

Institution	Location	President
Austin Theological Seminary	Austin, Tex	N. L. Anderson.
Columbia Seminary	Columbia, S. C	Thornton Whaling.
Divinity School, Southwestern Presbyterian University	Clarksville, Tenn	
Presbyterian Theological Sem. of Kentucky	Louisville, Ky	Charles R. Hemphill.
Union Theological Seminary	Richmond, Va	W. W. Moore.

For list of ministers with addresses see Minutes of the General Assembly, published at 6 North Sixth Street, Richmond, Va.

Orphans' Homes and Schools

Orphans' Home of the Synod of Alabama, Talladega, Ala., *Superintendent,* Geo. Dunglinson; *Grundy Presbyterian Orphans' Home,* Springfield, Ky., *Superintendent,* W. A. Waters; *Highland Orphans' Home,* Clay City, Ky., *Superintendent,* Miss Clementina Stamps; *Louisville Presbyterian Orphanage,* Anchorage, Ky., *Superintendent,* Miss Margaret F. Shaw; *Palmer Orphanage,* Columbus, Miss., *Superintendent,* W. V. Frierson, Sr.; *Mountain Orphanage,* Balfour, N. C., *Superintendent,* A. H. Temple; *Presbyterian Orphans' Home,* Barium Springs, N. C., *Superintendent,* W. T. Walker; *Thornwell Home and School for Orphans,* Clinton, S. C., *Superintendent,* W. P. Jacobs; *Monroe-Harding Children's Home,* Nashville, Tenn., *Superintendent,* Miss E. J. Fuller; *Southwestern Presbyterian Home and School for Orphans,* Itasca, Tex., R. F. D. No. 1, *Superintendent,* J. D. McLean; *Presbyterian Orphans' Home,* Lynchburg, Va., *Superintendent,* C. R. Warthen.

Periodicals

Christian Observer, Louisville, Ky., Editor, Rev. D. M. Sweets; *Presbyterian Standard,* Charlotte, N. C., Editor, Rev. J. R. Bridges; *Presbyterian of the South,* Richmond, Va., Editor, Rev. W. S. Campbell; *Presbyterian Journal,* New Orleans, La., Rev. George Summey.

REFORMED PRESBYTERIAN CHURCH, GENERAL SYNOD

General Synod, annual; next session in Philadelphia, Pa., May 16, 1917.

Officers of General Synod: *Moderator,* Rev. W. P. Harriman, Industry, Pa.; *Stated Clerk,* Rev. James L. Chesnut, Cedarville, Ohio.

Board of Foreign Missions. *Secretary,* Rev. James L. Chesnut, Cedarville, Ohio; *Treasurer,* A. B. McMillan, Sparta, Ill.

Board of Home Missions. *Treasurer,* W. J. Imbrie, New Galilee, Pa.

Sustentation Fund. *Treasurer,* W. J. Imbrie, New Galilee, Pa.

Disabled Ministers' Fund. *Treasurer,* F. A. Jurkat, Cedarville, Ohio.

Theological Seminary, Cedarville, Ohio. Dean, Rev. James L. Chesnut.

College, Cedarville, Ohio. *President,* Rev. W. R. McChesney.

UNITED PRESBYTERIAN CHURCH OF NORTH AMERICA

The General Assembly, annual; next session in Boston, Mass., May 23, 1917.

There are 75 presbyteries.

Officers of the General Assembly: *Moderator,* Rev. W. B. Smiley, Oneonta, N. Y.; *Stated Clerk,* Rev. David F. McGill, Ben Avon, Pa.

Board of Foreign Missions, Philadelphia, Pa. *Corresponding Secretary,* Rev. W. B. Anderson, 200 North Fifteenth Street, Philadelphia, Pa.; *Treasurer,* Mr. Robert L. Latimer, 24 North Front Street, Philadelphia, Pa.

Board of Home Missions, 703 Publication Building, Pittsburgh, Pa. *Corresponding Secretary,* Rev. R. A. Hutchison; *Treasurer,* Mr. J. Allison Reed, 519 Wood Street, Pittsburgh, Pa.

Board of Freedmen's Missions, 701 Publication Building, Pittsburgh, Pa. *Corresponding Secretary and Treasurer,* Rev. J. W. Witherspoon, 1703 Buena Vista Street, N. S., Pittsburgh, Pa.

Board of Church Extension, 701 Publication Building, Pittsburgh, Pa. *Corresponding Secretary,* Mr. J. J. Porter, 209 Ninth Street, Pittsburgh, Pa.; *Treasurer,* Mr. George C. Arnold, Monongahela National Bank, Pittsburgh, Pa.

Board of Education, Monmouth, Ill. *Educational Secretary,* Mr. Ralph D. Kyle; *Treasurer of Income Funds,* Mr. Hugh R. Moffett; *Treasurer of Permanent Funds,* Mr. R. L. Wray.

Board of Publication, Publication Building, 209 Ninth Street, Pittsburgh, Pa. *Business Manager,* Rev. E. M. Milligan; *Corresponding Secretary,* Rev. John McNaugher; *Editor of Sabbath School Periodicals,* Rev. R. J. Miller; *Chairman of Sabbath School Committee,* Mr. T. J. Gillespie; *Treasurer,* Mr. John D. Fraser.

Board of Ministerial Relief, Philadelphia, Pa. *Corresponding Secretary,* Rev. J. C. Scouller, 2441 Carpenter Street, Philadelphia, Pa.; *Treasurer,* Mr. James Walker, 1508 Christian Street, Philadelphia, Pa.

Women's Board, Publication Building, Pittsburgh, Pa. *Secretary,* Mrs. John S. Crawford, 95 Trenton Avenue, Wilkinsburg, Pa.; *Treasurer,* Mrs. J. B. Hill, 5630 Bartlett Street, Pittsburgh, Pa.

Young People's Work. *General Secretary,* Rev. C. R. Stevenson, 1912 Leland Avenue, Chicago, Ill.

Missionary and Efficiency Committee, Pittsburgh, Pa. *Chairman,* Rev. W. I. Wishart, 2333 Perrysville Avenue, N. S., Pittsburgh, Pa.; *Executive Secretary,* Rev. J. H. White, 209 Ninth Street, Pittsburgh, Pa.; *Treasurer,* Mr. J. Allison Reed.

Committee on Temperance and Other Reforms. *Chairman,* Rev. T. McCrory, 77 North Rodgers Avenue, Bellevue, Pa.

Colleges

Institution	Location	President
Assiut Training College	Assiut, Egypt	R. S. McClenahan.
Cooper Memorial College	Sterling, Kan.	Ross T. Campbell.
Gordon Mission College	Rawalpindi, India	E. L. Porter.
Knoxville College	Knoxville, Tenn.	R. W. McGranahan.
Monmouth College	Monmouth, Ill.	Thomas H. McMichael.
Muskingum College	New Concord, O.	J. Knox Montgomery.
Tarkio College	Tarkio, Mo.	Jos. Addison Thompson.
Westminster College	New Wilmington, Pa.	W. C. Wallace.

Theological Seminaries

Institution	Location	President
Pittsburgh Theological Seminary	Pittsburgh, Pa.	John McNaugher.
Theological Seminary	Cairo, Egypt	Andrew Watson.
Theological Seminary	Gujranwala, India	J. A. McConnelee.
United Presbyterian Theological Seminary	Xenia, O.	Joseph Kyle.

For list of ministers with addresses see Minutes of the General Assembly, published by the United Presbyterian Board of Publication, Pittsburgh, Pa.

Periodicals

Christian Instructor (weekly), Pittsburgh, Pa., Editor, Rev.

R. J. Miller; *United Presbyterian* (weekly), Pittsburgh, Pa., Editor, Rev. D. R. Miller.

WELSH PRESBYTERIAN CHURCH

General Assembly, triennial; holds its next meeting at Lake Crystal, Minn., September, 1917.

There are 6 synods.

Officers: *Moderator,* Rev. William E. Evans, Mankato, Minn.; *Secretary,* Rev. R. E. Williams, 56 North 53d Street, Philadelphia, Pa.; *Treasurer,* E. J. Jones, M.D., Oak Hill, O.

Board of Home and Foreign Missions. *President,* Mr. W. Owen Jones, 40 Miller Street, Pittsburgh, Pa.; *Secretary,* Rev. Edward Roberts, 408 Jackson Street, Oshkosh, Wis.

A Year Book containing names and addresses will be published soon it is expected; when ready, copies may be had of the Secretary.

Periodical

"Y Cyfaill" (The Friend), Utica, N. Y., Editor, Rev. Joseph Roberts, 519 West 152nd Street, New York City.

REFORMED CHURCH IN AMERICA

(For other Reformed Bodies, not constituent members of the Federal Council see Directory of other Religious Bodies, pages 149-151.)

General Synod, annual; next session at Asbury Park, N. J., May 31, 1917.

Four particular synods; 37 classes.

Officers: *President,* Rev. Peter Moerdyke, Holland, Mich.; *Stated Clerk,* Rev. Henry Lockwood, East Millstone, N. J.; *Treasurer,* Frank R. Van Nest, 25 East Twenty-second Street, New York City.

Board of Foreign Missions and The Arabian Missions, 25 East Twenty-second Street, New York City. *Foreign Secretary,* Rev. W. I. Chamberlain; *Home Secretary,* Rev. E. W. Miller; *Treasurer,* Howell S. Bennet.

Woman's Board of Foreign Missions, 25 East Twenty-second Street, New York City. *Corresponding Secretary,* Miss Olivia H. Lawrence; *Treasurer,* Miss Gertrude Dodd, 159 West Fiftieth Street, New York City.

Board of Domestic Missions, 25 East Twenty-second Street,

New York City. *Office Secretary,* Mr. William T. Demarest; *Treasurer,* Mr. Charles W. Osborne.

Women's Board of Domestic Missions, 25 East Twenty-second Street, New York City. *Corresponding Secretary,* Mrs. John S. Allen; *Treasurer,* Mrs. E. H. Peters.

Board of Publication and Bible School Work, 25 East Twenty-second Street, New York City. *Business Agent,* Louis E. Turk; *Treasurer,* John F. Chambers; *Educational Secretary,* Rev. Theodore F. Bayles.

Board of Education, 25 East Twenty-second Street, New York City. *Corresponding Secretary,* Rev. John G. Gebhard; *Treasurer,* Mr. John F. Berry.

Disabled Ministers' Fund and Widows' Fund, 25 East Twenty-second Street, New York City. *Field Secretary,* Rev. Denis Wortman, 40 Watson Avenue, East Orange, N. J.

Colleges

Institution	Location	President
Hope College	Holland, Mich	Ame Vennema.
Rutgers College (non-sectarian)	New Brunswick, N. J	W. H. S. Demarest.

Theological Seminaries

Institution	Location	Stated Clerk or Principal
Arcot Theological Seminary	Arcot Mission, India	J. H. Wyckoff.
Theological Seminary	New Brunswick, N. J	Jasper S. Hogan.
Western Theological Seminary	Holland, Mich	Peter Moerdyke.

For list of ministers with addresses see Acts and Proceedings of the General Synod, 1915, published by the Board of Publication and Bible School Work, 25 East Twenty-second Street, New York City.

Periodicals

Christian Intelligencer (weekly), New York City, Editor, Rev. A. DeWitt Mason.

Leader, Holland, Mich., Editor, Rev. James F. Zwemer.

De Hope, Holland, Mich., Editor, Rev. M. Kolyn.

REFORMED CHURCH IN THE UNITED STATES

The General Synod, triennial; next session to be held at Dayton, O., May 16, 1917.

There are 9 district synods, and 61 classes.

Officers: *Vice President,* Rev. C. E. Miller; *Stated Clerk,* Rev. J. Rauch Stein, 359 East Broad Street, Bethlehem, Pa.; *Treasurer,* E. A. Rice, York, Pa.

Board of Home Missions, Fifteenth and Race Street, Philadelphia, Pa. *President,* Rev. C. E. Miller, Tiffin, O.; *Recording Secretary,* Rev. J. Harvey Mickley; *Treasurer,* Mr. Joseph S. Wise, Fifteenth and Race Streets, Philadelphia, Pa.

Board of Foreign Missions, Fifteenth and Race Streets, Philadelphia, Pa. *President,* Rev. James I. Good, 3260 Chestnut Street, Philadelphia, Pa.; *Secretary,* Rev. Allen R. Bartholomew; *Treasurer,* Rev. A. S. Bromer.

Publication and Sunday School Board, Fifteenth and Race Streets, Philadelphia, Pa. *President,* Rev. C. Clever, Hagerstown, Md.; *General Secretary,* Rev. Rufus W. Miller; *Treasurer,* Calvin O. Althouse, Reformed Church Building, Philadelphia, Pa.

Board of Ministerial Relief of the Reformed Church in the United States. *President,* Dr. Philip Vollmer, 15 Seminary Avenue, Dayton, O.; *Secretary and Treasurer,* Dr. J. W. Meminger, 138 East Chestnut Street, Lancaster, Pa.

Officers of the Society for the Relief of Ministers and their Widows. *President,* Rev. H. N. Bassler, 1518 Green Street, Harrisburg, Pa.; *Secretary,* Rev. D. N. Dittmar, Mann's Choice, Pa.; *Treasurer,* Rev. Simon S. Miller, Frederick, Md.

Officers of the Society for the Support of Indigent Ministers and Teachers. *President,* Rev. C. J. Walenta, Reesville, Wis.; *Secretary,* Rev. A. Muehlmeier, Monticello, Wis.; *Treasurer,* Rev. J. W. Grosshuesch, R. F. D. 29, Plymouth, Wis.

Board of Directors of the Central Publishing House, 2969 West Twenty-fifth Street, Cleveland, O. *President,* Dr. J. H. Stepler, 1366 Sloan Avenue, Lakewood, O.; *Secretary,* Rev. F. W. Leich, 3305 Franklin Avenue, Cleveland, O.; *Business Manager,* Rev. A. Becker, Cleveland, O.

Women's Missionary Society of General Synod. *President,* Mrs. W. R. Harris, 434 Biddle Avenue, Wilkinsburg, Pa.; *Corresponding Secretary,* Mrs. B. B. Krammes, Tiffin, O.; *Statistical Secretary,* Mrs. Homer Miller, 98 South Avenue, Poughkeepsie, N. Y.; *Treasurer,* Mrs. Lewis L. Anewalt, 814 Walnut Street, Allentown, Pa.

Colleges

Institution	Location	President or Principal
Catawba College	Newton, N. C.	J. D. Andrew.
Claremont College	Hickory, N. C.	Joseph L. Murphy.
College for Women	Allentown, Pa.	William F. Curtis.
Franklin and Marshall College	Lancaster, Pa.	Henry Harbaugh Apple.
Heidelberg University	Tiffin, O.	Charles E. Miller.
Hood College	Frederick, Md.	Joseph H. Apple.
Massanutten Academy	Woodstock, Va.	Howard J. Benchoff.
Mercersburg Academy	Mercersburg, Pa.	William Mann Irvine.
North Japan College	Sendai, Japan	D. B. Schneder.
Ursinus College	Collegeville, Pa.	George Leslie Omwake.

Theological Seminaries

Institution	Location	President or Principal
Central Theological Seminary	Dayton, O.	Henry I. Christman.
Mission House (Theological Seminary and College Academy)	Plymouth, Wis.	E. A. Hofer.
Theological Seminary	Lancaster, Pa.	John C. Bowman.

Hospital, Homes for Aged, and Orphans' Homes

German Hospital, Cleveland, O., *Superintendent,* F. W. Leich; *Treasurer,* Mr. P. Wetzel, 2069 West Twenty-fifth Street, Cleveland, O.; *Phœbe Deaconess Home,* Allentown, Pa., *Superintendent, Secretary, and Treasurer,* Rev. Robert M. Kern; *German Protestant Home,* Lawndale, Pa., *President of Board of Trustees,* F. W. Berlemann, 341 Fairmount Avenue, Philadelphia, Pa.; *Deaconess House and Training School for Christian Workers of the Presbyterian and Reformed Churches,* 1122 Spruce Street, Philadelphia, Pa.; *President,* Rev. Wm. H. Roberts, Philadelphia, Pa.; *Secretary,* Mr. S. T. Kerr, 1907 Spruce Street, Philadelphia, Pa.; *Treasurer,* Mr. Thos. R. Patton, 1713 Sansom Street, Philadelphia, Pa.; *Bethany Orphans' Homes of the Reformed Church in the United States,* Womelsdorf, Pa., *Superintendent,* Wilson F. More; *Treasurer,* Christ. G. Gross, 879 North Forty-first Street, Philadelphia, Pa.; *St. Paul's Orphans' Home,* Greenville, Pa., *Superintendent,* A. M. Keifer; *Treasurer,* Rev. Lewis Robb, Wilkinsburg, Pa.; *Fort Wayne Orphans' Home,* Fort Wayne, Ind., *Superintendent,* J. F. Winter; *Treasurer,* H. H. Kattmann, Berne, Ind.; *Nazareth Orphans' Home,* Crescent, N. C., *Superintendent,* J. W. Bell; *Treasurer,* Geo. H. Moose, Gold Hill, N. C.; *The George W. and Agnes Hoffman Orphanage,* Near Littletown, Pa., *Superintendent,* J. Stewart Hartman; *Treasurer,* C. S. Slagle, Westminster, Md.

Periodicals

English: *Reformed Church Messenger* (weekly), Philadelphia, Pa., Editor, C. J. Musser; *Christian World* (weekly), Cleveland, O., Editor, J. H. Bomberger; *Reformed Church Review* (quarterly), Philadelphia, Pa., Editors, Theo. F. Herman and John S. Stahr; *Reformed Church Record* (weekly), Reading, Pa., Editor, I. M. Beaver; *Reformed Church Herald* (weekly), Tipton, Ia., Editors, D. F. Boomershine, J. F. Hawk, F. S. Bromer, D. H. Fouse, W. D. Marburger, S. S. Brown, S. R. Neiman; *Reformed Church Standard* (semi-monthly), Crescent, N. C., Editors, J. M. L. Lyerly and W. W. Rowe; *Heidelberg Teacher* (monthly), Editor, Rufus W. Miller; *Way* (weekly), Philadelphia, Pa., Editor, R. L. Gerhart; *Leaves of Light* (weekly), Philadelphia, Pa., Editor, R. L. Gerhart; *Sunshine* (weekly), Philadelphia, Pa., Editor, R. L. Gerhart; *Outlook of Missions* (monthly), Philadelphia, Pa., Editors, A. R. Bartholomew, C. E. Schaeffer, Mrs. Edward F. Evemeyer.

German: *Reformierte Kirchenzseitung* (weekly), Cleveland, O., Editor, G. Dolch; *Hungarian-American Reformed Sentinel* (weekly), New York City, Editor, Lad. Harsanyi; *Evangel* (weekly), Philadelphia, Editor, Lad. Harsanyi.

PROTESTANT EPISCOPAL CHURCH

General Convention, triennial; next session, in October, 1919, in Detroit, Mich.

Presiding Bishop of the Church, The Most Rev. Daniel S. Tuttle, Bishop of Missouri, 74 Vandeventer Place, St. Louis, Mo.

Officers of the House of Bishops: *Chairman,* Rt. Rev. T. F. Gailor, Bishop of Tennessee, Memphis, Tenn.; *Secretary,* (office vacant); *President of the House of Deputies,* Rev. Alexander Mann, Boston, Mass.; *Secretary,* Rev. Henry Anstice, New York City; *Treasurer of the Convention,* Mr. William W. Skiddy, 82 Wall Street, New York City.

There are 91 dioceses and missionary districts in the United States and 12 missionary districts abroad.

Bishops

Rt. Rev. Charles Minnigerode Beckwith, Bishop of Alabama, Montgomery, Ala.

Rt. Rev. Peter Trimble Rowe, Missionary Bishop of Alaska, 418 Mutual Life Building, Seattle, Wash.

Rt. Rev. Richard Henry Nelson, Bishop of Albany, 25 Elk Street, Albany, N. Y.

Rt. Rev. Julius W. Atwood, Missionary Bishop of Arizona, Phœnix, Ariz.

Rt. Rev. James Ridout Winchester, Bishop of Arkansas, 1222 Scott Street, Little Rock, Ark.

Rt. Rev. Junius Moore Horner, Missionary Bishop of Asheville, Asheville, N. C.

Rt. Rev. (office vacant), Bishop of Atlanta.

Rt. Rev. Ethelbert Talbot, Bishop of Bethlehem, South Bethlehem, Pa.

Rt. Rev. William Ford Nichols, Bishop of California, 1215 Sacramento Street, San Francisco, Cal.

Rt. Rev. Charles Tyler Olmsted, Bishop of Central New York, 1101 Park Avenue, Utica, N. Y.

Rt. Rev. Charles Palmerston Anderson, Bishop of Chicago, 1612 Prairie Avenue, Chicago, Ill.

Rt. Rev. Charles Sanford Olmsted, Bishop of Colorado, Saybrook, Conn.

Rt. Rev. Chauncey Bunce Brewster, Bishop of Connecticut, 98 Woodland Street, Hartford, Conn.

Rt. Rev. Alexander Charles Garrett, Bishop of Dallas, Dallas, Tex.

Rt. Rev. Frederick Joseph Kinsman, Bishop of Delaware, Bishopstead, Wilmington, Del.

Rt. Rev. James-Dow Morrison, Bishop of Duluth, 2131 East Superior Street, Duluth, Minn.

Rt. Rev. Thomas Campbell Darst, Bishop of East Carolina, Wilmington, N. C.

Rt. Rev. Theodore Payne Thurston, Bishop of Eastern Oklahoma, 743 Terrace Boulevard, Muskogee, Okla.

Rt. Rev. Robert Lewis Paddock, Bishop of Eastern Oregon, Hood River, Ore.

Rt. Rev. William Forbes Adams, Bishop of Easton, Easton, Md.

Rt. Rev. Rogers Israel, Bishop of Erie, 437 West Sixth Street, Erie, Pa.

Rt. Rev. Edwin Gardner Weed, Bishop of Florida, Jacksonville, Fla.

Rt. Rev. Reginald Heber Weller, Bishop of Fond du Lac, Fond du Lac, Wis.

Rt. Rev. Frederick Focke Reese, Bishop of Georgia, 2425 Bull Street, Savannah, Ga.

Rt. Rev. James Henry Darlington, Bishop of Harrisburg, 321 North Front Street, Harrisburg, Pa.

Rt. Rev. Henry Bond Restarick, Missionary Bishop of Honolulu, Honolulu, T. H.

Rt. Rev. James Bowen Funsten, Missionary Bishop of Idaho, Boise, Ida.

Rt. Rev. Joseph Marshall Francis, Bishop of Indianapolis, 1559 Central Avenue, Indianapolis, Ind.

Rt. Rev. Theodore Nevin Morrison, Bishop of Iowa, Davenport, Ia.

Rt. Rev. James Wise, Bishop of Kansas, Topeka, Kan.

Rt. Rev. Charles Edward Woodcock, Bishop of Kentucky, 1129 Third Street, Louisville, Ky.

Rt. Rev. Lewis William Burton, Bishop of Lexington, 436 West Sixth Street, Lexington, Ky.

Rt. Rev. Frederick Burgess, Bishop of Long Island, Garden City, L. I., N. Y.

Rt. Rev. Joseph Horsfall Johnson, Bishop of Los Angeles, 523 South Olive Street, Los Angeles, Cal.

Rt. Rev. David Sessums, Bishop of Louisiana, 2919 St. Charles Avenue, New Orleans. La.

Rt. Rev. Benjamin Brewster, Bishop of Maine, 143 State Street, Portland, Me.

Rt. Rev. Gershom Mott Williams, Bishop of Marquette, Marquette, Mich.

Rt. Rev. John Gardner Murray, Bishop of Maryland, Charles Street Avenue, and University Parkway, Baltimore, Md.

Rt. Rev. William Lawrence, Bishop of Massachusetts, 122 Commonwealth Avenue, Boston, Mass.

Rt. Rev. Charles David Williams, Bishop of Michigan, St. Paul's Cathedral, Detroit, Mich.

Rt. Rev. John Hazen White, Bishop of Michigan City, 319 West Colfax Avenue, South Bend, Ind.

Rt. Rev. William Walter Webb, Bishop of Milwaukee, 222 Juneau Avenue, Milwaukee, Wis.

Rt. Rev. (office vacant), Bishop of Minnesota.

Rt. Rev. Theodore DuBose Bratton, Bishop of Mississippi, Battle Hill, Jackson, Miss.

Rt. Rev. Daniel Sylvester Tuttle, Bishop of Missouri, 74 Vandeventer Place, St. Louis, Mo.

Rt. Rev. William Frederick Faber, Bishop of Montana, Helena, Mont.

Rt. Rev. Arthur Llewellyn Williams, Bishop of Nebraska, 1716 Dodge Street, Omaha, Neb.

Rt. Rev. George Coolidge Hunting, Missionary Bishop of Nevada, 505 Ridge Street, Reno, Nev.

Rt. Rev. Edwin Stevens Lines, Bishop of Newark, 21 Washington Street, Newark, N. J.

Rt. Rev. Edward Melville Parker, Bishop of New Hampshire, Concord, N. H.

Rt. Rev. Paul Matthews, Bishop of New Jersey, 107 Greenwood Avenue, Trenton, N. J.

Rt. Rev. Frederick Bingham Howden, Missionary Bishop of New Mexico, Albuquerque, N. M.

Rt. Rev. David Hummel Greer, Bishop of New York, Amsterdam Avenue and 110th Street, New York City.

Rt. Rev. Joseph Blount Cheshire, Bishop of North Carolina, Raleigh, N. C.

Rt. Rev. John Poyntz Tyler, Missionary Bishop of North Dakota, Fargo, N. D.

Rt. Rev. Edward Arthur Temple, Missionary Bishop of North Texas, Amarillo, Tex.

Rt. Rev. William Andrew Leonard, Bishop of Ohio, 3054 Euclid Avenue, Cleveland, O.

Rt. Rev. Francis Key Brooke, Missionary Bishop of Oklahoma, 427 West Ninth Street, Oklahoma, City, Okla.

Rt. Rev. Frederick William Keator, Bishop of Olympia, Tacoma, Wash.

Rt. Rev. Walter Taylor Sumner, Bishop of Oregon, 574 Elm Street, Portland, Ore.

Rt. Rev. Philip Mercer Rhinelander, Bishop of Pennsylvania, 251 South Twenty-second Street, Philadelphia, Pa.

Rt. Rev. Charles H. Brent, Missionary Bishop of the Philippine Islands, 567 Calle Isaac Peral, Manila, P. I.

Rt. Rev. Cortlandt Whitehead, Bishop of Pittsburgh, Shady Side, Pittsburgh, Pa.

Rt. Rev. Charles Blayney Colmore, Missionary Bishop of Porto Rico, Box 1115, San Juan, P. R.

Rt. Rev. M. Edward Fawcett, Bishop of Quincy, 1661 Jersey Street, Quincy, Ill.

Rt. Rev. James De Wolf Perry, Bishop of Rhode Island, 10 Brown Street, Providence, R. I.

Rt. Rev. William Hall Moreland, Bishop of Sacramento, Sacramento, Cal.

Rt. Rev. (office vacant), Missionary Bishop of Salina, Salina, Kan.

Rt. Rev. Louis Childs Sanford, Missionary Bishop of San Joaquin, 733 Peralta Way, Fresno, Cal.

Rt. Rev. William Alexander Guerry, Bishop of South Carolina, Charleston, S. C.

Rt. Rev. Hugh Latimer Burleson, Missionary Bishop of South Dakota, Sioux Falls, S. D.

Rt. Rev. Camerón Mann, Missionary Bishop of Southern Florida, Orlando, Fla.

Rt. Rev. Boyd Vincent, Bishop of Southern Ohio, 223 West Seventh Street, Cincinnati, O.

Rt. Rev. Alfred Magill Randolph, Bishop of Southern Virginia, 226 West Freemason Street, Norfolk, Va.

Rt. Rev. Herman Page, Missionary Bishop of District of Spokane, 2303 First Avenue, Spokane, Wash.

Rt. Rev. (office vacant), Bishop of Springfield, 519 East Edwards Street, Springfield, Ill.

Rt. Rev. Thomas Frank Gailor, Bishop of Tennessee, Memphis, Tenn.

Rt. Rev. George Herbert Kinsolving, Bishop of Texas, Austin, Tex.

Rt. Rev. Paul Jones, Missionary Bishop of District of Utah, 444 East First South Street, Salt Lake City, Utah.

Rt. Rev. Arthur Crawshay Alliston Hall, Bishop of Vermont, Burlington, Vt.

Rt. Rev. Robert Atkinson Gibson, Bishop of Virginia, 906 Park Avenue, Richmond, Va.

Rt. Rev. Alfred Harding, Bishop of Washington, Mt. St. Alban, Washington, D. C.

Rt. Rev. Frank Hale Touret, Missionary Bishop of Western Colorado, Glenwood Springs, Colo.

Rt. Rev. Thomas Frederick Davies, Bishop of Western Massachusetts, 1154 Worthington Street, Springfield, Mass.

Rt. Rev. John Newton McCormick, Bishop of Western Michigan, 43 Lafayette Avenue, S. E., Grand Rapids, Mich.

Rt. Rev. Sidney Catlin Partridge, Bishop of West Missouri, 14 West Armour Boulevard, Kansas City, Mo.

Rt. Rev. George Allen Beecher, Missionary Bishop of Western Nebraska, Hastings, Neb.

Rt. Rev. William David Walker, Bishop of Western New York, 367 Elmwood Avenue, Buffalo, N. Y.

Rt. Rev. William Theodotus Capers, Bishop of West Texas, 106 French Place, San Antonio, Tex.

Rt. Rev. William Loyall Gravatt, Bishop of West Virginia, Charlestown, W. Va.

Rt. Rev. Nathaniel Seymour Thomas, Missionary Bishop of Wyoming, Cheyenne, Wyo.

Rt. Rev. (office vacant), Missionary Bishop of Liberia, Monrovia, Liberia, West Africa.

Rt. Rev. Frederick Rogers Graves, Missionary Bishop of Shanghai, Shanghai, China.

Rt. Rev. Logan H. Roots, Missionary Bishop of Hankow, Hankow, China.

Rt. Rev. Daniel Trumbull Huntington, Missionary Bishop of Anking, Anking, China.

Rt. Rev. John McKim, Missionary Bishop of Tokyo, Tokyo, Japan.

Rt. Rev. Henry St. George Tucker, Missionary Bishop of Kyoto, Kyoto, Japan.

Rt. Rev. Hiram Richard Hulse, Missionary Bishop of Cuba, Havana, Cuba.

Rt. Rev. Henry Damerel Aves, Missionary Bishop of Mexico, Apartado, 151 Guadalajara, Jal., Mexico.

Rt. Rev. Lucien Lee Kinsolving, Missionary Bishop of Southern Brazil, Caixa, 174 Porto Alegro, Brazil.

Rt. Rev. A. W. Knight, Bishop in Charge of Panama Canal Zone, Sewanee, Tenn.

Rt. Rev. G. Mott Williams, Bishop in Charge of European Churches, Marquette, Mich.

PROVINCES OF THE CHURCH

First, New England. Dioceses of Me., N. H., Vt., Mass., Western Mass., R. I., and Conn. Rt. Rev. William Lawrence, *President;* Rev. Philip Schuyler, 121 State Street, Portland, Me., *Secretary.*

Second, New York and New Jersey. Dioceses of N. Y., L. I., Albany, Central N. Y., Western N. Y., Newark, N. J., and Mis. Dist. of Porto Rico. Rt. Rev. E. S. Lines, *President;* Rev. Roy F. Duffield, Garden City, L. I., *Secretary.*

Third, Washington. Dioceses of Pa., Harrisburg, Bethlehem, Pittsburgh, Erie, Del., Md., Easton, Wash., Va., and So. Va. Rt. Rev. John G. Murray, *President;* Rev. Wm. C. Hicks, 810 Woodward Building, Washington, D. C., *Provincial Secretary.*

Fourth, Sewanee. Dioceses of Ala., N. C., East Carolina, S. C., Ga., Atlanta, Fla., Miss., La., Tenn., Ky., Tex., and Missionary Dists. of Asheville and So. Fla. Presidency vacant; Rev. Mercer P. Logan, Charlestown, S. C., *Secretary.*

Fifth, Mid-West. Dioceses of Ohio, So. O., Mich. City, Indianapolis, Chicago, Quincy, Springfield, Mich., W. Mich., Marquette, Fond du Lac, and Milwaukee. Rt. Rev. Wm. A. Leonard, *President;* Rev. Charles G. Reade, 223 W. Seventh St., Cincinnati, O., *Secretary.*

Sixth, Northwest. Dioceses of Minn., Duluth, Ia., Neb., Col., Mon., and Mis. Dists. of W. Neb., W. Col., S. D., N. D., and Wyo. Presidency vacant. Rev. C. C Rollitt, Minneapolis, Minn., *Provincial Secretary.*

Seventh, Southwest. Dioceses of Mo., W. Mo., Ark., Tex., Dallas, Kan., and Mis. Dists. of W. Tex., N. Tex., Salina, Okla., E. Okla., and N. M. Rt. Rev. D. S. Tuttle, *President;* Rev. Henry N. Hyde, Joplin, Mo., *Secretary.*

Eighth, Pacific. Dioceses of Olympia, Ore., Cal., Los Angeles, and Mis. Dists. of Idaho, Utah, Spokane, E. Ore., Nev., San Joaquin, Alaska, Honolulu, Philippines. Rt. Rev. W. F. Nichols, *President;* Rev. Alfred Lockwood, Spokane, Wash., *Secretary.*

Domestic and Foreign Missionary Society, 281 Fourth Avenue, New York City. *President of the Board of Missions,* Rt.

Rev. Arthur S. Lloyd; *Secretaries,* John Wilson Wood, Rev. Arthur R. Gray, Rev. Franklin J. Clark, Rev. Charles E. Betticher, Dr. W. C. Sturgis; *Treasurer,* George Gordon King; Assistant Treasurer, E. Walter Roberts.

Woman's Auxiliary to the Board of Missions, Church Missions House, 281 Fourth Avenue, New York City. *Secretary,* Miss M. G. Lindley.

American Church Building Fund Commission, 281 Fourth Avenue, New York City. Presidency vacant; *Treasurer,* Mr. George Gordon King; *Corresponding Secretary,* Rev. Charles L. Pardee.

General Clergy Relief Fund, The Church House, Twelfth and Walnut Streets, Philadelphia, Pa. *Treasurer and Financial Agent,* Rev. Alfred J. P. McClure.

General Board of Religious Education, 289 Fourth Avenue, New York City. *President,* ex officio, the Most Rev. Daniel S. Tuttle, Presiding Bishop; *Secretary,* Rev. Charles H. Boynton; *General Secretary,* Rev. Wm. E. Gardner; *Treasurer,* Mr. William Fellowes Morgan.

Joint Commission on Social Service, 281 Fourth Avenue, New York City. *Executive Secretary,* Rev. F. M. Crouch.

Brotherhood of St. Andrew, Church House, Twelfth and Walnut Streets, Philadelphia, Pa. *President,* Edward H. Bonsall; *General Secretary and Editor* St. Andrew's Cross (official organ), Franklin S. Edmunds; *Executive Secretary,* George H. Randall; *Treasurer,* Alexander M. Hadden.

Society for the Increase of the Ministry. *President,* Rt. Rev. C. B. Brewster; *Corresponding Secretary,* Rev. F. D. Hoskins, 86 Buckingham Street, Hartford, Conn.; *Treasurer,* Elijah C. Johnson, National Exchange Bank, Hartford, Conn.

Clergyman's Retiring Fund Society, 281 Fourth Avenue, New York City. *President,* Rt. Rev. Frederick Burgess; *Secretary,* Mr. J. Van Vechten Olcott; *Treasurer* and *Financial Secretary,* Rev. Henry Anstice.

Clerical Union for the Maintenance and Defence of Catholic Principles. *President,* Rt. Rev. R. H. Weller, Bishop of Fond du Lac; *Secretary,* Rev. Wm. H. A. Hall, 90 Morningside Drive, New York.

American Church Union. *President,* Mr. Clinton Rogers Woodruff, 707 North American Building, Philadelphia, Pa. *Corresponding Secretary,* Rev. Eliot White, 1625 Locust Street, Philadelphia, Pa.; *Treasurer,* Rev. E. S. Lane, 5541 Morris Street, Germantown, Pa.

New York Bible and Common Prayer Book Society. *President*, Rt. Rev. David H. Greer; *Secretary*, Edwin S. Gorham, 11 West Forty-fifth Street, New York City; *Treasurer*, Frank B. Warburton, 68 Wall Street, New York City.

Association for Promoting the Interests of Church Schools, Colleges, and Seminaries. *President*, Rev. Lawrence T. Cole; *Secretary*, Charles F. Hoffman, 258 Broadway, New York City; *Treasurer*, George Zabriskie, 49 Wall Street, New York City.

Church Association for the Advancement of the Interests of Labor, 416 Lafayette Street, New York City. *President*, the Rt. Rev. David H. Greer; *Executive Secretary*, Miss Harriette A. Keyser; *Treasurer*, Mr. H. B. Livingston.

Church Socialist League in America. *National Secretary*, Rev. A. L. Byron-Curtiss, 11 Liberty Street, Utica, N. Y.

Church Temperance Society, Church Missions House, New York City. *President*, Rt. Rev. Frederick Courtney; *General Secretary*, Miss H. K. Graham; *Treasurer*, Mr. Irving Grinnell.

Christian Unity Foundation, 143 East Thirty-seventh Street, New York City. *President*, Rt. Rev. Frederick Courtney; *Chairman Executive Committee*, Hon. Lawson Purdy; *Chairman of Committee on Research*, Rev. Rockland Tyng Homans; *Secretary*, Rev. Arthur Lowndes; *Treasurer*, Origen S. Seymour, 54 William Street, New York City.

Church Unity Society. *Acting President*, the Rt. Rev. E. Talbot; *General Secretary*, Rev. G. Woolsey Hodge, Philadelphia; *Recording Secretary*, Mr. David Goodbread; *Treasurer*, Mr. William J. Dickson.

Association for the Promotion of the Unity of Christendom. *General Secretary for the United States*, Rev. Calbraith Bourn Perry, Cambridge, N. Y.

Anglican and Eastern-Orthodox Churches Union (International). American Branch: *Presidents*, the Rt. Rev. F. M. Parker and Rev. Demetrius Patrides; *Secretary*, Rev. Arthur Lowndes, 143 East Thirty-seventh Street, New York.

Confraternity of the Blessed Sacrament of the Body and Blood of Christ. *Superior General*, the Rt. Rev. R. H. Weller; *Secretary General*, Rev. C. P. A. Burnett, 14 East 109th Street, New York City; *Treasurer General*, Rev. Charles H. Young, 6451 Woodlawn Avenue, Chicago, Ill.

Church Congress in the United States. *General Chairman*, Rev. C. L. Slattery, 804 Broadway, New York City; *General Secretary*, Rev. G. A. Carstensen, Riverdale-on-the-Hudson, N. Y.; *Treasurer*, William Foulke, 6 Bible House, New York City.

Church Endowment Society. *President Board of Trustees,* Rt. Rev. W. F. Adams; *Secretary General,* Rev. E. W. Hunter, Rector of St. Ann's Church, New Orleans, La.

Free and Open Church Association, 2353 East Cumberland Street, Philadelphia, Pa. *President,* R. Francis Wood, Philadelphia, Pa.; *General Secretary,* Rev. J. A. Goodfellow, 2353 East Cumberland Street, Philadelphia, Pa.; *Treasurer,* George Hall, Franklin Building, Philadelphia, Pa.

Society of Mission Priests of St. John the Evangelist. *Superior,* Rev. F. C. Powell, 33 Bowdoin Street, Boston, Mass.

Order of the Holy Cross. *Father Superior,* O. H. C., West Park, N. Y.

Congregation of the Companions of the Holy Savior. *Master of the Congregation,* Rev. F. D. Ward, 1606 Mifflin Street, Philadelphia, Pa.

Order of Deaconesses Central Committees. *Chairman,* Henrietta R. Goodwin; *Secretary,* Anna G. Newell, Christ Church Cathedral, St. Louis, Mo.

Schools of Arts and Sciences

Institution	Location	President
Racine College	Racine, Wis	B. Talbot Rogers.
St. Stephen's College	Annandale, N. Y	William C. Rodgers.

Non-Sectarian Colleges

Institution	Location	President
Hobart College	Geneva, N. Y	Lyman P. Powell.
Trinity College	Hartford, Conn	Flavel S. Luther.

Theological Seminaries

Institution	Location	President or Dean
Berkeley Divinity School	Middletown, Conn	Samuel Hart.
Bishop Payne Divinity School	Petersburg, Va	C. B. Bryan.
Church Divinity School of the Pacific	San Francisco, Cal	W. F. Nichols.
Divinity School of the Prot. Epis. Ch	Philadelphia, Pa	George G. Bartlett.
Episcopal Theological School	Cambridge, Mass	George Hodges.
General Theological Seminary	New York City	Hughell E. W. Fosbrooke
Nashotah House	Nashotah, Wis	E. A. Larrabee.
Seabury Divinity School	Faribault, Minn	Samuel C. Edsall.
Virginia Theological Seminary	Theological Sem., Va	Berryman Green.
Western Theological Seminary	Chicago, Ill	William C. DeWitt.

Schools of Theology and Arts

Institution	Location	President or Dean
Kenyon College	Gambier, O	William F. Peirce.
University of the South	Sewanee, Tenn	Cleveland K. Benedict.

For list of clergy, with addresses, see Living Church Annual and Churchman's Almanac, published by Young Churchman Co., Milwaukee, Wis., and American Church Almanac, published by Edwin S. Gorham, New York City.

Periodicals

General: *Churchman* (weekly), New York City; *Living Church* (weekly), Milwaukee, Wis.; *Parish Leaflet* (weekly), Hobart, Ind.; *Southern Churchman* (weekly), Richmond, Va.

Diocesan: *Church Record*, Montgomery, Ala.; *Alaskan Churchman*, Fairbanks, Alaska; *Bethlehem Churchman*, Box 291, Reading, Pa.; *Pacific Churchman*, San Francisco, Cal.; *Gospel Messenger*, Utica, N. Y.; *Diocese of Chicago*, Chicago, Ill.; *Colorado Churchman*, Fort Collins, Colo.; *Connecticut Churchman*, Hartford, Conn.; *Mission Herald*, Kinston, N. C.; *Eastern Oklahoma*, Muskogee, Okla.; *Church Herald*, Pensacola, Fla.; *Church Outlook*, Antigo, Wis.; *Missions in Georgia*, Americus, Ga.; *Harrisburg Churchman*, Harrisburg, Pa.; *Hawaiian Church Chronicle*, Honolulu, Hawaii; *Indianapolis Churchman*, Indianapolis, Ind.; *Iowa Churchman*, Des Moines, Ia.; *Kansas Churchman*, Topeka, Kan.; *Bishop's Letter*, Louisville, Ky.; *Diocesan News*, Lexington, Ky.; *Los Angeles Churchman*, Santa Monica, Cal.; *Diocese of Louisiana*, New Orleans, La.; *North-East*, Portland, Me.; *Maryland Churchman*, Baltimore, Md.; *Church Militant*, Boston, Mass.; *Michigan Churchman*, Detroit, Mich.; *Church Times*, Milwaukee, Wis.; *Church Record*, Minneapolis, Minn.; *Church News*, Yazoo City, Miss.; *Church News*, St. Louis, Mo.; *Montana Churchman*, Helena, Mont.; *Crozier*, Omaha, Neb.; *Newark Churchman*, Newark, N. J.; *Church Fly Leaf*, Concord, N. H.; *Diocese of New Jersey*, Trenton, N. J.; *Carolina Churchman*, Charlotte, N. C.; *North Dakota Sheaf*, Fargo, N. D.; *Mission Churchman*, Amarillo, Tex.; *Church Life*, Cleveland, O.; *Oregon Churchman*, Portland, Ore.; *Church News*, Philadelphia, Pa.; *Church News*, Pittsburgh, Pa.; *Light*, Macomb, Ill.; *Diocesan Record*, Providence, R. I.; *Sacramento Missionary*, Sacramento, Cal.; *South Dakota Churchman*, Mitchell, S. D.; *Anpao Kin*, Cheyenne Agency, S. D.; *Palm Branch*, Orlando, Fla.; *Church Messenger*, Cincinnati, O.; *Diocesan Journal*, Portsmouth, Va.; *Cathedral Chimes*, Spokane, Wash.; *Springfield Churchman*, Springfield, Ill.; *Mountain Echo*, Brandon, Vt.; *Western Colorado Evangel*, Durango, Colo.; *Pastoral Staff*, Westfield, Mass.; *Church Helper*, Grand Rapids, Mich.; *Western Nebraska Churchman*, Kearney, Neb.; *Church News*, San Antonio, Tex.; *Church News*, Wheeling, W. Va.; *Wyoming Churchman*, Cheyenne, Wyo.

Periodicals Devoted to Special Interests

American Church S. S. Magazine, Sunday Schools, Philadelphia, Pa.; *Church Advocate*, Colored Work, Baltimore, Md.; *Cross*, Italian work, Port Richmond, L. I.; *St. Andrew's Cross*,

St. Andrew's Brotherhood, Philadelphia, Pa.; *Spirit of Missions,* Missions (Monthly), 281 Fourth Avenue, New York; *Shepherd's Arms,* Sunday Schools, Milwaukee, Wis.; *Silent Churchman,* Deaf Mutes, Chicago, Ill.; *Young Churchman,* Sunday Schools, Milwaukee, Wis.

REFORMED EPISCOPAL CHURCH

General Council, triennial; last session held in New York City, in May, 1915.

There are three synods, including one in Canada, and three missionary jurisdictions.

Officers of General Council: *President and Presiding Bishop,* Samuel Fallows, 2344 Monroe Street, Chicago, Ill.; *Secretary,* Rev. Walter E. Oakford, 3528 Ainslie Street, Philadelphia, Pa.; *Treasurer,* George W. Wagner, 4418 Pine Street, Philadelphia, Pa.

Bishops

Samuel Fallows, 2344 Monroe Street, Chicago, Ill.

Robert L. Rudolph, 103 South Thirty-sixth Street, Philadelphia, Pa.

Arthur L. Pengelley, 75 Charlotte Street, Charleston, S. C.

Willard Brewing, 373 Crawford Street, Toronto, Ontario, Can.

Board of Foreign Missions. *President,* Rev. William Tracy, 4400 Chestnut Street, Philadelphia, Pa.; *Secretary,* H. H. Sinnamon, West End Trust Building, Philadelphia, Pa.

Board of Home Missions. *Secretary,* William Spence, 1231 Tasker Street, Philadelphia, Pa.

Committee on Sunday Schools. *Secretary,* Rev. Wm. Tracy, 4400 Chestnut Street, Philadelphia, Pa.

Committee on Education and Publication. *Secretary,* Rev. Robert W. Peach, 271 Parker Street, Newark, N. J.

Sustentation Fund. *Treasurer,* The Provident Life and Trust Company, Philadelphia, Pa.

Woman's Foreign Missionary Society. *President,* Mrs. William A. Freemantle, 1617 Oxford Street, Germantown, Philadelphia, Pa.; *Corresponding Secretary,* Mrs. Samuel B. Ray, Philadelphia, Pa.

Woman's Home Missionary Society. *President,* Mrs. Charles F. Hendricks, 4236 Old York Road, Philadelphia, Pa.; *Corresponding Secretary,* Mrs. Walter E. Oakford, 3528 Ainslie Street, Falls of Schuykill, Philadelphia, Pa.

Theological Seminary. Theological Seminary, Philadelphia, Pa. *Chairman,* Rev. Joseph D. Wilson, 4401 Sansom Street, Philadelphia, Pa.

Periodical. *Episcopal Recorder* (weekly), Philadelphia, Pa.

UNITED BRETHREN IN CHRIST

(For the other body bearing this name see Directory of Other Religious Bodies, page 153.)

General Conference, quadrennial; next session in 1917; 40 annual conferences.

Bishops

N. Castle (emeritus), Philomath, Ore.

G. M. Mathews, 130 Oxford Avenue, Dayton, O.

W. M. Weekley, 1038 Murdock Avenue, Parkersburg, W. Va.

W. M. Bell, 227 West Fifty-first Street, Los Angeles, Cal.

H. H. Fout, 945 Middle Drive, Woodruff Place, Indianapolis, Ind.

C. J. Kephart, 3936 Harrison Avenue, Kansas City, Mo.

A. T. Howard, 821 Summers Street, Dayton, O.

United Brethren Publishing House, Dayton, O. *Publishing Agent,* Rev. W. R. Funk.

Foreign Missionary Society, Dayton, O. *President,* Bishop W. M. Bell, 227 West Fifty-first Street, Los Angeles, Cal.; *General Secretary,* Rev. S. S. Hough, 1003 United Brethren Building, Dayton, O.

Home Missionary Society, Dayton, O. *General Secretary,* Rev. C. Whitney, 904 United Brethren Building, Dayton, O.; *Secretary of the Educational Department,* Miss Lyda B. Wiggim, Dayton, O.

Church Erection Society, Dayton, O. *President,* Bishop W. M. Weekley, Parkersburg, W. Va.; *Secretary,* Rev. A. C. Siddall, 1007 United Brethren Building, Dayton, O.; *Treasurer,* L. O. Miller, 901 United Brethren Building, Dayton, O.

Woman's Missionary Association, Dayton, O. *President,* Mrs. L. R. Harford, 1550 Georgia Avenue, Omaha, Neb.; *General Secretary and Treasurer,* Mrs. Alva Kauffman, 1104 United Brethren Building, Dayton, O.

Board of Control of Sunday School, Brotherhood, and Young People's Work, United Brethren Building, Dayton, O. *General Secretary Sunday School and Brotherhood Work,* Rev. Charles W. Brewbaker; *Secretary,* (emeritus), Col. Robert Cowden; *Director Religious Education,* M. A. Honline; *Superin-*

tendent Elementary Division, Miss Ida M. Koontz; *General Secretary Young People's Work,* Rev. O. T. Deever; *Editor Sunday School Literature,* Rev. W. O. Fries, 39 Warder Street, Dayton, O.

Sunday School and Brotherhood Executive Committee, Dayton, O. *Chairman,* Col. Robert Cowden; *Secretary,* Rev. Ira D. Warner.

Christian Endeavor Executive Committee, Dayton, O. *Chairman,* Rev. J. G. Huber; *Secretary,* Rev. A. R. Clippinger.

Board of Education, United Brethren Building, Dayton, O. *President,* Bishop C. J. Kephart, Kansas City, Mo.; *General Secretary,* William E. Schell; *Treasurer,* L. O. Miller.

Colleges and Theological Seminary

Institution	Location	President
Indiana Central University	University Heights, Ind.	I. J. Good.
Kansas City University	Kansas City, Kan.	John H. Lucas.
Leander Clark College	Toledo, Ia.	M. R. Drury.
Lebanon Valley College	Annville, Pa.	G. D. Gossard.
Otterbein University	Westerville, O.	W. G. Clippinger.
Philomath College	Philomath, Ore.	Lloyd L. Epley.
York College	York, Neb.	M. O. McLaughlin.
Bonebrake Theological Seminary	Dayton, O.	J. P. Landis.

List of ministers with addresses will be found in the United Brethren Year Book, published at The Otterbein Press, Dayton, O. W. R. Funk, Editor and Publisher.

Periodicals

Religious Telescope, Dayton, O., Editor, Rev. J. M. Phillippi; *Watchword,* Dayton, O., Editor, Rev. H. F. Shupe; *Friend of Boys and Girls,* Dayton, O., Editors, Rev. W. O. Fries and Rev. J. W. Owen; *Woman's Evangel,* Dayton, O., Editor, Miss Mabel Drury.

CONSTITUENT BODIES OF THE FEDERAL COUNCIL, JANUARY, 1917

Denominations	Ministers	Churches	Communicants
Baptist Churches, North	8,572	9,542	1,289,909
Free Baptist	*805	*1,110	*65,440
National Baptist Convention†	13,806	16,842	2,133,635
Seventh-Day Baptist	98	82	8,255
Christian Church	1,066	1,360	106,159
Congregational	5,974	6,106	790,488
Disciples of Christ	6,324	8,533	1,177,792
Evangelical Association	1,056	1,625	120,387
United Evangelical	516	948	89,530
Friends	1,287	748	97,514
German Evangelical Synod	1,089	1,389	274,787
Lutheran, General Synod	1,425	1,847	360,749
Mennonite, General Conference	180	116	15,451
Methodist Episcopal	18,763	28,360	3,743,031
Methodist Episcopal, South	7,320	16,993	2,123,785
African Methodist Episcopal	5,000	6,000	620,000
African Methodist Episcopal Zion	3,552	3,180	568,608
Colored Methodist Episcopal	3,072	3,196	240,798
Methodist Protestant	1,410	2,400	201,110
Moravian	144	126	20,859
Presbyterian in U. S. A.	9,585	9,784	1,543,027
Presbyterian in U. S. (South)	1,861	3,437	348,223
United Presbyterian	973	992	156,954
Welsh Presbyterian	91	142	14,668
Reformed Presbyterian (General Synod)	16	17	3,300
Protestant Episcopal, Commissions on Christian Unity and Social Service	5,598	8,054	1,066,970
Reformed Church in America	775	724	131,724
Reformed Church in U. S.	1,245	1,773	326,112
Reformed Episcopal	82	80	11,465
United Brethren	1,937	3,577	345,705
Totals for 1916	103,622	139,083	17,996,435
Totals for 1915	103,113	139,091	17,742,509

* Largely merged with Baptist Churches, North.

† Statistics include both Conventions, the incorporated and the unincorporated.

Note—The difference between the totals for 1916 and 1915 does not represent the actual increase of 1916, for the reason that there has been one extraordinary change. The figures for membership of the Disciples of Christ have been reduced by the denominational statisticians by about 185,000, and those for membership of the National Baptist Convention have been increased by adjustment by about 115,000.—*Editor.*

DIRECTORY OF RELIGIOUS BODIES OTHER THAN THOSE IN THE FEDERAL COUNCIL*

For statistics see General tables, beginning on page 184.

Adventists

ADVENT CHRISTIAN CHURCH

General Conference, biennial; 52 subordinate conferences. *President,* Rev. O. R. Jenks; *General Superintendent,* Rev. Finn Murra, 160 Warren Street, Boston, Mass.; *Secretary,* Rev. Charles F. King, 21 Devonshire Street, Portland, Me.; *Treasurer,* Charles H. Woodman, 13 Carmel Street, Chelsea, Mass.

American Advent Mission Society, 160 Warren Street, Boston, Mass. *President,* Rev. Henry Stone; *Secretary-Treasurer,* Rev. Geo. E. Tyler.

Woman's Home and Foreign Missions Society, 5 Whiting Street, Boston, Mass. *President,* Mrs. Maude M. Chadsey; *Clerk,* Mrs. Nellie E. Fellows; *Treasurer,* Mrs. Maude M. Chadsey.

Young People's Society of Loyal Workers. *President,* Rev. L. F. Reynolds, 93 Messer Street, Providence, R. I.; *Corresponding Secretary,* Miss Charlotte Whitman, Old Orchard, Me.

College

Institution	Location	President
Aurora College	Aurora, Ill.	O. R. Jenks.

For list of ministers with addresses see Advent Christian Manual, published by the Advent Christian Publication Society; *Manager,* Rev. L. F. Reynolds, 160 Warren Street, Boston, Mass.

Periodicals

World's Crisis (weekly), Boston, Mass., Editor, Rev. F. L. Piper; *Our Hope* (weekly), Mendota, Ill., Editor, Rev. Henry Pollard; *Messiah's Advocate* (weekly), Oakland, Cal., Editor,

---

*For Directory of the Constituent Bodies of the Federal Council of the Churches of Christ in America, see pages 43-109.

Rev. J. J. Schaumburg; *Present Truth Messenger* (weekly), Live Oak, Fla., Editor, Rev. B. A. L. Bixler.

CHURCH OF GOD, ADVENTIST

No general organization; 7 district conferences, annual.

Periodicals

The Restitution, Cleveland, O.; *The Restitution Herald,* Oregon, Ill.

SEVENTH-DAY ADVENTISTS

General Conference, quadrennial; 12 union conferences in the United States and Canada. *President,* A. G. Daniells; *Secretary,* W. A. Spicer; *Treasurer,* W. T. Knox.

Headquarters, Takoma Park, Washington, D. C.

There are no separate boards; but publishing, educational, medical, and other general activities are under the charge of a General Conference Committee, with a secretary for each department.

Colleges

Institution	Location	President
Clinton German Seminary	Clinton, Mo.	F. R. Isaac
Emmanuel Missionary College	Berrien Springs, Mich.	O. J. Graf.
Loma Linda Medical College	Loma Linda, Cal.	N. G. Evans.
Pacific Union College	St. Helena, Cal.	C. W. Irwin.
Union College	College View, Neb.	H. A. Morrison.
Walla Walla College	College Place, Wash.	E. C. Kellogg.
Washington Missionary College	Takoma Park, Washington, D. C.	B. F. Machlan.

There are 18 sanitariums, the chief of which are at Loma Linda, Cal.; St. Helena, Cal.; Boulder, Colo.; Melrose, Mass.; and Takoma Park, Washington, D. C.

The Year Book, published by the Review and Herald Publishing Association, Takoma Park, Washington, D. C., contains list of ministers with addresses.

Periodicals

Advent Review and Sabbath Herald, Washington, D. C., Editor, F. M. Wilcox; *Signs of the Times,* Mountain View, Cal., Editor, A. O. Tait; *Watchman,* Nashville, Tenn., Editor, L. A. Smith.

Baptists

SOUTHERN BAPTIST CONVENTION

Annual; last session held in Asheville, N. C., in May, 1916. The Convention, according to its constitution, consists "(1) of brethren who contribute funds, or are delegated by Baptist bodies contributing funds for the regular work of the Convention, on the basis of one delegate for every $250 actually paid into the treasuries of the Board during the fiscal year ending the 30th day of April next preceding the meeting of the Convention; (2) of one representative from each of the district associations which cooperate with this Convention, such representatives to furnish credentials of their election."

There is also in each State a State Convention or General Association. The Southern Baptist Convention, the State Conventions, and the district associations are composed of ministerial and lay members.

Officers: *President,* Rev. Lansing Burrows, Americus, Ga.; *Secretaries,* Rev. Oliver Fuller Gregory, Baltimore, Md., and Rev. Hight C. Moore, Raleigh, N. C.; *Treasurer,* Mr. George W. Norton, Louisville, Ky.

Foreign Mission Board, Richmond, Va. *President,* Rev. J. B. Hutson; *Corresponding Secretary,* Rev. J. F. Love; *Treasurer,* R. R. Gwathmey; *Assistant Secretary,* Rev. T. B. Ray.

Home Mission Board, Atlanta, Ga. *President,* Rev. John F. Purser; *Corresponding Secretary,* Rev. B. D. Gray; *Treasurer,* P. H. Mell.

Sunday School Board, Nashville, Tenn. *President,* Rev. E. E. Folk; *Corresponding Secretary and Treasurer,* J. Van Ness (acting).

Laymen's Movement, Chattanooga, Tenn. *Chairman Executive Committee,* Newell Sanders; *General Secretary,* J. T. Henderson; *Treasurer,* Charles Hood.

Baptist Young People's Union of the South, Louisville, Ky. *President,* W. W. Hamilton, Lynchburg, Va.; *Corresponding Secretary and Treasurer,* Thomas J. Watts, Columbia, S. C.

Woman's Missionary Union (auxiliary to Southern Baptist Convention), Baltimore, Md. *President* Mrs. W. J. James, Richmond, Va.; *Corresponding Secretary,* Miss Kathleen Mallory; *Treasurer,* Mrs. W. C. Lowndes, Baltimore, Md.

Colleges and Universities

Institution	Location	President or Secretary
Anderson College	Anderson, S. C	James E. White.
Baptist University of Oklahoma	Shawnee, Okla	W. B. Taylor.
Baylor Female College	Belton, Tex	J. C. Hardy.
Baylor University	Waco, Tex	Samuel P. Brooks.
Bessie Tift College	Forsyth, Ga	J. H. Foster.
Bethel College	Russellville, Ky	H. G. Brownell:
Bethel Female College	Hopkinsville, Ky	C. M. Thompson (acting)
Blue Mountain College	Blue Mountain, Miss	W. T. Lowrey.
Burleson College	Greenville, Tex	John S. Humphreys
Carson-Newman College	Jefferson City, Tenn	J. M. Burnett.
Central College	Conway, Ark	John W. Conger.
Chowan College	Murfreesboro, N. C	G. E. Lineberry.
Clark Memorial College	Newton, Miss	M. O. Patterson.
Clinton College	Clinton, Ky	G. W. Duncan.
Coker College	Hartsville, S. C	S. W. Garrett.
Columbia College (of Florida)	Lake City, Fla	A. P. Montague.
Cumberland College	Williamsburg, Ky	E. E. Wood
Doyle College	Doyle, Tenn	J. C. Ammons.
Furman University	Greenville, S. C	E. M. Poteat.
Georgetown College	Georgetown, Ky	M. B. Adams.
Grand River College	Gallatin, Mo	E. W. Dow.
Greenville Female College	Greenville, S. C	D. M. Ramsay.
Hardin College	Mexico, Mo	John W. Million.
Hillman College	Clinton, Miss	M. P. L. Berry.
Hollins College	Hollins, Va	Miss Matty L. Cocke.
Howard College	East Lake, Birmingham, Ala	James M. Shelburne.
Howard Payne College	Brownwood, Tex	
Jacksonville College	Jacksonville, Tex	J. V. Vermillion.
John B. Stetson University	De Land, Fla	Lincoln Hulley.
Judson College for Young Ladies	Marion, Ala	Paul V. Bomar.
Lagrange College	Lagrange, Mo	J. T. Muir.
Lexington College for Young Ladies	Lexington, Mo	M. W. Hatton.
Limestone College	Gaffney, S. C	Lee Davis Lodge.
Louisiana College	Pineville, La	C. Cottingham.
Mars Hill College	Mars Hill, N. C	R. L. Moore.
Mercer University	Macon, Ga	W. L. Pickard.
Meredith College	Raleigh, N. C	C. E. Brewer.
Mississippi College	Clinton, Miss	J. W. Provine.
Mississippi Woman's College	Hattiesburg, Miss	J. L. Johnson, Jr.
Ouashita College	Arkadelphia, Ark	C. E. Dicken.
Oxford College for Girls	Oxford, N. C	F. P. Hobgood.
Richmond College	Richmond College, Va	F. W. Boatwright.
Shorter College	Rome, Ga	A. W. Van Hoose.
Simmons College	Abilene, Tex	J. D. Sandefer.
Southern Female College	Lagrange, Ga	James E. Ricketson.
Southwest Baptist College	Bolivar, Mo	C. W. Fisher.
Stephens College	Columbia, Mo	James M. Wood.
Tennessee College for Women	Murfreesboro, Tenn	George J. Burnett.
Union University	Jackson, Tenn	G. M. Savage.
Virginia Intermont College	Bristol, Va	H. G. Noffsinger.
Wake Forest College	Wake Forest, N. C	W. L. Poteat.
Westhampton College	Richmond College, Va	May Lansfield Keller.
William Jewell College	Liberty, Mo	John P. Greene.
Will Mayfield College	Marble Hill, Mo	A. F. Hendricks.
Woodland College	Jonesboro, Ark	W. M. Harrell.

Theological Seminaries

Institution	Location	President
Southern Baptist Theological Sem	Louisville, Ky	E. Y. Mullins.
Southwestern Baptist Theological Sem	Fort Worth, Tex	L. R. Scarborough,

Hospitals, Homes for Aged, and Orphans' Homes

Baptist Hospital, Columbia, S. C.; *Baptist Hospital,* Jackson, Miss.; *Baptist Hospital,* Memphis, Tenn.; *Baptist Hospital,* St. Louis, Mo.; *Georgia Baptist Hospital,* Atlanta, Ga.; *Memorial Sanitarium,* Dallas, Tex.; *Missouri Baptist Sanitarium,* St. Louis, Mo.; *Oklahoma Baptist Hospital,* Muskogee, Okla.; *Oklahoma Baptist Sanitarium,* Oklahoma City, Okla.; *Baptist Home for Aged Women,* Richmond, Va.; *Missouri Home for Aged Baptists,* Ironton, Mo.; *Baptist Widows' and Orphans' Home,* Evergreen, Ala.; *Buckner Orphans' Home,* Dallas, Tex.; *Connie Maxwell Orphanage,* Greenwood, S. C.; *Georgia Baptist Orphans' Home,* Hopeville, Ga.; *German Orphans' Home,* Louisville, Ky.; *Kentucky Baptist Orphans' Home,* Louisville, Ky.; *Maryland Baptist Orphanage,* Baltimore, Md.; *Mississippi Baptist Orphanage,* Jackson, Miss.; *Missouri Baptist Orphans' Home,* St. Louis, Mo.; *Tennessee Baptist Orphans' Home,* Nashville, Tenn.

Periodicals

Alabama Baptist (weekly), Birmingham, Ala., Editor, Rev. F. W. Barnett; *Baptist Advance* (weekly), Little Rock, Ark., Editor, Rev. E. J. A. McKinney; *Baptist and Reflector* (weekly), Nashville, Tenn., Editor, Rev. E. E. Folk; *Baptist Chronicle* (weekly), Alexandria, La., Editor, E. O. Ware; *Baptist Courier* (weekly), Greenville, S. C., Editor, Rev. Z. T. Cody; *Baptist Flag* (weekly), Fulton, Ky., Editor, Rev. T. F. Moore; *Baptist Messenger* (weekly), Oklahoma City, Okla., Editor, Rev. C. P. Stealy; *Baptist Record* (weekly), Jackson, Miss., Editor, Rev. P. I. Lipsey; *Baptist Review and Exposition* (quarterly), Louisville, Ky., Editor, Rev. E. Y. Mullins; *Baptist Standard* (weekly), Dallas, Tex., Editor, Rev. E. C. Routh; *Baptist World* (weekly), Louisville, Ky., Editor, Rev. E. Y. Mullins; *Biblical Recorder* (weekly), Raleigh, N. C., Editor, Rev. H. C. Moore; *Child's Gem* (weekly), Nashville, Tenn., Editor, Rev. I. J. Van Ness; *Christian Index* (weekly), Atlanta, Ga., Editor, B. J. W. Graham; *Convention, Southern, Publications* (quarterly), Nashville, Tenn., Editor, Rev. I. J. Van Ness; *Kind Words* (weekly, semi-monthly, monthly), Nashville, Tenn., Editor, Rev. I. J. Van Ness; *Missionary Worker* (semi-monthly), Dallas, Tex., Editor, Rev. J. B. Gambrell; *Home and Foreign Fields* (monthly), Sunday School Board, Nashville, Tenn.; *Our Missionary Helper* (monthly), Decatur, Ga., Editor, Mrs. C. E. Kerr; *News and Truths* (weekly), Murray, Ky., Editor, Rev. H. B. Taylor; *Religious Herald* (weekly), Richmond, Va., Editor, Rev. R. H. Pitt; *Western Evangel* (weekly), Abilene, Tex., Editor, W. F. Fry;

Western Recorder (weekly), Louisville, Ky., Editor, Rev. J. W. Porter; *Word and Way* (weekly), Kansas City, Mo., Editor, Rev. S. M. Brown; *Florida Baptist Witness,* Arcadia, Fla., Editor, Rev. A. J. Holt.

NATIONAL BAPTIST CONVENTION, UNINCORPORATED

This body separated from the National Baptist Convention (Incorporated) in Chicago in September, 1915. Its annual session was held in Kansas City, Kan., in September, 1916. Its next annual meeting will be held in Atlanta, Ga., Wednesday after the first Sunday in September, 1917.

Officers of the National Convention, unincorporated, *President,* Rev. Edward P. Jones, Vicksburg, Miss.; *Recording Secretary,* J. L. King, Wytheville, Va.; *Treasurer,* Rev. J. F. Thomas, Chicago, Ill.

Foreign Mission Board. *Secretary,* R. Kemp, Charleston, S. C.

Home Mission Board. *Secretary,* J. D. Brooks, Aiken, S. C.

Educational Board. *Secretary,* D. Abner, Conroe, Tex.

Publishing Board. *Secretary,* Rev. R. H. Boyd, Nashville, Tenn.

Baptist Young People's Union. *Secretary,* Rev. S. R. Prince, Ft. Worth, Tex.

Benefit Board. *Secretary,* S. T. Floyd, Sherman, Tex.

Evangelical Board. *Corresponding Secretary,* Rev. J. S. Anderson, Sherman, Tex.

Laymen's Movement. *National Organizer,* C. T. Hume.

Woman's Auxiliary. *Corresponding Secretary,* Mrs. M. A. B. Fuller, Austin, Texas.

It is not possible at present to give a list of the institutions and periodicals belonging to each Convention.

Periodical of National Baptist Convention, unincorporated, *Union-Review,* weekly, Nashville, Tenn.

GENERAL BAPTISTS

General Association; annual. *Secretary-Treasurer,* J. P. Cox, Owensville, Ind. There are 35 district associations.

Foreign Mission Board. *President,* Rev. A. B. Stone, Dixon, Ky. *Secretary,* J. P. Cox, Owensville, Ind.

Home Mission Board. *President,* B. E. Whitmer, Boonville, Ind.

Sunday School Board. *President,* A. E. Powers, Evansville, Ind.; *Secretary,* Rev. Claud Neal, Howell, Ind.

Oakland College, Oakland City, Ind., *President,* W. P. Dearing.

Periodical. *The Messenger* (weekly), Owensville, Ind.

SIX PRINCIPLE BAPTISTS

(Known also as The International Old Baptist Union)

There are two annual conferences in the United States.

Presiding Bishop of International Old Baptist Union, Rev. Thomas H. Squire, Allisonville, Ontario, Can.

President or Bishop of Rhode Island Conference, Rev. D. L. Bennett, Washington, R. I.; *President of Pennsylvania Conference,* J. H. Billings, Nicholson, Pa.

Brethren

CHURCH OF THE BRETHREN

(Conservative Dunkards)

The next meeting of the General Conference, annual, will be held at Wichita, Kan., early in June, 1917.

There are 47 district conferences.

Officers of the General Conference: *Moderator,* Elder I. W. Taylor, Neffsville, Pa.; *Secretary,* Elder A. C. Wieand, 3435 Van Buren Street, Chicago, Ill.; *Treasurer,* J. B. Deeter, West Milton, O.

General Mission Board. *Chairman,* H. C. Early, Penn Laird, Va.; *Secretary-Treasurer,* Rev. Galen B. Royer, Elgin, Ill.

General Sunday School Board. *Chairman,* H. K. Ober, Elizabethtown, Pa.; *Secretary,* J. E. Miller, Elgin, Ill.; *Treasurer,* Jas. M. Mohler, Leeton, Mo.; *Editor Sunday School Publications,* J. E. Miller, Elgin, Ill.

General Educational Board. *Chairman,* D. W. Kurtz, McPherson, Kan.; *Secretary-Treasurer,* J. H. B. Williams, Elgin, Ill.

Temperance Committee. *Chairman,* P. J. Blough, Hooversville, Pa.; *Secretary,* J. J. John, New Windsor, Md.; *Treasurer,* J. Carson Miller, Moores Store, Va.

Peace Committee. *Chairman,* J. Kurtz Miller, 664 Forty-fourth Street, Brooklyn, N. Y.

Homeless Children Committee. *President,* Frank Fisher, Mexico, Ind.

Sisters' Aid Societies. *President,* Mrs. J. H. Brubaker, Virden, Ill.; *Secretary-Treasurer,* Mrs. Levi Minnich, Greenville, O.

Colleges

Institution	Location
Blue Ridge College	New Windsor, Md.
Bridgewater College	Bridgewater, Va.
Daleville College	Daleville, Va.
Elizabethtown College	Elizabethtown, Pa.
Juniata College	Huntingdon, Pa.
Lordsburg College	Lordsburg, Cal.
Manchester College	North Manchester, Ind.
McPherson College	McPherson, Kan.
Mount Morris College	Mount Morris, Ill.

Theological Seminary

Institution	Location
Bethany Bible School	3435 West Van Buren Street, Chicago, Ill.

For list of ministers, with addresses, see the Brethren Family Almanac, published at Elgin, Ill.

Periodical. *Gospel Messenger,* Elgin, Ill., Editor, D. L. Miller.

OLD GERMAN BAPTIST CHURCH

(Old Order Dunkards)

Yearly Meeting; next meeting, Camden, Ind., May, 1917.

Officers of Yearly Meeting: *Foreman,* Elder Michael Montgomery, Fairview, Mo.; *Clerk,* Elder Ezra M. Senseney, Union Bridge, Md.

List of ministers with addresses published in the November number of the *Vindicator.*

Periodical. *Vindicator* (monthly), Brookville, O. *Publishing Agent,* J. M. Kimmel.

THE BRETHREN CHURCH

(Progressive Dunkards)

The General Conference; annual, meets at Winona Lake, Ind., August 27, 1917.

Moderator, J. M. Tombaugh, D.D., Hagerstown, Md.; *Secretary,* Rev. Dyoll Belote, Canton, O.

General Missionary Board. *Secretary,* Horace Kolb, 1603 Butler Street, Philadelphia, Pa.

Foreign Missionary Society. *Secretary,* L. S. Bauman, Long Beach, Cal.

College and Seminary, Ashland, Ohio. W. D. Furry, *President.*

Brethren Publishing Company, Ashland, Ohio, publishes *Brethren Evangelist, Woman's Outlook,* and Sunday school supplies.

GERMAN SEVENTH-DAY BAPTISTS
(Dunkards)

Annual meeting.

President, C. L. King, New Enterprise, Bedford County, Pa.; *Secretary,* Emma Monn, Quincy, Franklin County, Pa.

Missionary Board. *Secretary,* Rev. J. A. Peutz, Waynesboro, Pa.

THE BRETHREN (PLYMOUTH)

No ordained ministers, no ecclesiastical organization; societies usually worship in halls. For literature write Loizeaux Brothers, publishers, No. 1 East Thirteenth Street, New York.

Eastern Churches
ARMENIAN APOSTOLIC CHURCH IN AMERICA

General Assembly.

There are 13 state and district sub-dioceses.

Prelate, Rt. Rev. A. E. Vehouni, 65 Laurel Street, Worcester, Mass.

Central Church Committee: *Chairman,* Rev. D. Rijagion, 10 Brookdale Street, Roslindale, Mass.; *Secretary,* M. Berberian; *Treasurer,* Dr. P. Adamian.

Periodical. *Local Church Calendar* (Armenian).

GREEK ORTHODOX CHURCH

Rev. Methodias Kourkolis, 154 East Seventy-second Street, New York City.

RUSSIAN ORTHODOX CHURCH

Most Rev. Archbishop Eudokin; Rt. Rev. Bishop Alexander, 15 East Ninety-seventh Street, New York City.

North American Ecclesiastical Consistory. *Secretary*, Rev. Peter I. Popoff, 15 East Ninety-seventh Street, New York City.

Six districts, including one in Canada and one in Alaska.

Theological Seminary, Tenafly, N. J.

SERBIAN ORTHODOX CHURCH

Rt. Rev. Sebastian Dabovitch, Archimandrite, 2610 Tenth Avenue, Oakland, Cal.

SYRIAN ORTHODOX CHURCH

Rt. Rev. Alexander Nemelovsky, Bishop, 15 East Ninety-seventh Street, New York City.

Western Churches

AMERICAN OLD CATHOLIC CHURCH

Headquarters, Waukegan, Ill.

POLISH NATIONAL CATHOLIC CHURCH OF AMERICA

General Synod, quinquennial; next session, 1919.

There are four provinces: Eastern, Central, Western, and Northern.

Bishops

Rt. Rev. Francis Hodur, 529 Locust Street, Scranton, Pa.
Rt. Rev. Francis Bonczak, Milwaukee, Wis.
Rt. Rev. Valenty Gawrychowski, Buffalo, N. Y.
Rt. Rev. Joseph Plaga, Chicago, Ill.
Rt. Rev. Valenty Cichy, Toledo, O.
Theological Seminary. Theological Seminary at Plymouth, Pa.
Periodical. *Straz* (Guard), Scranton, Pa.

ROMAN CATHOLIC CHURCH IN THE UNITED STATES

Apostolic Delegate, the Most Rev. John Bonzano, 1811 Biltmore Street, Washington, D. C.

Cardinals

James Cardinal Gibbons, Archbishop of Baltimore, Baltimore, Md.

John Cardinal Farley, Archbishop of New York, New York City.

William Cardinal O'Connell, Archbishop of Boston, Boston, Mass.

According to the Official Catholic Directory for 1916, covering the year 1915, there are 14 provinces in the United States, 14 Archbishops and 97 Bishops. Of dioceses there are 86 besides the 14 archdioceses, two Vicariates Apostolic, and one Prefecture Apostolic. In the United States possessions there are nine dioceses in the Philippines, including the archdiocese of Manila and one Prefecture Apostolic. There is also a diocese in Porto Rico and Vicariates Apostolic in Guam and the Samoan Islands. The Panama Canal Zone is included in the diocese of Panama, Central America.

There are in the United States, not including the insular possessions, 19,572 clergy, 15,163 churches, including missions, and an aggregate Catholic population of 16,564,109. There is besides, in Alaska, 11,500 Catholic population; in Guam, 12,995; in Samoa, 1,000; in Hawaii, 42,000; in Porto Rico, 1,000,000; in the Canal Zone, 5,000; and in the Philippines, 7,284,458; making a grand total of 24,921,062 Catholic population in the United States and its possessions.

The Church has 85 seminaries with 6,200 theological students, 210 colleges for boys, 685 academies for girls, 5,588 parochial schools, with 1,497,949 pupils, 283 orphanages with 48,089 orphans, and 112 homes for the aged.

Among the organizations doing home missionary work are the following:

Catholic Church Extension Society, McCormick Building, Chicago, Ill. *Director,* Very Rev. Francis C. Kelley.

Catholic Missionary Union, Brookland Station, Washington, D. C. *Director,* Rev. Walter Elliott.

Bureau of Catholic Indian Missions, 1326 New York Avenue, Washington, D. C. *Director,* Rev. William H. Ketcham.

Catholic Board for Mission Work among Colored People, 1 Madison Avenue, New York City. *Director,* Right Rev. John E. Burke.

St. Joseph's Society for Colored Missions, St. Joseph's Seminary, Baltimore, Md. *Director,* Very Rev. Justin McCarthy.

It is estimated that about $1,000,000 a year is raised by the above named and other organizations.

There are also various societies interested in foreign missions, including: Society for the Propagation of the Faith, a branch of the Society whose headquarters are Lyons, France; 627 Lexington Avenue, New York City, *General Director,* Rt. Rev. Joseph Freri. This society also has numerous diocesan branches: Association of the Holy Childhood for the Redemption of the Children of Infidels, Pittsburgh, Pa., *Director,* Rev. Edward J. Knaebel. Commissariat of the Holy Land, Brookland Station, Washington, D. C., *Director,* Rev. Godfrey Schilling. Catholic Foreign Missionary Society, Mary Knoll, Ossining, N. Y., *Director,* Very Rev. James A. Walsh. There are also other similar societies. It is estimated that about $750,000 a year is raised for foreign missions.

Of religious orders of men and women there are a great number—seventy or more of different orders for men, and of different orders for women nearly a hundred more than for men.

CHRISTADELPHIANS

Have no conferences, general officers, boards or colleges. The *Christadelphian Advocate,* Waterloo, Ia., represents this congregational body, which has no ordained ministers.

CHURCH OF CHRIST, SCIENTIST

Governing Board, The Christian Science Board of Directors. *President of the Denomination,* Calvin A. Frye, Boston, Mass.; *Clerk,* John V. Dittemore, Boston, Mass.

Christian Science Publishing Society, Falmouth and St. Paul Streets, Boston, Mass.

Periodicals

Christian Science Journal (monthly), Boston, Mass., Editor, Archibald McLellan; *Christian Science Sentinel,* Boston, Mass., Editor, Archibald McLellan; *Christian Science Monitor* (daily), Boston, Mass., Editor, Frederick Dixon; Christian Science Quarterly Bible Lessons, Boston, Mass., Edited by a Committee.

CHRISTIAN UNION

General Council meets quadrennially; next meeting in Iowa.

There are 11 state councils.

Officers: *President,* Rev. A. C. Thomas, Milo, Ia.; *Secretary,* Rev. W. H. Baker, Findlay, Ohio; *Corresponding Secretary,* Rev. D. L. Vandament, Greencastle, Ind.; *Treasurer,* Rev. A. F. Dorrell, Tryon, Okla.

List of ministers, with addresses, in the annual minutes of the various state councils.

Periodicals

Christian Union Messenger, Greencastle, Ind., Editor, Rev. D. L. Vandament; *Christian Union Herald,* Excelsior Springs, Mo., Editor, J. W. Hyder.

CHURCH OF THE NEW JERUSALEM—GENERAL CONVENTION

General Convention, annual; 11 associations meeting annually or semiannually.

Officers: *President,* Rev. Julian K. Smyth, 230 West Fifty-ninth Street, New York City; *Recording Secretary,* Mr. Benjamin A. Whittemore, 134 Bowdoin Street, Boston, Mass.; *Treasurer,* Mr. James Richard Carter, 246 Devonshire Street, Boston, Mass.

Board of Home and Foreign Missions. *President,* Mr. Ezra Hyde Alden, 1217 Commercial Trust Building, Philadelphia, Pa.; *Secretary,* Rev. Paul Sperry, 1437 Q Street, N. W., Washington, D. C.; *Treasurer,* Lloyd A. Frost, 716 Old South Building, Boston, Mass.

Board of Publication, 3 West Twenty-ninth Street, New York City. *President,* Robert Alfred Shaw; *Secretary,* Rev. Adolph Roeder; *Treasurer,* John F. Seekamp.

Committee on Education. *Chairman,* Rev. Lewis F. Hite, 42 Arlington Street, Cambridge, Mass.

Committee of the American New-Church Sunday School Association. *President,* Mr. Richard B. Carter, Newtonville, Mass.; *Secretary-Treasurer,* Mr. John V. Horr, Cleveland, O.

National Alliance of New-Church Women. *President,* Mrs. James R. Carter, 235 Mount Vernon Street, West Newton, Mass.; *Corresponding Secretary,* Miss Mary E. Howes, Fenway Post Office, Boston, Mass.; *Treasurer,* Mrs. E. A. Munger, 3307 Rhodes Avenue, Chicago, Ill.

Social Service Commission. *Chairman,* Rev. C. W. Harvey, 214 North Thirty-fourth Street, Philadelphia, Pa.; *Executive Secretary,* Rev. John W. Stockwell, 4304 Frankford Avenue, Philadelphia, Pa.

Theological School. New-Church Theological School, Cambridge, Mass., *President,* William L. Worcester.

For list of ministers, with addresses, see Journal of the General Convention, published by the Massachusetts New-Church Union, 134 Bowdoin Street, Boston, Mass.

Periodicals

New-Church Review (quarterly), Boston, Mass., Editor, Rev. H. C. Hay; *New-Church Messenger* (weekly), Chicago, Ill., Editor, Rev. John S. Saul.

CHURCH OF THE NEW JERUSALEM—GENERAL CHURCH

General Assembly, triennial.

There are also district assemblies.

General Officers: *Bishop,* Rev. N. D. Pendleton, *Secretary,* Rev. C. Th. Odhner, Bryn Athyn,. Pa.; *Treasurer,* Rev. W. H. Alden.

Publishing House, Bryn Athyn, Pa.

Academy of the New Church, with collegiate department and theological school, Bryn Athyn, Pa. *President,* N. D. Pendleton.

List of ministers, with addresses, in *New Church Life,* for August, 1915.

Periodical. *New Church Life* (monthly), Bryn Athyn, Pa.

SOCIETY OF FRIENDS (HICKSITE)

General Conference, biennial; next meeting will be held in 1918, place to be selected.

Seven Yearly Meetings.

Officers of the General Conference: *Chairman,* O. Edward Janney, 825 Newington Avenue, Baltimore, Md.; *General Secretary,* J. Barnard Walton, 140 North 15th Street, Philadelphia, Pa.; *Recording Secretary,* Josephine H. Tilton, Mount Vernon, N. Y.; *Treasurer,* Harry A. Hawkins, 57 Pierrepont Avenue, West, Rutherford, N. J.

Headquarters of Sunday School Committee, Central Bureau of Philadelphia Yearly Meeting, 150 North Fifteenth Street, Philadelphia, Pa. Miss Jane P. Rushmore, *Secretary.*

There are no denominational theological schools or colleges. Friends generally patronize Swarthmore College.

Friends' School for Religious and Social Education, Woolman House, Swarthmore, Pa.

There is no official list of ministers.

Periodical. *Friends' Intelligencer,* Philadelphia, Pa., Editor, Henry Ferris.

JEWISH CONGREGATIONS

Union of Orthodox Jewish Congregations in America.

Seventh Convention held at Arverne, L. I., N. Y., in 1914.

President, Bernard Drachman; *Secretary,* Albert Lucas, 56 West 105th Street, New York City.

United Orthodox Rabbis of America. *President,* Bernard L. Levinthal, 716 Pine Street, Philadelphia, Pa.

Union of American Hebrew Congregations. Twenty-fourth Council held in Chicago, Ill., in 1915. *President,* J. Walter Freiberg; *Secretary,* Lipman Levy, Fourth National Bank Building, Cincinnati, O.

Central Conference of American Rabbis. Convention, annual. *Corresponding Secretary,* Joseph S. Kornfield, 1428 Fair Avenue, Columbus, O.

Eastern Council of Reform Rabbis. *Secretary,* Clifton H. Levy, 2 Duane Street, New York City.

Jewish Publication Society of America, Girard Avenue and Broad Street, Philadelphia, Pa. *President,* Simon Miller; *Secretary,* Benjamin Alexander.

Colleges and Theological Seminary

Institution	Location	President
Dropsie Col. for Hebrew & Cognate Learning	Philadelphia, Pa	Cyrus Adler.
Hebrew Union College	Cincinnati, O	Edward L. Heinsheimer.
Jewish Theological Seminary of America	New York City	(acting) Cyrus Adler.

American Jewish Year Book, Jewish Publication Society, Philadelphia, Pa.

Latter Day Saints

CHURCH OF JESUS CHRIST OF LATTER DAY SAINTS

Headquarters, Salt Lake City, Utah.

REORGANIZED CHURCH OF JESUS CHRIST OF LATTER DAY SAINTS

General Conference, annual; next session, April 6-20, 1917, Lamoni, Iowa.

There are 4 stakes, 65 state or district conferences, in the United States, and 25 district conferences in foreign countries.

General officers: *President,* Frederick M. Smith; *First Counselor,* Elbert A. Smith; *President* of Quorum of Twelve Apostles, G. T. Griffiths; *Presiding Bishop,* Benjamin R. McGuire; *Secretary,* R. S. Salyards; *Recorder,* C. I. Carpenter; *Historian,* Heman C. Smith.

General Sunday School Association. *Superintendent,* G. R. Wells, Lamoni, Iowa; *Secretary,* E. D. Moore, Lamoni, Iowa.

Religio-Literary Society—young people's organization: *President,* G. S. Trowbridge, St. Louis, Mo.; *Secretary,* A. E. McKim, Independence, Mo.

Woman's Auxiliary for Social Service. *President,* Mrs. F. M. Smith, Independence, Mo.; *Secretary,* Mrs. Carrie Maitland, Des Moines, Iowa:

College. Graceland College, Lamoni, Iowa; George N. Briggs, *President.*

For list of ministers, with addresses, see General Conference Minutes, Publishing House, Lamoni, Ia.

Homes for aged people, and for orphans, at Lamoni, Ia., and at Independence, Mo., and at Kirtland, O.

Periodical. *Saints' Herald,* official organ, Lamoni, Ia.

Evangelical Lutheran Bodies

There are five general bodies of Lutherans in the United States with fifty-two synods, of which four are in Canada, and sixteen independent synods. The General Bodies are as follows: General Synod, organized in 1820, with twenty-four synods, General Council, organized in 1867, with fourteen synods, the United Synod South, organized in 1886, with eight synods, the Synodical Conference, organized in 1872, with six synods, and the United Norwegian Synod.

For directory of General Synod, Lutheran, see Constituent Bodies, pages 61, 62.

LUTHERAN GENERAL COUNCIL

General Council, biennial; holds its next meeting in Philadelphia, Pa., 1917.

There are 14 District Synods.

Officers: *President,* Rev. Theodore E. Schmauk, Lebanon, Pa.; *Recording Secretaries:* English, Rev. William K. Frick, 2505 Cedar Street, Milwaukee, Wis.; German, Rev. Gottlieb C. Berkemeier, Mount Vernon, N. Y.; Swedish, Rev. Lars G. Abrahamson, 3949 Seventh Avenue, Rock Island, Ill.; *Corresponding Secretaries:* English, Rev. Frederick A. Kaehler, 998 Main Street, Buffalo, N. Y.; German, Prof. Henry Offerman, Mount Airy, Philadelphia, Pa.; Swedish, Rev. Alfred Appell, Burlington, Ia.; *Treasurer,* Mr. A. G. Anderson, Augustana Book Concern, Rock Island, Ill.

Board of English Home Missions, 807 Drexel Building, Philadelphia, Pa. *General Superintendent and Secretary,* Rev. Jacob C. Kunzmann.

Board of German Home Missions, Emigrant House, 21 Pearl Street, New York City. *Corresponding Secretary,* Rev. P. Ludwig, Camden, N. J.

Board of Swedish Home Missions, Rock Island, Ill. *Secretary and Treasurer,* Mr. Christian A. Larson, Augustana Book Concern, Rock Island, Ill.

Board of Foreign Missions, 1716 Arch Street, Philadelphia, Pa. *General Secretary,* Rev. George Drach, Trappe, Pa.; *Treasurer,* Mr. James M. Snyder, 401 Chestnut Street, Philadelphia, Pa.

Board of Missions for Porto Rico and Latin America, Pittsburgh, Pa. *Secretary,* Rev. Benjamin F. Hankey, 576 Orchard Street, Bellevue, Pa.

Board of Publication, 1716 Arch Street, Philadelphia, Pa. *Business Manager,* Mr. Charles B. Opp.

Board of Immigrant Missions, Emigrant House, 21 Pearl Street, New York City. *Secretary,* Rev. D. W. Peterson, Maspeth, N. Y.; *Treasurer,* F. Kracke, 2848 Briggs Avenue, New York, N. Y.

Board of Slav and Hungarian Missions, 45 South Thirteenth Street, Allentown, Pa. *Superintendent,* Rev. A. L. Ramer, Allentown, Pa.

Board of Education, 415 South Forty-fourth Street, Philadelphia, Pa. *Corresponding Secretary,* Rev. Ernst P. H. Pfatteicher.

Committee on Sunday School Work, 1716 Arch Street, Philadelphia, Pa. *Secretary,* Rev. William L. Hunton.

Mission and Church Extension Society, 805 Drexel Building, Philadelphia, Pa. *General Secretary,* Rev. Charles L. Fry.

Colleges

Institution	Location	President
Augustana College	Rock Island, Ill	G. A. Andreen.
Bethany College	Lindsborg, Kan	E. F. Pihlblad.
Evangelical Lutheran College	Saskatoon, Sask., Can	J. Goos.
Gustavus Adolphus College	St. Peter, Minn	O. J. Johnson.
Luther College	Wahoo, Neb	A. T. Seashore.
Muhlenberg College	Allentown, Pa	J. A. W. Haas.
Thiel College	Greenville, Pa	H. W. Elson.
Upsala College	Kenilworth, N. J	Peter Froeberg.
Wagner Memorial College	Rochester, N. Y	J. A. W. Kirsch.
Weidner Institute	Mulberry, Ind	A. H. Arbaugh.

Theological Seminaries

Institution	Location	President
Augustana Theological Seminary	Rock Island, Ill	G. A. Andreen.
Evangelical Lutheran Theological Sem	Maywood, Ill	E. F. Krause.
Evangelical Lutheran Theological Sem	Waterloo, Ont., Can	P. A. Laury.
Lutheran Theological Seminary	Philadelphia, Pa	H. E. Jacobs.
Pacific Lutheran Theological Seminary	Seattle, Wash	P. W. H. Frederick.

For a list of ministers of all Lutheran bodies in the United States see Lutheran Church Year Book, 1716 Arch Street, Philadelphia, Pa.

Hospitals

Augustana, Chicago, Ill., *Superintendent,* Rev. M. Wahlstrom; *Bethesda,* St. Paul, Minn., *Superintendent,* Rev. J. A. Krantz; *Children's,* Philadelphia, Pa., *Superintendent,* Rev. E. F. Bachmann; *Emanuel,* Portland, Ore., *Superintendent,* H. E. Sandstedt; *Milwaukee,* Milwaukee, Wis., *Superintendent,* Rev. H. L.

Fritschel; *Passavant Memorial,* Chicago, Ill., *Superintendent,* Miss C. Christian; *Swedish,* Kansas City, Mo., *Superintendent,* Miss E. Bergman; *Iowa Lutheran,* Des Moines, Ia., *Superintendent,* Rev. F. O. Hanson; *Lutheran,* Moline, Ill.; *Immanuel,* Omaha, Neb., *Superintendent,* Rev. P. M. Lindberg; *Rajahmundry,* Rajahmundry, India, *Superintendent,* B. A. Nilsson.

Homes for Aged

Evangelical Lutheran, Philadelphia, Pa., *Superintendent,* Mrs. G. C. Eisenhardt; *Mary J. Drexel,* Philadelphia, Pa., *Superintendent,* E. F. Bachman; *Lutheran Church Home,* Buffalo, N. Y., *Superintendent,* Miss L. E. Kaehler; *Nazareth,* Omaha, Neb., *Superintendent,* P. M. Lindberg; *Bethesda,* Chisago City, Minn., *Superintendent,* C. A. Hultkrans; *Salem,* Joliet, Ill., *Superintendent,* A. W. Stark; *Lutheran,* Erie, Pa., *Superintendent,* Sister Frieda; *Lutheran,* Madrid, Ia., *Superintendent,* Sister Anna Johnson; *Old People's Kansas Conference,* Lindsborg, Kan., *Superintendent,* Francis Johnson; *Old People's,* Zelienople, Pa., *Superintendent,* Sister K. Foerster; *Swedish Augustana,* Brooklyn, N. Y., *Superintendent,* J. H. Benson; *Good Shepherd,* Allentown, Pa., *Superintendent,* J. H. Raker; *Augustana,* Chicago, Ill., *Superintendent,* J. N. Brandelle; *Old People's,* Story City, Ia., *Superintendent,* R. L. Gutteboe.

Homes for Defectives

Passavant Memorial for Epileptics, Rochester, Pa., *Superintendent,* F. W. Kohler; *Good Shepherd for Crippled Orphans,* Allentown, Pa., *Superintendent,* J. H. Raker.

Bethphage for Epileptics, Axtell, Neb., *Superintendent,* Rev. K. G. W. Dahl.

Deaconess Motherhouses

Mary J. Drexel, Philadelphia, Pa., *Superintendent,* E. F. Bachmann; *Immanuel,* Omaha, Neb., *Superintendent,* P. M. Lindberg; *Bethesda,* St. Paul, Minn., *Superintendent,* J. A. Krantz; *Lutheran,* Milwaukee, Wis., *Superintendent,* H. L. Fritschel.

Orphans' Homes

Augustana Children's Home, Minneapolis, Minn., *Superintendent,* Sister Bathilda Svenson; *Bethany,* Bridgewater, Nova Scotia, Can., *Superintendent,* Peter A. Ernst; *Bethany,* Duluth, Minn., Mrs. C. O. Cassell; *Children's Friend,* Jersey City, N. J., *Superintendent,* G. Doering; *Bethlehem,* Omaha, Neb., Rev. P. M. Lindberg; *Evangelical Lutheran,* Philadelphia, Pa., *Superintend-*

ent, Mrs. G. C. Eisenhardt; *Evangelical Lutheran Kansas Conference,* Cleburne, Kan., *Superintendent,* Rev. N. H. Youngberg; *Good Shepherd Home,* Allentown, Pa., *Superintendent,* Rev. J. H. Raker; *Gustavus Adolphus,* Jamestown, N. Y., *Superintendent,* J. S. Swensson; *Home and Farm School,* Zelienople, Pa., *Superintendent,* Rev. C. W. White; *Home and Farm School,* Lynn Center, Ill., *Superintendent,* Sister Emily Clareen; *Lutheran,* Joliet, Ill., *Superintendent,* Rev. A. W. Stark; *Lutheran,* Topton, Pa., *Superintendent,* Rev. J. O. Henry; *Lutheran,* Avon, Mass., *Superintendent,* A. Rabenius; *St. John's,* Buffalo, N. Y., *Superintendent,* O. Ehlers; *Swedish Evangelical Lutheran,* Stanton, Ia., *Superintendent,* S. P. Olin; *Swedish Evangelical Lutheran,* Stromsburg, Neb., *Superintendent,* Rev. C. A. Sward; *Vasa,* Vasa, Minn., *Superintendent,* P. Johnson.

Home Finding and Children's Friend Societies

Allentown, Pa., *Superintendent,* J. H. Raker; Chicago, Ill., *Superintendent,* J. Jesperson.

Miscellaneous Institutions

Augustana Nursery, Chicago, Ill., *Superintendent,* J. Jesperson; *Bethesda Invalids' Home,* St. Paul, Minn., *Superintendent,* Rev. J. A. Krantz; *Good Shepherd for Infants,* Allentown, Pa., *Superintendent,* J. H. Raker; *Memorial for Infants,* Philadelphia, Pa., *Superintendent,* Mrs. G. C. Eisenhardt; *Settlement of the Inner Mission,* Philadelphia, Pa., *Superintendent,* Rev. G. H. Bechtold.

Hospices

Augustana Central Home, Chicago, Ill., *Superintendent,* J. Jesperson; *Augustana Missionary Cottage,* Minneapolis, Minn., *Superintendent,* Sister Bathilda Svenson; *German Lutheran,* New York, N. Y., *Superintendent,* G. C. F. Haas; *Immanuel Women's Home,* Chicago, Ill., *Superintendent,* Sister Frieda Haff; *Luther,* Philadelphia, Pa., *Superintendent,* Rev. Jos. S. Schantz; *Lutheran For Women,* Brooklyn, N. Y., *Superintendent,* Miss E. Pape; *Swedish Lutheran Missionary Home,* Chicago, Ill., *Superintendent,* Miss Matilda Carlson; *Swedish Lutheran,* Denver, Colo., *Superintendent,* Sister Olga Wangblad.

Immigrant and Seamen's Missions

German Lutheran Emigrant, New York City, *Superintendent,* G. F. Haas; *Lutheran Seamen's Home,* Philadelphia, Pa., *Superintendent,* H. Robean; *Immigrant and Sailors' Home,* Boston,

Mass., *Superintendent,* Iwar Loren; *Swedish Lutheran Immigrant Home,* New York City, *Superintendent,* A. C. Helander.

Periodicals

Canadian Lutheran (monthly), Hamilton, Ontario, Can.; *Foreign Missionary* (monthly), Philadelphia, Pa., Editor, Rev. Geo. Drach; *Home Missionary* (monthly), Philadelphia, Pa., Editor, Rev. J. C. Kunzman; *Lutheran, The,* (weekly), Philadelphia, Pa., Editor, Rev. Geo. W. Sandt; *Lutheran Companion* (weekly), Rock Island, Ill., Editor, Rev. C. J. Bengston; *Lutheran Church Review* (quarterly), Philadelphia, Pa., Editor, Rev. T. E. Schmauk; *Lutheran Church Year Book,* Philadelphia, Pa., Editor, Rev. W. M. Kopenhaver; *Lutheran Messenger* (monthly), Philadelphia, Pa., Editor, Rev. W. L. Hunton; *Lutheran Mission Worker* (quarterly), Philadelphia, Pa., Editor, Mrs. C. L. Fry; *Nova Scotia Lutheran* (monthly), Bridgewater, Nova Scotia, Can.; *Deutsche Lutheraner* (weekly), Philadelphia, Pa., Editor, Gottlieb C. Beckemeier; *Lutherische Kirchenbote* (weekly), Philadelphia, Pa.; *Lutherische Kalender* (annually), Philadelphia, Pa., Editor, Rev. W. Wackernagel; *Missionsbote* (monthly), Philadelphia, Pa., Editor, Rev. R. G. C. Belinske; *Augustana* (weekly), Rock Island, Ill., Editor, Rev. L. G. Abrahamson; *Almanak.* (annually), Rock Island, Ill., Editor, Rev. O. V. Holmgram; *Barnens Tidning* (semi-monthly), Rock Island, Ill., Editor, Rev. T. A. Conrad; *Dorkas* (annually), Omaha, Neb., Editor, Rev. P. M. Lindberg; *Korsbaneret* (annually), Rock Island, Ill., Editor, Rev. O. H. Ardahl; *Lindsborgs Posten* (weekly), Lindsborg, Kan., Editor, Rev. D. Nystorem; *Lutheranen* (monthly), Chicago, Ill., Editor, Rev. V. H. Hegstrom; *Minnesota Stats Tidning* (weekly), St. Paul, Minn., Editor, O. P. Ohlson; *Missions Tidning* (monthly), Rock Island, Ill.; *Ungdomsvannen* (monthly), Rock Island, Ill., Editor, E. W. Olson.

LUTHERAN UNITED SYNOD, SOUTH

Next session of Synod, biennial, will be held in Roanoke, November, 1918.

There are 8 district synods.

Officers: *President,* Rev. M. G. G. Scherer, Charleston, S. C.; *Vice President,* Rev. M. M. Kinard, Salisbury, N. C.; *Secretary,* Rev. S. T. Hallman, Spartanburg, S. C.; *Treasurer,* Mr. J. E. Cooper, Winchester, Va.

Colleges and Seminary

Institution	Location	President
Lenoir College	Hickory, N. C.	R. L. Futz.
Newberry College	Newberry, S. C.	J. A. Harms.
Roanoke College	Salem, Va.	J. A. Morehead.
Lutheran Theological Seminary	Columbia, S. C.	A. G. Voight.

Theological Seminary, Kumamoto, Japan. Orphan's Home, Salem, Va., *Superintendent,* Prof. T. J. Crabtree.

Periodical. *Lutheran Church Visitor* (weekly), Columbia, S. C.

LUTHERAN SYNODICAL CONFERENCE

The next session of the Synodical Conference, biennial, will be held in August, 1918.

There are 6 synods, subdivided into districts.

Officers: *President,* Rev. C. Gausewitz, 620 Broadway, Milwaukee, Wis.; *Secretary,* Prof. J. Meyer, Oconomowoc, Wis.; *Treasurer,* Mr. H. H. Christiansen, Detroit, Mich.

Board of Colored Missions, St. Louis, Mo. *President,* Rev. C. F. Drewes, 4108 Natural Bridge Avenue, St. Louis, Mo.; Mr. J. H. Schulze, 2211 Holly Avenue, St. Louis, Mo. This is the only general board under the direction of the synodical conference.

The Synod of Missouri, Ohio, and other States, has a Board of Missions embracing home missions in foreign countries, home missions in North America, foreign missions, deaf-mute missions, missions to people of foreign tongues in America, Jewish missions, Indian missions, and immigrant missions.

Home Missions in Foreign Countries. Rev. Karl Schmidt, Chicago, Ill.

Home Missions in North America. Rev. C. F. Dietz, 1122 Garfield Avenue, Milwaukee, Wis.

Foreign Missions. Prof. L. Fuerbringer, 2619 Winneb Street, St. Louis, Mo.; *Director,* Rev. Jul. Friedrich, St. Charles, Mo.

Deaf-Mute Missions. Rev. H. A. Kuntz, St. Paul, Minn.

Missions to People of Foreign Tongues in America. Rev. J. D. Matthius, 510 East Ohio Street, Indianapolis, Ind.

Jewish Missions. Rev. H. C. Steup, 229 East 124th Street, New York City.

Indian Missions. Rev. F. H. Siebrandt, Tigerton, Wis.

Immigrant Missions. Rev. A. Beyer, 197 Maujer Street, Brooklyn, N. Y.

Relief of Invalid Professors, and their Indigent Widows and

Orphans. Rev. F. J. Keller, 3271 Forty-third Street, South West, Cleveland, O.

Relief of Invalid Pastors, Teachers, and their Indigent Widows and Orphans. Rev. A. Lange, 131 Walton Avenue, Fort Wayne, Ind.

Church Extension Board. Rev. H. Bartels, 3738 Morganford Street, St. Louis, Mo.

Colleges and Theological Seminaries

Institution	Location	President
Bethany Ladies' College	Mankato, Minn	W. F. Georg.
California Concordia College	East Oakland, Cal	Th. Brohm, Jr.
Concordia College	Bronxville, N. Y	H. Feth.
Concordia College	Conover, N. C	A. Haentzschel.
Concordia College	Fort Wayne, Ind	M. Luecke.
Concordia College	Milwaukee, Wis	M. J. F. Albrecht.
Concordia College	New Orleans, La	C. Niermann.
Concordia College	Portland, Ore	F. Sylwester.
Concordia College	Porto Alegre, Brazil	E. C. Wegehaupt.
Concordia College	St. Paul, Minn	Th. Buenger.
Concordia Teachers' College	River Forest, Ill	W. C. Kohn.
Immanuel Lutheran College	Greensboro, N. C	F. Berg.
Michigan Lutheran Seminary	Saginaw, West Side, Mich	O. J. R. Hoenecke.
Northwestern University	Watertown, Wis	A. F. Ernst.
St. John's Lutheran College	Winfield, Kan	A. W. Meyer.
St. Paul's College	Concordia, Mo	J. H. C. Kaeppel.
Teachers' College	Seward, Neb	G. Weller.
Teachers' Sem. and Dr. Martin Luther Coll.	New Ulm, Minn	A. Ackermann.
Walther College	St. Louis, Mo	E. Harms.
Concordia Theological Seminary	St. Louis, Mo	F. Pieper.
Concordia Theological Seminary	Springfield, Ill	R. Pieper.
Theological Seminary	Wauwatosa, Wis	J. Schaller.

Charitable Institutions

Lutheran Hospital, St. Louis, Mo., *Superintendent, F. M. Rudi; Lutheran Orphan Home*, Des Peres, Mo., *President*, C. Kellermann; *Lutheran Hospital*, East New York, N. Y., *President*, F. Rabbe; *Wartburg Home*, Brooklyn, N. Y., *President*, W. Braasch; *Bethlehem Orphan Home*, College Point, L. I., N. Y., *President*, D. Lankenau; *Martin Luther Orphan Home*, West Roxbury, Mass., *Superintendent*, Th. Keyl; *Lutheran Orphan Home*, Addison, Ill., *Superintendent*, H. Merz; *Bethlehem Orphan Home*, New Orleans, La., *Superintendent*, H. L. Huettmann; *Concordia Orphan Home*, Marwood, Pa., *Superintendent*, H. W. Lensner; *Lutheran Orphan Home*, Indianapolis, Ind., *Superintendent*, H. Hankemeier; *Dr. Martin Luther Orphan Home*, San Francisco, Cal., *President*, J. Schwerdt; *Lutheran Home for the Aged*, Monroe, Mich., *President*, R. Smukal; *Lutheran Home for the Aged*, Arlington Heights, Ill., *Secretary*, W. Both; *Augsburg Orphan Home and Home for the Aged*, Baltimore, Md., *President*, C. Spilman; *Lutheran Hospital*, Cleveland, O., *Super-*

intendent, Miss E. Manuel; *Lutheran Hospital,* Springfield, Ill., *Superintendent,* Miss R. Waltke; *Lutheran Hospital,* Sioux City, Ia., *President,* H. Wehking; *Lutheran Hospital,* Fort Wayne, Ind., *Superintendent,* Mrs. L. Rolf; *Lutheran Sanitarium,* Edgewater, Colo., *Manager,* J. Schley; *Immanuel Lutheran Hospital,* Mankato, Minn., *Superintendent,* Miss A. Bauer; *Lutheran Home for the Aged,* Wauwatosa, Wis., *Secretary,* H. L. Wedekind, 699 Lapham Street, Milwaukee, Wis.; *Lutheran Home for the Aged,* St. Louis, Mo., *Secretary,* A. P. Feddersen; *Evangelical Lutheran Deaf-Mute Institute,* North Detroit, Mich., *President,* W. Gielow; *Evangelical Lutheran Home for Feeble-Minded and Epileptics.* Watertown, Wis., *President,* H. Tetslaff; *Lutheran Home for the Aged,* St. Louis, Mo., Mr. A. H. Kanning.

Lutheran Hospice, New York City, *Superintendent,* O. H. Restin; *Walther League Hospice,* Milwaukee, Wis., *Matron,* Miss Amanda Wietzke; *Lutheran Hospice,* Detroit, Mich., *Secretary,* Miss Elsie Werfelmann; *Lutheran Hospice,* Buffalo, N. Y., *Superintendent,* C. H. Franke; *Chairman of Hospice Committee of Walther League,* Mr. Henry G. Pfeifer, 1202 East Wayne Street, Fort Wayne, Ind.

Periodicals

Lutheraner (bi-weekly), St. Louis, Mo.; *Lehre u. Wehre* (monthly), St. Louis, Mo.; *Magazin für Evangelical Lutheran Homiletik* (monthly), St. Louis, Mo.; *Theological Quarterly,* St. Louis, Mo.; *Lutheran Witness* (bi-weekly), St. Louis, Mo.; *Lutherische Botschafter,* Oakland, Cal., Publisher, Rev. J. H. Theiss; *Zeuge und Anzeiger* (weekly), Publisher, G. Kaufmann, 24 North William Street, New York City; *Missouri Lutherliga-Bote* (monthly), Publisher, Mr. W. Reschke, 16 Adams Street, Holyoke, Mass.; *Southern Lutheran,* Publisher, J. H. Schoenhardt, 124 South Jefferson Davis Parkway, New Orleans, La.; *Ev. Luth. Gemeindeblatt* (semi-monthly), Milwaukee, Wis.; *Theologische Quartalschrift* (quarterly), Milwaukee, Wis.

LUTHERAN UNITED NORWEGIAN SYNOD

Next session of the Synod is to be held in St. Paul, Minn., June 6-15, 1917.

Officers: *President,* Rev. T. H. Dahl, 3117 Park Avenue, Minneapolis, Minn.; *Secretary,* Rev. J. C. Roseland, Silverton, Ore.; *Treasurer,* Mr. E. Waldeland, Minneapolis, Minn.

Colleges and Theological Seminary

Institution	Location	President
Augustana College	Canton, S. D.	P. M. Glasoe.
Camrose College	Camrose, Alta., Can	J. R. Lavik.
Concordia College	Moorhead, Minn	J. A. Aasgaard.
Columbia College	Everett, Wash	Rev. Bogstad.
Pleasant View Luther College	Ottawa, Ill	H. M. Thompson.
St. Olaf College	Northfield, Minn	L. A. Vigness.
Spokane College	Spokane, Wash	A. O. Ulvestad.
Waldorf College	Forest City, Ia	M. Hegland.
Theological Seminary	St. Paul, Minn	M. O. Boeckmann.

Periodicals

Folke Kalender (annual), Minneapolis, Minn.; *Lutheraneren* (weekly), Minneapolis, Minn., Editor, Rev. Th. Eggen; *Luthersk Börneblad* (weekly), Minneapolis, Minn., Editor, Rev. John Peterson; *United Lutheran* (weekly), Minneapolis, Minn., Editor, Rev. Olaf Lysnes.

Lutheran Independent Synods

(Not connected with any of the General Bodies.)

LUTHERAN OHIO JOINT SYNOD

Meets biennially; next session in August, 1918.

Officers: *President,* Rev. C. H. L. Schuette, 62 Wilson Avenue, Columbus, O.; *Secretary,* A. Pflueger, Clyde, O.; *Treasurer,* Mr. C. Nagel, Springfield, O.

University and Seminaries

Institution	Location	President
Capital University	Columbus, O.	Otto Mees.
Luther Seminary	St. Paul, Minn	H. Ernst.
Theological Seminary	Columbus, O.	F. W. Stellhorn.

Periodicals

Lutheran Standard (weekly), Columbus, O.; *Evangelical Lutheran Kalender* (annual), Columbus, O.; *Lutheran Kirchen-Zeitung* (weekly), Columbus, O.

LUTHERAN BUFFALO SYNOD

Officers: *President,* Rev. E. Nemeschy, Niagara Falls, N. Y.; *Secretary,* Rev. O. Bruss, La Salle, N. Y.; *Treasurer,* Mr. P. Maul.

Seminary. German Martin Luther Seminary (Theological), Buffalo, N. Y. *President,* R. Grabau.

Periodicals

Wachsende Kirche (semi-monthly), Buffalo, N. Y., Editor, Rev. K. Hoessel, Milwaukee, Wis.; *Forward,* Buffalo, N. Y., Editor, Rev. H. Beutler, Sherkston, Ontario, Can.

LUTHERAN HAUGE'S SYNOD (NORWEGIAN)

Officers: *Vice-President,* Rev. J. J. Ekse, Hendricks, Minn.; *Secretary,* Rev. N. J. Loehre, 518 Walnut Street, Grand Forks, N. D.; *Treasurer,* Mr. O. A. Ulvin.

Home Mission Board. *President,* Rev. T. J. Oppedahl, Sacred Heart, Minn.

Foreign Mission Board. *President,* Rev. C. J. Eastvold, Dawson, Minn.

Inter-synodical Lutheran Orient Missions Society. *President,* Rev. N. J. Loehre, 518 Walnut Street, Grand Forks, N. D.; *Secretary,* Rev. H. Mackensen, 196 Berlin Street, Detroit, Mich.

College and Seminary

Institution	Location	President
Jewell Lutheran College	Jewell, Ia.	K. O. Eittreim.
Red Wing Seminary (College and Theological Departments)	Red Wing, Minn.	E. W. Schmidt.

Periodicals

Budbäreren (weekly), Red Wing, Minn., Editor, Rev. C. C. Holter; *Börnevennen* (weekly), Red Wing, Minn., Editor, Rev. C. C. Holter; *Tidskrift* (monthly), Red Wing, Minn., Editor, Prof. M. O. Wee.

LUTHERAN EILSEN'S SYNOD (NORWEGIAN)

Officers: *President,* Rev. S. M. Stenby, Clear Lake, Ia.; *Secretary,* Rev. A. L. Wiek, 2818 Cedar Avenue, Minneapolis, Minn.; *Treasurer,* Mr. L. Paterson, Centerville, S. D.

Board of Home Missions. *President,* I. T. Erickson, Dawson, Minn.; *Treasurer,* T. P. Thompson, Dawson, Minn.

Board of Indian Missions. *President,* S. O. Overby, Taylor, Wis.; *Treasurer,* W. T. Peterson, Taylor, Wis.

Periodical. *Den Kristelige Legmand* (monthly), Minneapolis, Minn., Editor, Rev. A. L. Wiek.

LUTHERAN IOWA SYNOD (GERMAN)

Seven districts; meets triennially; next session August, 1917.

Officers: *President,* Rev. F. Richter, 634 Fourth Avenue, Clinton, Ia.; *Secretary,* Rev. E. H. Caselman, Charles City, Ia.; *Treasurer,* Rev. J. Haefner, Muscatine, Ia.

Home Mission Board. *President,* Rev. F. Zimmerman, Oelwein, Ia.

Luther League and Sunday School Board. *President,* Rev. M. Reu, Dubuque, Ia.

Church Extension Board. *President,* Rev. H. Fretschel, Milwaukee, Wis.

Colleges and Theological Seminary

Institution	Location	President
Luther College	Eureka, S. D.	R. H. Bunge.
Seminary and College	Seguin, Tex.	C. Weeber.
Wartburg College	Clinton, Ia.	J. Fritschel.
Wartburg Teachers' Seminary and Academy	Waverly, Ia.	A. Engelbrecht
Wartburg Theological Seminary	Dubuque, Ia.	M. Fritschel.

Periodicals

Anstalts Bote, Der (monthly), Muscatine, Ia., Editor, Rev. H. Foelsch, Defiance, Ia.; *Kirchliche Zeitschrift,* Editor, Rev. M. Reu, Dubuque, Ia.; *Kirchenblatt,* Waverly, Ia., Editor, Rev. F. Richter, Clinton, Ia.; *Lutheran Herald* (monthly), Waverly, Ia., Editor, Rev. E. H. Rausch; *Missions Stunde* (monthly), Waverly, Ia., Editor, Prof. M. Wiederaenders, Eureka, S. D.; *Vereine Bote* (monthly), Waverly, Ia., Editor, G. A. Grossman; *Wartburg Kalender* (annually), Waverly, Ia., Editor, Rev. H. Bergstaedt, Princeton, Ill.; *Wartburg Quarterly,* Editor, Prof. J. Fritschel, Clinton, Ia.

LUTHERAN NORWEGIAN SYNOD

Meets triennially; next session will be held at St. Paul, Minn., June 6-15, 1917.

Officers: *President,* Rev. H. G. Stub, 806 Sheldon Avenue, St. Paul, Minn.; *Secretary,* Rev. O. J. Kvale, Orfordville, Wis.; *Treasurer,* Rev. H. B. Hustvedt, Decorah, Ia.

Foreign Mission Board. Dr. J. R. Birkelund, 4530 Monticello Avenue, Chicago, Ill.

Home Mission Board. Rev. L. C. Foss, 779 Lake View Boulevard, Seattle, Wash.

Colleges and Theological Seminary

Institution	Location	President
Luther College	Decorah, Ia.	C. K. Preus.
Park Region Luther College	Fergus Falls, Minn	Knut Gjerset.
Luther Theological Seminary	St. Paul, Minn	E. Hove.

Periodicals

Lutheran Herald (weekly), Decorah, Ia., Editor, Prof. G. T. Lee, Fergus Falls, Minn.; *Our Friend* (weekly), Decorah, Ia., Editor, Rev. Lauritz Larsen, 460 Seventy-fourth Street, Brooklyn, N. Y.; *Boerneblad* (weekly), Decorah, Ia., Editor, Rev. Kr. Kvamme, Ossian, Ia.; *Evangelical Lutheran Kirketidende* (weekly), Decorah, Ia., Editor, Rev. R. Malmin.

LUTHERAN DANISH SYNOD IN AMERICA

Last session at Newell, Ia., June, 1916.

Officers: *President,* Rev. N. P. Gravengaard, Marquette, Neb.; *Secretary,* Rev. Aug. Faber, Newell, Ia.; *Treasurer,* Mr. H. P. Rasmussen, 17 North La Salle Street, Chicago, Ill.

Board of Foreign Missions. Rev. Adam Dan, 510 East Sixty-fourth Street, Chicago, Ill.

Colleges

Institution	Location	President
Ashland College	Grant, Mich	P. Rasmussen.
Attarday College	Soliang, Cal.	B. Th. Nordentoft.
Grand View College (Theological Dept.)	Des Moines, Ia	C. T. Hojbjerg.

Charitable Institutions

Danish Lutheran Orphan Home, Chicago, Ill.; *Danish Lutheran Orphan Home,* Perth Amboy, N. J.; *Danish Lutheran Orphan Home,* Tyler, Minn.; *Danish Lutheran Home for Old People,* Des Moines, Ia.

Periodicals

Boernevennen (weekly), Cedar Falls, Ia.; *Dannevirke* (weekly), Cedar Falls, Ia.; *Kirkelig Samler* (weekly), Des Moines, Ia.; *Ungdom* (semi-monthly), Cedar Falls, Ia.

LUTHERAN ICELANDIC SYNOD

Next session will be held in June, 1917.

Officers: *President,* Rev. B. B. Jonsson, 650 William Avenue, Winnipeg, Manitoba, Can.; *Secretary,* Rev. F. Hallgrimsson, Baldur, Manitoba, Can.; *Treasurer,* Mr. J. J. Vopni, 597 Bannatyne Avenue, Winnipeg, Manitoba, Can.

Board of Home Missions. *Chairman,* Rev. Johann Bjarnason Arborg, Manitoba, Can.

Board of Foreign Missions. *Chairman,* Rev. K. K. Olafsson, Mountain, N. D.

Board of Directors for Old Folks' Home. *Chairman,* Dr. B. J. Brandsson, 776 Victor Street, Winnipeg, Manitoba, Can.

Periodical. *Sameiningin* (monthly organ), Winnipeg, Manitoba, Can., Editor, Rev. B. B. Jonsson.

LUTHERAN IMMANUEL SYNOD (GERMAN)

Next session to be held in August, 1917.

Officers: *President,* Rev. W. E. Rommell, 58 Grinnell Street, Greenville, Mass.; *Secretary,* Rev. H. A. F. Kern, Turners Falls, Mass.; *Treasurer,* Rev. G. A. Fischer, 320 Chadwick Avenue, Newark, N. J.

Seminary. Immanuel's Theological Seminary, Turners Falls, Mass., *President,* H. A. F. Kern. (Closed.)

Periodical. *Quellwasser,* Turners Falls, Mass.

LUTHERAN FINNISH SUOMI SYNOD

Next session, June, 1917.

Officers: *President,* Rev. J. K. Nikander, 503 Finn Street, Hancock, Mich.; *Secretary,* Rev. F. W. Kava, 213 Mitchell Avenue, Negaunee, Mich.; *Treasurer,* Mr. I. Vargelin.

College. College and Theological Seminary, Hancock, Mich. *President,* J. K. Nikander.

Periodicals

(Published at the Finnish Lutheran Book Concern, Hancock, Mich.)

Amerikan Suometar (tri-weekly), Editor, Emil Saastamoinen; *Aura* (monthly), farmers' paper; *Lasten Lehti* (monthly), children's paper; *Nuorten Ystava* (monthly), The Young People's Friend; *Paimen Sanomia* (weekly), Editor, Rev. M. J. Kunsi, South Range, Mich.

LUTHERAN NORWEGIAN FREE SYNOD

Next meeting at Willmar, Minn., June, 1917.

Officers: *President,* Rev. J. Mattson, Ellendale, Minn.; *Secretary,* Rev. J. M. Halvorsen, Northwood, N. D.; *Treasurer,* Miss Ragna Sverdrup, Minneapolis, Minn.

Board of Foreign Missions. *President,* Rev. E. E. Gynild, Willmar, Minn.; *Secretary,* Prof. A. Helland, Minneapolis, Minn.; *Treasurer,* Prof. J. H. Blegen, Minneapolis, Minn.

Board of Home Missions. *President,* Prof. E. P. Harbo, Minneapolis, Minn.; *Treasurer,* Rev. O. H. Sletten, Minneapolis, Minn.

Colleges and Seminary

Institution	Location	President
Augsburg College	Minneapolis, Minn	George Sverdrup, Jr.
Bethany College	Everett, Wash	L. B. Saetern.
Theological Seminary	Minneapolis, Minn	George Sverdrup, Jr.

Periodicals

Folkebladet (weekly), Minneapolis, Minn., Editor, I. Hain; *Barncts Ven* (weekly), Minneapolis, Minn., Editor, Prof. J. Nydahl.

LUTHERAN UNITED DANISH SYNOD

Next meeting, Neenah, Wis., June, 1917.

Officers: *President,* Rev. G. B. Christiansen, Audubon, Ia.; *Secretary,* Rev. S. Provensen, 904 Bluff Street, Cedar Falls, Ia.; *Treasurer,* Mr. O. Hansen, Blair, Neb.

The president and secretary are also president and secretary of both home and foreign mission boards.

Educational Board. *President,* Rev. H. P. Jensen, Minden, Neb.; *Secretary,* Mr. H. Skov. Nielsen, Blair, Neb.

Publication Board. *Manager,* Mr. H. Skov. Nielsen.

SWEDISH EVANGELICAL MISSION COVENANT

One of two Swedish Evangelical bodies in the U. S. The movement dates back to a spiritual awakening in Sweden the middle of the nineteenth century.

Headquarters, 56 West Washington Street, Chicago, Ill.

President of Executive Board, Rev. E. G. Hjerpe; *Secretary,* Rev. D: Marcelius; *Editor,* Rev. D. Marcelius.

Mennonites*

(Oldest and largest of the Mennonite bodies)

General Conference, biennial; next session in 1917.

Board of Missions and Charities. *President,* C. Z. Yoder, Wooster, O.; *Secretary,* J. S. Shoemaker, Freeport, Ill.; *Treasurer,* G. L. Bender, Elkhart, Ind.

Board of Education. *President,* H. Frank Reist, Scottdale, Pa.; *Secretary,* D. D. Miller, Middlebury, Ind.; *Treasurer,* S. C. Yoder, Kalona, Ia.

Publication Board. *President,* J. S. Shoemaker, Freeport, Ill.; *Secretary,* S. H. Miller, Shanesville, O.; *Treasurer,* Abram Metzler, Martinsburg, Pa. Mennonite publishing house, Scottdale, Pa.

Colleges

Institution	Location	President or Principal
Goshen College	Goshen, Ind	J. E. Hartzler.
Hesston Academy and Bible School	Hesston, Kan	D. H. Bender.

Charitable Institutions

Orphans' Home, West Liberty, O.; *Superintendent,* A. Metzler; *Old People's Home,* Marshallville, O.; *Superintendent,* P. R. Lantz; *Sanitarium,* La Junta, Colo., *Superintendent,* Allen H. Erb; *Home,* Lancaster, Pa., *Superintendent,* Tobias E. Moyer; *Children's Home,* Millersville, Pa., *Superintendent,* Levi Sauder.

For list of ministers, with addresses, see Mennonite Year Book, published at Scottdale, Pa.; also Bundesbote Kalendar, published by Mennonite Book Concern at Berne, Ind.

Periodicals. *Mennonite,* official, weekly, Berne, Ind.; *Christliches Bundesbote* (weekly), Berne, Ind.; *Kinderbote* and Sunday School *Lessons* at Berne, Ind.

AMISH MENNONITES

Three Annual Conferences: Eastern, Indiana-Michigan, and Western.

United with the Mennonites in supporting Goshen College, Goshen, Ind. Represented on Charitable, Missionary and Publishing Boards of the Mennonites.

For list of ministers, with addresses, see Mennonite Year Book, Scottdale, Pa.

---

*For Mennonite General Conference branch, see Directory of Constituent Bodies of the Federal Council, pages 64, 65.

AMISH MENNONITES (OLD ORDER)

They have no annual conference and no church buildings. The older forms of worship, usually in German, are strictly adhered to.

For list of ministers, with addresses, see Mennonite Year Book, Scottdale, Pa.

AMISH MENNONITES (CONSERVATIVE)

They have an annual conference, to which, however, only a part of them belong.

For list of ministers with addresses, see Mennonite Year Book, Scottdale, Pa.

MENNONITES (OLD ORDER, OR WISLER)

A conservative body, using generally the German. They have no conference.

For list of ministers with addresses, see Mennonite Year Book, Scottdale, Pa.

DEFENSELESS MENNONITES

An annual conference. *Moderator,* D. E. Harder, Hillsboro, Kan.; *Secretary,* Jacob G. Barkman, Hillsboro, Kan.

They support an orphanage in Flanagan, Ill., and a missionary in Africa.

For list of ministers with addresses, see Mennonite Year Book, Scottdale, Pa.

MENNONITE BRETHREN IN CHRIST

General Conference meets in Kitchener, Ontario, Can., in October, 1920.

There are 5 district conferences in the United States and 2 in Canada.

Officers of the General Conference: *President,* Rev. C. S. Scott, Shambaugh, Ia.; *Secretary,* Rev. A. B. Yoder, Wakarusa, Ind.; *Treasurer,* A. D. Hoke, New Carlisle, O.; *Editor of Sunday School Literature,* Rev. J. A. Huffman, Bluffton, O.

Publication Headquarters, Gospel Banner, Office, New Carlisle, O., and The Bethel Publishing Co., New Carlisle, O.

Periodical. *The Gospel Banner,* New Carlisle, O., Editor, Rev. J. A. Huffman, Bluffton, O.

Methodists

For Methodist denominations connected with the Federal Council of the Churches of Christ in America, see Directory of Constituent Bodies, pages 65-80.

WESLEYAN METHODIST CONNECTION OF AMERICA

General Conference, quadrennial; next session in 1919.

Annual Conferences, 23, with a mission conference in India and one in Africa.

President of General Conference, Rev. Eber Teter, Sheridan, Ind.; *Secretary,* Rev. E. F. McCarty, Pittsford, Mich. The Book Committee is the Board of Managers of all the Connectional Societies; Publishing, Missionary, Superannuated, Educational, and Sunday School. Headquarters, Syracuse, N. Y. *President,* E. G. Dietrich; *Secretary,* E. D. Carpenter, Glens Falls, N. Y.

Missionary Society of the Wesleyan Methodist Connection of America. *Secretary,* Rev. Eber Teter, Sheridan, Ind.

Woman's Home and Foreign Missionary Society. *President,* Mrs. Francene McMillan, Houghton, N. Y.; *Corresponding Secretary,* Miss Eva McMichael, Arlington, Ind.

Colleges

Institution	Location	President
Central College	Central, S. C	H. C. Bedford.
Houghton College	Houghton, N. Y	J. S. Luckey.
Miltonvale College	Miltonvale, Kan	H. W. McDowell.

List of ministers, with addresses, in the *Wesleyan Methodist* and in Minutes of Annual Conferences.

Publishing House, 330 East Onondaga Street, Syracuse, N. Y.

Periodical. *The Wesleyan Methodist* (weekly), Syracuse, N. Y., Editor, F. A. Butterfield.

FREE METHODIST CHURCH OF NORTH AMERICA

General Conference, quadrennial; next session, 1919. There are 43 annual conferences.

Bishops

Burton R. Jones, 44 East Peoria Street, Pasadena, Cal.
Walter A. Sellew, Jamestown, N. Y.
Wilson T. Hogue, Michigan City, Ind.
William Pearce, 4532 Chestnut Street, Philadelphia, Pa.

Officers of the General Conference: *President,* Bishop Walter A. Sellew; *Secretary,* Mendal B. Miller, Franklin, Pa.; *Treasurer,* George W. Saunders.

Board of Education, 1132 Washington Boulevard, Chicago, Ill. *President,* Bishop W. T. Hogue; *Corresponding Secretary,* M. B. Miller, Franklin, Pa.

General Missionary Board, 1132 Washington Boulevard, Chicago, Ill. *President,* Bishop W. A. Sellew; *Secretary,* J. S. MacGeary.

The Woman's Foreign Missionary Society, 1132 Washington Boulevard, Chicago, Ill. *President,* Mrs. Mary L. Coleman, Greenville, Ill.; *Corresponding Secretary,* Mrs. Charlotte T. Bolles, Oneida, N. Y.; *Treasurer,* Mrs. Lillian C. Jensen, Chicago, Ill.

Church Extension Society, 1132 Washington Boulevard, Chicago, Ill. *President,* Bishop W. Pearce; *Secretary,* J. S. MacGeary.

General Sunday School Board, 1132 Washington Boulevard, Chicago, Ill. *President,* Jacob Moyer; *General Secretary,* W. B. Olmstead.

Board of Charities and Benevolences, 1132 Washington Boulevard, Chicago, Ill. *President,* Bishop W. Pearce; *Secretary,* J. S. MacGeary.

Board of Conference Claimants, 1132 Washington Boulevard, Chicago, Ill. *President,* Bishop B. R. Jones; *Secretary,* M. B. Miller, Franklin, Pa.

Colleges

Institution	Location	President
The Central Academy and College	McPherson, Kan	L. Glenn Lewis.
Evansville Seminary and Junior College	Evansville, Wis	Richard R. Blews.
Greenville College	Greenville, Ill	Eldon G. Burritt.
Seattle Pacific College	Seattle, Wash	O. E. Tiffany.

The Annual Minutes, published by W. B. Rose, Agent,

1132 Washington Boulevard, Chicago, Ill., give list of min·isters, with addresses.

Charitable Institutions

Gerry Homes, Gerry, N. Y., *Superintendent,* Jarvis K. Wilson; *Old People's Rest Home,* Woodstock, Ill., *Superintendent,* J. D. Kelsey; *Chicago Industrial Home for Children,* Woodstock, Ill., *Superintendent,* W. P. Ferries.

Periodicals

Free Methodist, Chicago, Ill., Editor, J. T. Logan; *Light and Life Evangel,* Chicago, Ill., Editor, David S. Warner; *Missionary Tidings,* Chicago, Ill., Editor, Mrs. Tressa R. Arnold.

PRIMITIVE METHODIST CHURCH

General Conference, quadrennial; there are 3 annual conferences.

Officers: *President,* Rev. H. G. Russell, Nanticoke, Pa.; *Secretary,* Rev. A. Humphries, Methuen, Mass.; *Treasurer,* Rev. J. T. Barlow, New Bedford, Mass.

Board of Foreign Missions. *President,* Rev. W. F. Nicholls, Tamaqua, Pa.; *Secretary,* Rev. J. Iley, Plymouth, Pa.

Board of Education. *President,* Rev. S. T. Nicholls, 2609 Lehigh Avenue, Philadelphia, Pa.; *Secretary,* Rev. J. Proude, Providence, R. I.

List of ministers with addresses will be found in the Annual Conference Year Book; *Publisher,* Mr. B. R. Acomley, Fall River, Mass.

Periodical. *Primitive Methodist Journal,* 378 New York Avenue, Brooklyn, N. Y., Editor, Rev. E. Humphries.

CONGREGATIONAL METHODIST CHURCH

General Conference, quadrennial; next session at Laurel, Miss., in 1917.

There are 13 state conferences.

Officers of the General Conference: *President,* Rev. N. E. Fair; *Secretary,* John Phinazee, Jackson, Ga.

Educational Board—*Chairman,* T. W. Collins, Ellisville, Miss.

Board of Publication, Laurel, Miss. *Chairman,* G. W. Blacklidge, Laurel, Miss.; *Secretary-Treasurer,* C. C. Pearson.

Periodical. *Messenger* (semi-monthly), Ellisville, Miss.; Editor, Rev. G. C. VanDevender.

REFORMED METHODIST UNION EPISCOPAL CHURCH

General Conference, quadrennial; 2 state conferences.

General Officers: *Bishop,* Rt. Rev. E. Russell Middleton, Sumter, S. C.; *Financial Secretary,* Rev. J. M. Seabrook; *Secretary of Education,* Rev. F. R. Young; *Sunday School Secretary,* John Richardson; *Missionary Secretary,* Rev. Thomas Chisolm; *Manager of Publications,* Rev. John Heywood.

PENTECOSTAL CHURCH OF THE NAZARENE

General Assembly, quadrennial; last session held at Kansas City, Mo., September, 1915.

There are 33 district assemblies.

General Assembly: *General Secretary,* Rev. F. H. Mendell, 1000 Main Street, Newton, Kan.; *Statistical Secretary,* Rev. C. A. Kinder, 2109 Troost Avenue, Kansas City, Mo.

General Missionary Board, 2109 Troost Avenue, Kansas City, Mo. *Superintendent and General Secretary,* Rev. H. F. Reynolds.

Board of Publication, 2109 Troost Avenue, Kansas City, Mo. *President,* Rev. J. C. Kinne; *Secretary and Treasurer,* J. F. Sanders.

Board of Education. *President,* DeLance Wallace, Walla Walla, Wash.

Colleges and Universities

Institution	Location	President
Arkansas Holiness College	Vilonia, Ark	C. A. Imhoff.
Central Nazarene University	Hamlin, Tex	J. E. L. Moore.
Nazarene University	Pasadena, Cal	H. O. Wiley.
Olivet University	Olivet, Ill	E. F. Walker.
Peniel University	Peniel, Tex	J. A. Chapman.
Southeastern Holiness University	Donalsonville, Ga	Z. B. Whitehurst.

The Minutes of the district assemblies furnish the names of ministers, with addresses, and may be obtained at the Pentecostal Nazarene Publishing House, Kansas City, Mo.

Periodicals

Herald of Holiness, Kansas City, Mo., Editor, Dr. B. F. Haynes; *Other Sheep,* Kansas City, Mo., Editor, C. A. Mc-

Connell; *Youth's Comrade,* Kansas City, Mo., Editor, C. A. McConnell.

INTERNATIONAL APOSTOLIC HOLINESS CHURCH

(A Pentecostal Body.)

General Assembly, quadrennial; next session at Nelsonville, O., November, 1919.

General Superintendent, Rev. George B. Kulp, 112 Battle Creek Avenue, Battle Creek, Mich.; *Secretary and Treasurer,* Jay E. Strong, 147 South Jefferson Avenue, Battle Creek, Mich.

There are State or District organizations in Pennsylvania, Oklahoma, Kansas, New Mexico and Colorado. The denomination has two Bible schools, two rescue homes, and missions in the British West Indies, South America, Africa, Japan and Korea.

Periodicals. *Apostolic Messenger,* Greensboro, S. C.; *Bethel Herald,* Milton, Pa.; *Apostolic Visitor,* Lansing, Mich.

CUMBERLAND PRESBYTERIAN CHURCH

General Assembly, annual; meets at Lincoln, Ill., May 17, 1917.

There are 12 synods and 71 presbyteries.

Officers: *Moderator,* Rev. J. J. Price, Campbell, Mo.; *Stated Clerk and Treasurer,* Rev. D. W. Fooks, Paducah, Ky.

Board of Missions and Church Erection. *President,* Rev. A. M. Buchanan, Moberly, Mo.; *Treasurer,* Rev. J. W. Duvall, Moberly, Mo.

Board of Education. *President,* J. H. Copeland, Wingate, Ky.; *Corresponding Secretary and Treasurer,* Rev. W. B. Cunningham, Union City, Tenn.

Board of Publication, Sunday School and Young People's Work, Nashville, Tenn. *President,* Prof. H. J. Graf, Evansville, Ind.; *Secretary and Treasurer,* Rev. T. Asburn, Knoxville, Tenn.

Board of Ministerial Relief. *Corresponding Secretary and Treasurer,* Rev. John A. McLane, Chandler, Ind.

Committee on Prohibition. *Chairman,* Rev. J. B. Eshman, Hopkinsville, Ky.

Charitable Institution. Cumberland Presbyterian Orphans' Home and Home for Old Ministers, Their Widows and Missionaries, Bowling Green, Ky.

College and Theological Seminary

Institution	Location	Dean
Cumberland College	Leonard, Tex	
Cumberland Presbyterian Theological Seminary	McKenzie, Tenn	P. F. Johnson

For list of ministers, with addresses, see Minutes of the General Assembly, furnished by Rev. D. W. Fooks, Paducah, Ky.

Periodicals

Cumberland Presbyterian, Nashville, Tenn., Editor, Rev. J. L. Hudgins; *Cumberland Banner,* Tullahoma, Tenn., Editor, Hon. T. A. Haveron.

ASSOCIATE PRESBYTERIAN CHURCH

Last meeting of the Synod, annual, was at Minneola, Kan., May, 1916.

There are 3 presbyteries.

President of the Synod, Rev. D. J. Masson; *Secretary,* Rev. H. S. Atchison, Beaver Falls, Pa.; *Treasurer,* Rev. D. J. Masson.

Board of Missions. *President,* A. J. Dawson; *Secretary,* Rev. A. M. Malcolm, Albia, Ia.

Board for Freedmen. *President,* Rev. W. P. Gilkey; *Secretary,* Rev. D. J. Masson, Washington, Ia.

Board of Relief. *President,* Rev. A. M. Malcolm; *Secretary,* A. J. Dawson, Washington, Ia.

Board of Publication. *Business Manager,* Rev. R. K. Atchison, Rimersberg, Pa.

Board of Education. *Treasurer,* Rev. D. J. Masson, Washington, Ia.

Theological Seminary. Theological Seminary, Beaver Falls, Pa.; Professor, H. S. Atchison.

For list of ministers with addresses see the June number of the Associate Presbyterian Magazine, published by the Associate Presbyterian Synod; *Business Manager,* Rev. R. K. Atchison, Rimersburg, Pa.

Periodical. *Associate Presbyterian Magazine* (monthly), Rimersburg, Pa., Editor, Rev. R. K. Atchison.

ASSOCIATE REFORMED PRESBYTERIAN SYNOD

The Synod, annual, meets November 14, 1917, at York, S. C.

There are 6 presbyteries, and one in Mexico. .

Officers of Synod, *Moderator,* Rev. W. M. Hunter, Little Rock, Ark.; *Principal Clerk,* Rev. A. S. Rogers, Rock Hill, S. C.

Board of Foreign Missions, Due West, S. C. *Chairman,* Rev. F. Y. Pressly; *Secretary,* Rev. G. G. Parkinson, *Treasurer,* A. S. Kennedy.

Board of Home Missions and Church Extension. *Chairman,* Rev. J. C. Galloway, Gastonia, N. C.; *Corresponding Secretary,* Rev. R. G. Miller, Charlotte, N. C., R. F. D. 1; *Treasurer,* Rev. G. R. White, Charlotte, N. C., R. F. D.

Sabbath School and Young People's Work. *General Secretary,* Rev. J. W. Carson, Newburg, S. C.

Junior Christian Work. *General Secretary,* Mrs. W. B. Lindsay, Charlotte, N. C.

Woman's Work. *General Secretary,* Mrs. Iva Cook Bryson, Clinton, S. C.

Board of Ministerial Relief. *Secretary,* Rev. R. W. Carson, Brunswick, Tenn.

Colleges and Theological Seminary

College	Location	President
Erskine College	Due West, S. C.	Rev. J. S. Moffatt.
Woman's College	Due West, S. C.	Rev. Richard L. Robinson.
Theological Seminary	Due West, S. C.	Rev. F. Y. Pressly.

Institution. Dunlap Orphanage, *Superintendent,* Kerr Oates, Brighton, Tenn., R. F. D.

Periodical. *Associate Reformed Presbyterian,* Due West, S. C.

REFORMED PRESBYTERIAN CHURCH SYNOD

Synod, annual; next meeting at Sterling, Kas., June 6, 1917. There are 11 presbyteries. '

Officers of the Synod: *Moderator,* Rev. J. K. Robb, Tak Hing, China; *Clerk,* Rev. G. A. Edgar, Selma, Ala.; *Stated Clerk and Treasurer,* James S. Tibby, 408 Penn Building, Pittsburgh, Pa.

Foreign Mission Board. *President,* Henry O'Neill, 740 Riverside Drive, New York City; *Secretary,* Rev. F. M. Wilson, Philadelphia, Pa.

Home Mission Board, 408 Penn Building, Pittsburgh, Pa. *President,* S. Connor; *Secretary,* James S. Tibby.

Jewish Mission Board, Eighth and Catherine Streets, Philadelphia, Pa. *President,* Dr. J. C. McFeeters; *Secretary,* Rev. F.· M. Wilson.

Board of Church Erection. *President,* R. J. Bole, 170 Broadway, New York City; *Secretary,* Rev. R. C. Montgomery, Philadelphia, Pa.

Board of Relief. *President,* O. L. Samson, Washington, Ia.; *Secretary,* Rev. S. E. Greer, Washington, Ia.

College and Theological Seminary

Institution	Location	President
Geneva College	Beaver Falls, Pa	R. H. Martin.
Theological Seminary	Pittsburgh, Pa	R. C. Wylie.

List of ministers, with addresses, will be found in the minutes of the Synod, James S. Tibby, 408 Penn Building, Pittsburgh, Pa.

Aged People's Home, Burgess Street, North Side, Pittsburgh, Pa. *Superintendent,* Miss Etta Jamison.

Periodicals

Christian Nation, New York City, Editor, J. H. Pritchard; *Olive Trees,* Philadelphia, Pa., Editor, Rev. M. M. Pearce.

CHRISTIAN REFORMED CHURCH IN NORTH AMERICA

Next meeting of the Synod, biennial, June 19, 1918, Grand Rapids, Mich.

There are 13 classes.

Synodical Officers: *Synodical Committee,* Prof. J. Timmermann, Rev. W. P. Van Wyk and Rev. F. Fortuin; *Stated Clerk,* Rev. Henry Beets, 2050 Francis Avenue, S. E., Grand Rapids, Mich.; *Treasurer,* Rev. J. Noordewier, 617 Bates Street, Grand Rapids, Mich.

Home Mission Committee. *President,* Rev. K. Poppen; *Secretary and Treasurer,* Rev. I. Van Dellen, 1804 South Emerson Street, Denver, Colo.

Church Erection Committee. *Secretary and Treasurer,* Rev. J. Manni, 525 Superior Avenue, Sheboygan, Wis.

Home Mission Committee in the East. *President,* Rev. J. A. Westervelt; *Treasurer,* Mr. J. VanderPlaat, Garfield, N. J.;

150   Federal Council Year Book

Seamen's Home, 310 Hudson Street, Hoboken, N. J. In charge of *Immigration Work* at Ellis Island and Hoboken, Rev. J. J. Hiemenga, 219 Myrtle Avenue, Passaic, N. J.

Immigration Committee in the West. *Secretary,* Mr. W. Aardappel, Orange City, Ia.; *Treasurer,* Mr. W. Bierma, Sioux Center, Ia.

Jewish Mission Committee. *Treasurer,* Rev. J. I. Fles, Muskegon, Mich.

Board of Heathen Missions. *President,* Rev. J. Manni; *Secretary,* Rev. Y. P. DeJong, 19 LeGrand Street, Grand Rapids, Mich.; *Corresponding Secretary,* Rev. Henry Beets, 2050 Francis Avenue, S. E., Grand Rapids, Mich.; *Treasurer,* Rev. J. Dolfin, 155 Terrace Street, Muskegon, Mich.

Board of Ministerial Relief. *Secretary,* Rev. M. VanVessem, Zeeland, Mich.; *Treasurer,* Rev. J. Smitter, Oostburg, Wis.

Board of Publication. *President,* Rev. J. Manni; *Secretary,* Hon. H. A. Bosch, Hudsonville, Mich.

Missions

Paterson Hebrew Mission, Paterson, N. J., *Superintendent,* H. Bregman; *Star of Hope Mission,* Paterson, N. J., *Superintendent,* P. Stam; *Helping Hand Gospel Mission,* 850 West Madison Street, Chicago, Ill., *Assistant Superintendent,* J. VandeWater; *Mission to the Mormons, Superintendent,* W. Van Westenbrugge, Ogden, Utah.

Colleges and Theological Seminary

Institution	Location	Principa lor Rector
Calvin College	Grand Rapids, Mich.	A. J. Rooks.
Theological Seminary (with Calvin College)	Grand Rapids, Mich.	F. M. TenHoor.
Christian Reformed College	Grundy Center, Ia.	Dr. W. Bode (Pres.).

For list of ministers, with addresses, see "Year Book of the Christian Reformed Church," published by the Eerdmans-Sevensma Co., Grand Rapids, Mich.

Periodicals

The Banner (weekly), Grand Rapids, Mich., Editor, Rev. Henry Beets; *De Wachter* (weekly), Holland, Mich., Editor, Rev. A. Keizer; *Der Reformierte Bote* (monthly), Wellsburgh, Ia., Editor, Rev. G. L. Hoefker.

HUNGARIAN REFORMED CHURCH IN AMERICA

General Convention of the Reformed Church in Hungary. *Presidents,* Rt. Rev. Bishop Bela Kenessey, Kolozsvar,

Hungary, and Count Joseph Degenfeld, Debrecen, Hungary.

There are two classes in America: the Eastern, *President*, Rev. Z. Kuthy, New York City; and the Western, *President*, Rev. Alex. Kalassay, Pittsburgh, Pa.

For list of ministers, with addresses, see Reformatus Hirado, New York City.

Periodicals. *Reformatus Hirado* (weekly), New York City, Editor, Rev. Z. Kuthy; *Egyhasi Elet* (monthly), McKeesport, Pa., Editor, Rev. J. Mclegh.

THE SALVATION ARMY

National Headquarters, 122 West Fourteenth Street, New York City.

General Officers: Commander Evangeline C. Booth, leader of Salvation Army forces in the U. S. A.; Commissioner Thomas Estill, Territorial Leader for the Western States; Chief Secretary, Colonel William Peart.

Colleges

Institution	Location
Training College (men and women)	130 West Fourteenth Street, New York City.
Training College (for men)	1230 West Adams Street, Chicago, Ill.
Training College (for women)	116 South Ashland Boulevard, Chicago, Ill.

For list of officers, with addresses, see "Disposition of the Forces," monthly, for private use, at National Headquarters.

Periodicals. *War Cry* (weekly), *Strids Ropet* (weekly), *Young Soldier* (weekly), *Social News* (monthly), 122 West Fourteenth Street, New York City, Editor-in-Chief, Lt.-Col. W. F. Jenkins.

VOLUNTEERS OF AMERICA

Separate body from Salvation Army. Headquarters, 34 West Twenty-eighth Street, New York City. *Presidents*, General and Mrs. Ballington Booth.

SCHWENKFELDERS

General Conference, semi-annual.

Moderator, Edwin K. Schultz; *Secretary*, Jesse H. Snyder, Jr.; *Treasurer*, Amos S. Anders.

Board of Publication, Norristown, Pa. *President,* Edwin K. Schultz; *Secretary,* Rev. O. S. Kriebel.

Board of Home and Foreign Missions, Norristown, Pa. *President,* John H. Schultz; *Secretary,* Rev. H. K. Heebner.

Board of Managers of the Charity Fund. *President,* William H. Anders; *Secretary,* Wayne C. Meschter.

For list of ministers, with addresses, see The Schwenkfeldian, Norristown, Pa.

Periodical. *The Schwenkfeldian* (monthly), Norristown, Pa., Editor, S. K. Brecht.

NATIONAL SPIRITUALISTS' ASSOCIATION OF THE UNITED STATES

Annual convention, Oct., 1917, in N. Y. City.

There are 22 state associations.

Officers: *President,* Dr. George B. Warne, Chicago, Ill.; *Secretary,* George W. Kates, Washington, D. C.; *Treasurer,* Cassius L. Stevens, Pittsburgh, Pa.

Periodicals

Progressive Thinker (weekly), Chicago, Ill., Editor, Mrs. M. E. Cadwallader; *Banner of Life* (weekly), Boston, Mass., Editor, H. C. Berry; *Sunflower* (weekly), Hamburg, N. Y., Editor, Frank Walker; *Reason* (monthly), Los Angeles, Cal., Editor, Dr. B. F. Austin.

AMERICAN SECTION OF THE THEOSOPHICAL SOCIETY

Annual Convention meets at St. Louis, Mo., in August, 1916.

National President, A. P. Warrington; *National Vice-President,* Mrs. Marie B. Russak; *National Secretary,* Miss Isabel B. Holbrook, Krotona, Hollywood, Los Angeles, Cal.

Periodical. *Messenger* (monthly), Krotona, Hollywood, Los Angeles, Cal., Editor, Mrs. May S. Rogers.

Order of the Star of the East. In preparation of the coming of the Christ. *National Representative,* Miss Marjorie Tuttle, Los Angeles, Cal.

Official Journal: *Herald of the Star,* London, Eng.

UNITED BRETHREN IN CHRIST

(Old Constitution)

General Conference, quadrennial.

There are 23 Annual Conferences, including one in Canada.

Bishops

C. L. Wood, Alma, Mich.

F. L. Hoskins, Albion, Wash.

O. G. Alwood, Hillsdale, Mich.

Domestic, Frontier, and Foreign Missionary Society. *General Secretary,* Rev. J. Howe, Huntington, Ind.

Sunday Schools. *General Secretary,* J. W. Burton, Chambersburgh, Pa.

United Brethren Christian Endeavor Society. *General Secretary,* Miss M. M. Titus, Ubee, Ind.

Woman's Missionary Association. *General Secretary,* Mrs. F. A. Loew, Ubee, Ind.

Publishing Establishment, Huntington, Ind., *Agent* E. C. Mason.

Board of Education. *Secretary,* C. A. Mummart, Ubee, Ind.

Missionary, Church Erection, Educational and General Sabbath School. *Treasurer,* S. A. Stemen, Ubee, Ind.

General Preacher's Aid Board. *Secretary,* Rev. O. G. Alwood.

Colleges

Institution	Location	President
Albion College	Albion, Wash	F. L. Hoskins.
Central College	Huntington, Ind	C. W. H. Banga
Philomath College	Philomath, Ore	O. G. Alwood.

For list of ministers and addresses see Year Book, published at the United Brethren Publishing Establishment, Huntington, Ind., E. C. Mason, Agent.

Periodicals

Christian Conservator (weekly), Editor, Rev. William Dillon
Missionary Monthly, Editor, Parent Board Department, Rev. J. Howe; Editor Woman's Missionary Association Department, Mrs. F. A. Loew.

UNITARIAN CHURCHES

General Conference of Unitarian and Other Christian Churches meets biennially.

President, Hon. William H. Taft, New Haven, Conn.; *General Secretary,* Rev. Walter F. Greenman, 684 Astor Street, Milwaukee, Wis.; *Treasurer,* Percy A. Atherton, 30 State Street, Boston, Mass.

American Unitarian Association, 25 Beacon Street, Boston, Mass. *President,* Rev. Samuel A. Eliot; *Secretary,* Rev. Louis C. Cornish; *Treasurer,* Henry M. Williams; *Assistant Secretary,* W. Forbes Robertson. ,

Department of Social and Public Service, 25 Beacon Street, Boston, Mass. *Secretary,* Rev. Elmer S. Forbes.

Department of Religious Education, 25 Beacon Street, Boston, Mass. *Secretary,* Rev. William I. Lawrance; *Associate Secretary,* Rev. Florence Buck.

Field Secretaries: Rev. W. Channing Brown, 25 Beacon Street, Boston, Mass.; Charles O. Murdock, San Francisco, Cal.; Rev. Frank W. Pratt, Richmond, Va.; Rev. Samuel B. Nobbs, Boston, Mass.

Publication Agent, W. Forbes Robertson.

Unitarian Sunday School Society. *President,* Rev. William I. Lawrance, Boston, Mass.; *Clerk,* Miss Frances M. Dadmun, Cambridge, Mass.; *Treasurer,* Rev. Frederick M. Eliot, Cambridge, Mass.

Alliance of Unitarian and Other Liberal Christian Women. *President,* Miss Anna M. Bancroft, Hopedale, Mass.; *Corresponding Secretary,* Mrs. Mary B. Davis, 226 Windermere Avenue, Wayne, Pa.; *Treasurer,* Mrs. Lucia Clapp Noyes, 11 St. John Street, Jamaica Plain, Mass.

Committee to confer with the American Unitarian Association. *Chairman,* Miss Anna M. Bancroft.

Committee on Appeals. *Chairman,* Mrs. Prescott Keyes, Concord, Mass.

Committee on Finance. *Chairman,* Miss Lucy Lowell, Boston, Mass.

Committee on Study Classes. *Chairman,* Mrs. E. L. Houghton, Whitman, Mass.

Post Office Mission Committee. *Chairman,* Mrs. E. L. Osgood, Boston, Mass.

Committee on Cheerful Letter Exchange. *Chairman,* Mrs. George G. Saville, Quincy, Mass.

Committee on Southern Missionary Work. *Chairman,* Mrs. Abby A. Peterson, Jamaica Plain, Mass.

Sunday School Committee. *Chairman,* Mrs. John J. Donahue, Manchester, N. H.

International Committee. *Chairman,* Miss Elizabeth Marquand, Newburyport, Mass.

Junior Fellowship Committee. *Chairman,* Mrs. W. L. Voigt, New York City.

Committee on College Centers. *Chairman,* Miss Mary H. Bellows, Walpole, N. H.

Social Service Committee. *Chairman,* Mrs. Alva Roy Scott, Bangor, Me.

Young People's Religious Union. *President of the Executive Board,* Rev. Frederick W. Eliot, Cambridge, Mass.; *Secretary,* Miss Grace R. Torr, Peabody, Mass.; *Treasurer,* O. Arthur McMurdie, Belmont, Mass.

National League of Unitarian Laymen. *Honorary President,* Hon. William H. Taft; *President,* Charles E. Ware, Fitchburg, Mass.; *Secretary and Treasurer,* Elmer S. Forbes, 25 Beacon Street, Boston, Mass.

Unitarian Historical Society. *President,* Henry H. Edes; *Secretary,* Rev. George H. Reed, Fairhaven, Mass.; *Librarian,* Rev. Louis C. Cornish.

Unitarian Temperance Society. Headquarters, 25 Beacon Street, Boston, Mass. *President,* Rev. Edgar Swan Wiers, Montclair, N. J.; *Secretary,* Rev. Chester A. Drummond, Somerville, Mass.; *Treasurer,* Charles H. Stearns, Brookline, Mass.

Social Service Council of Unitarian Women. *President,* Mrs. Stella R. Root, Winchester, Mass.; *Secretary,* Mrs. Samuel S. Symmes, Winchester, Mass.; *Treasurer,* Mrs. Sara A. Robbins, Belmont, Mass.

Society for Ministerial Relief, Boston, Mass. *President,* Rev. Prof. F. G. Peabody, D.D., Cambridge, Mass. *Secretary,* Rev. Henry Wilder Foote, 22 Highland Street, Cambridge, Mass.; *Treasurer,* Mr. Stephen W. Philips, 10 Post Office Square, Boston, Mass.

Society for Promoting Theological Education, Boston, Mass. *President,* Rev. Howard N. Brown, D.D., Boston, Mass.; *Secretary,* Rev. Benjamin R. Bulkeley, Leominster, Mass.; *Treasurer,* William P. Fowler, Boston, Mass.

Society for Propagating the Gospel among the Indians and Others in North America, Boston, Mass. *President,* Rev. William W. Fenn, D.D.; *Secretary,* Rev. Charles E. Park, 347 Marlborough Street, Boston, Mass.; *Treasurer,* Francis H. Brown, M.D.

Union for Christian Work, Providence, R. I. *President,*

Prescott O. Clarke; *Secretary,* Rev. Arthur H. Winn, 3 Bell Street, Providence, R. I.

Unitarian Service Pension Society. *President,* James P. Parmenter; *Secretary,* Rev. Robert S. Loring, Ann Arbor, Mich.; *Treasurer,* Rev. J. H. Applebee, Syracuse, N. Y.

Divinity Schools

Institution	Location	President
Divinity School of Harvard University	Cambridge, Mass	Abbott Lawrence Lowell.
The Meadville Theological School	Meadville, Pa	Franklin C. Southworth.
Pacific Unitarian School for the Ministry	Berkeley, Cal	Earl M. Wilbur.

For a list of ministers with addresses see Unitarian Year Book, published at 25 Beacon Street, Boston, Mass.

Periodicals

Christian Register, Boston, Mass.; *Beacon* (weekly), Children's Paper, Boston, Mass.; *Unitarian Advance* (monthly), Chicago, Ill., Editor, George H. Badger; *The Pacific Unitarian* (monthly), San Francisco, Cal., Editor, Charles A. Murdock; *Unitarian Word and Work* (monthly), Boston, Mass.; *Unity* (weekly), Chicago, Ill., Editor, Jenkin Lloyd Jones.

UNIVERSALISTS

General Convention, biennial; next meeting in October, 1917.

Twenty-eight state conventions, 8 state conferences.

President, Rev. Lee S. McCollester, Tufts College, Mass.; *Secretary,* Rev. W. H. Skeels, 22 Cleveland Building, Watertown, N. Y.

General Superintendent of the Universalist Church. Position vacant.

Foreign Mission Board. *Chairman,* Rev. Lee C. McCollester, Tufts College, Mass.; *Secretary,* Rev. W. H. Skeels, Watertown, N. Y.

General Sunday School Association. *Secretary,* Rev. Frank Lincoln Masseck, Arlington, Mass.

Women's National Missionary Association. *President,* Mrs. Minnie J. Ayres, Woonsocket, R. I.; *Secretary,* Mrs. Agnes R. Canklin, Charlotte, Mich.

Commission on Social Service. *Chairman,* Rev. Frank Oliver Hall, 4 West Seventy-sixth Street, New York City; *Secretary,* Rev. Clarence R. Skinner, Tufts College, Mass.

Commission on Foreign Relations. *Chairman,* Rev. F. A. Bisbee, 359 Boylston Street, Boston, Mass.

National Y. P. C. U. *National Secretary,* Carl F. Elsner, 359 Boylston Street, Boston, Mass.; *President,* Rev. G. A. Gay, Little Falls, N. Y.

National Universalist Brotherhood. *President,* Samuel C. Kerr, 214 North Elmwood Avenue, Oak Park, Ill.

Universalist Publishing Houses: 359 Boylston Street, Boston, Mass.; 3011 Prairie Avenue, Chicago, Ill. *General Agent,* Melvin S. Nash.

Colleges and Theological Seminaries

Institution	Location	Dean or President
Lombard College	Galesburg, Ill	R. M. Barton.
St. Lawrence University	Canton, N. Y	J. Murray Atwood.
Tufts College	Tufts College, Mass	Herman Carey Bumpus.
Canton Theological Seminary	Canton, N. Y	J. Murray Atwood.
Crane Divinity School	Tufts College, Mass	Lee S. McCollester.
Ryder Divinity School	Chicago, Ill	Lewis B. Fisher.

The Universalist Register gives list of ministers, with addresses, published at the Universalist Publishing House, Boston, Mass.

Benevolent Institutions

Washburn Memorial Home, Minneapolis, Minn.; *Unity House,* Minneapolis, Minn.; *Parish House of St. Paul's Church,* Chicago, Ill.; *Bethany Union,* Boston, Mass.; *Franklin Square House,* Boston, Mass.; *Sheridan Cobb Hospital,* St. Paul, Minn.; *Thompson Home,* Waldron, Ind.; *Messiah Universalist Home,* Philadelphia, Pa.; *Chapin Home,* Jamaica, L. I., N. Y.

Periodicals

Universalist Leader (weekly), Boston, Mass., Editor, Frederick A. Bisbee; *Universalist Herald,* Cannon, Ga., Editor A. J. Owens; *Universalist,* Watertown, N. Y., Editor, Rev. G. D. Walker.

U. S. CHAPLAINS IN THE ARMY AND NAVY

CHAPLAINS IN THE ARMY

These chaplains have military rank from First Lieutenant up to and including Major.

Name	Denomination	Address
Bateman, C. C.	Baptist	Del Rio, Texas.
Groves, Leslie R.	Presbyterian in U. S. A.	Pasadena, Cal., R. F. D. 1, Box 376.
Gavitt, Halsey C.	Methodist Episcopal	Douglas, Ariz.
Randolph, John A.	Methodist Episcopal, South	Columbus, N. Mex.
Easterbrook, E. P.	Methodist Episcopal	Fort Flagler, Wash.

Hillman, James W	Presbyterian in U. S. A	Columbus, N. Mex.
Perry, Barton	Presbyterian in U. S. A	Eagle Pass, Texas.
Pruden, Aldred A	Protestant Episcopal	Fort Monroe, Va.
Rice, George D	Unitarian	Nogales, Ariz.
Stull, George C	Methodist Episcopal	Douglas, Ariz.
Dickson, Thomas J	Christian	Douglas, Ariz.
Newsom, Ernest P	Methodist Episcopal, South	Ft. Winfield Scott, Cal.
O'Keefe, Timothy P	Roman Catholic	Columbus, N. Mex.
Doherty, Francis B	Roman Catholic	Mercedes, Texas.
Smith, Samuel J	Methodist Episcopal	Fort Bliss, Texas.
Marvine, Walter	Protestant Episcopal	Fort Du Pont, Del.
Freeland, Charles W	Protestant Episcopal	Marfa, Texas.
Prioleau, George W	African Methodist Episcopal	Schofield Bks., Hawaii.
Griffes, James L	Presbyterian in U. S. A	Fort Bliss, Texas.
Brander, William W	Protestant Episcopal	Fort Bliss, Texas.
Clemens, Joseph	Methodist Episcopal	Fort Bliss, Texas.
Moose, John M	Methodist Episcopal, South	Columbus, N. Mex.
Ossewaarde, James	Reformed in America	U. S. Disciplinary Bks., Alcatraz, Cal.
Yates, Julian E	Baptist	Fort Hancock, N. J.
Hunter, Joseph L	Presbyterian in U. S. A	Fort Barrancas, Fla.
Axton, John T	Congregational	Fort Bliss, Texas.
Fleming, David L	Protestant Episcopal	Plattsburg Bks., N. Y.
Waring, George J	Roman Catholic	U. S. Disciplinary Bks., Fort Jay, N. Y.
Joyce, Francis P	Roman Catholic	U. S. Disciplinary Bks., Fort Leavenworth, Kan.
Lutz, Simon M	Lutheran	Fort Bayard, N. Mex.
Smith, Herbert S	Protestant Episcopal	Eagle Pass, Texas.
Gladden, W. W. E	Colored Baptist	Columbus, N. Mex.
Scott, Oscar J. W	African Methodist Episcopal	Columbus, N. Mex.
Chenoweth, John F	Methodist Episcopal	Fort Slocum, N. Y.
Chouinard, Horace A	Protestant Episcopal	El Paso, Texas.
Lloyd, Walter K	Protestant Episcopal	Columbus, N. Mex.
Wood, Stephen R	Congregational	Camp Gaillard, Canal Zone.
Ramsden, Stanley C	Baptist	Fort Ringgold, Texas.
Scott, William R	Protestant Episcopal	Fort Shafter, Hawaii.
Feinler, Franz J	Roman Catholic	care of Military Attache, Am. Embassy, Tokyo, Japan.
Fleming, Robert R., Jr	Baptist	Fort Sam Houston, Texas.
Londahl, Marinius M	Lutheran	Eagle Pass, Texas.
Livingston, Thomas	Congregational	Manila, P. I.
Houlihan, James F	Roman Catholic	Manila, P. I.
Carter, Louis A	Colored Baptist	Manila, P. I.
Brophy, Edward F	Roman Catholic	Fort Rosecrans, Cal.
Webb, James M	Presbyterian in U. S. A	Manila, P. I.
Watts, Wallace H	Protestant Episcopal	Tientsin, China.
Kangley, Joseph M	Roman Catholic	Fort Williams, Maine.
Lenehan, Jeremiah A	Roman Catholic	Schofield Bks., Hawaii.
Brasted, Alva J	Baptist	Manila, P. I.
Aiken, William A	Congregational	Schofield Bks., Hawaii.
Wood, Ernest W	Protestant Episcopal	Laredo, Texas.
Arnold, William R	Roman Catholic	Manila, P. I.
Sutherland, Alexander D	Presbyterian in U. S. A	Manila, P. I.
Rochford, John E	Roman Catholic	Camp E. S. Otis, Canal Zone.
Fealy, Ignatius	Roman Catholic	Schofield Bks., Hawaii.
Winter, Haywood L	Protestant Episcopal	Douglas, Ariz.
Maddox, John L	Presbyterian in U. S. A	Columbus, N. Mex.
Kelly, Thomas L	Roman Catholic	San Juan, P. R.
Schliesser, Adolf J	Lutheran	Warren, Ariz.
Miller, Clifford L	Universalist	Empire, Canal Zone.
Beebe, Milton O	Methodist Episcopal	Columbus, N. Mex.
Breden, John G	United Brethren	Fort Morgan, Ala.
Griffin, Edmond J	Roman Catholic	Fort Jay, N. Y.
Cohee, O. J	Disciples of Christ	Fort Bliss, Texas.
Silver, Horace Percy	Protestant Episcopal	Military Academy, West Point, N. Y.

CHAPLAINS IN THE NAVY
Address Chaplains in Navy, in care of the Postmaster, New York City.
These chaplains have rank from Lt. Junior grade up to and including Captain.

Name	Denomination
Thompson, Frank	Protestant Episcopal.
Wright, Carroll Q.	Disciples of Christ.
Isaacs, Walter G.	Methodist Episcopal, South.
Frazier, John B.	Methodist Episcopal, South.
Cassard, William G.	Protestant Episcopal.
Dickins, Curtis H.	Protestant Episcopal.
Charlton, Charles M.	Methodist Episcopal.
Patrick, Bower R.	Baptist.
Fleming, John F.	Baptist.
McDonald, Eugene L.	Roman Catholic.
Bayard, George L.	Protestant Episcopal.
Stone, Arthur W.	Protestant Episcopal.
Gleeson, Matthew C.	Roman Catholic.
Scott, Evan W.	Congregational.
Stevenson, George E. T.	Baptist.
Evans, Sydney K.	Protestant Episcopal.
Pearce, Hugh M. T.	Protestant Episcopal.
MacNair, James D.	Methodist Episcopal.
Brodman, Edmund A.	Roman Catholic.
Taylor, LeRoy N.	Methodist Episcopal.
Thompson, Thomas B.	Presbyterian in U. S. A.
Brady, John J.	Roman Catholic.
Bouffard, Irenee J. (Act. Chap.)	Roman Catholic.
Workman, Robert D. (Act. Chap.)	Presbyterian in U. S. A.
Anderson, William E. (Act. Chap.)	Disciples of Christ.
Alexander, Milton O. (Act. Chap.)	Baptist.
Burke, Eugene S. (Act. Chap.)	Roman Catholic.
Hayes, Allison J. (Act .Chap.)	Methodist Episcopal.
Ellis, Charles V. (Act. Chap.)	Baptist.
Behrens, Oscar W. (Act. Chap.)	Presbyterian in U. S. A.
Kranz, George B. (Act. Chap.)	Roman Catholic.
Dumstrey, Herbert (Act. Chap.)	Reformed in U. S.
Duff, Edward A. (Act. Chap.)	Roman Catholic.
Lewis, Roy L. (Act. Chap.)	Methodist Episcopal.
Elder, William W. (Act. Chap.)	Christian.
Riddle, Truman P. (Act. Chap.)	Protestant Episcopal.
Seidler, Paul E. (Act. Chap.)	Lutheran, Synodical Conference
Parks, Albert N. (Act. Chap.)	Presbyterian in U. S. A.
Short, Joseph C. (Act. Chap.)	Roman Catholic.
Hastings, Charles H. (Act. Chap.)	Methodist Episcopal.

DIRECTORY OF INTERCHURCH CONFERENCES, SOCIETIES, AND ORGANIZATIONS

FOREIGN MISSIONS CONFERENCE OF NORTH AMERICA

Purpose: To provide for an annual conference of North American foreign boards, to provide for the study of missionary problems, to promote a true science of missions, and to do work of interest to boards.

Embracing various denominational and interdenominational boards of the United States and Canada. Last annual meeting was held at Garden City, New York, in January, 1917. *Chairman of the 1917 conference,* Bishop W. R. Lambuth; *Secretaries,* Mr. W. Henry Grant and Rev. George Heber Jones. Office: 25 Madison Avenue, New York City.

Officers: *Chairman,* Rev. Paul de Sweinitz; *Vice-Chairmen,* Rev. F. D. Chown and Rev. B. H. Niebel; *Secretary,* Rev. George Heber Jones; *Honorary Secretary,* Mr. W. Henry Grant; *Treasurer,* Mr. Alfred Marling.

Committee of Reference and Counsel. *Chairman,* Rev. James L. Barton; *Secretary,* Rev. Charles R. Watson; *Treasurer,* Alfred E. Marling. Members, Mrs. Anna R. Atwater, Rev. Allen R. Bartholomew, Rev. James L. Barton, Rev. Arthur J. Brown, Rev. William I. Chamberlain, Rev. Ed F. Cook, Rev. Stephen J. Corey, Rev. James Endicott, Rev. James H. Franklin, Rev. Principal Alfred Gandier, Rev. John F. Goucher, Rev. Canon S. Gould, Rev. A. Woodruff Halsey, Miss Margaret E. Hodge, Rev. George Johnson, Rt. Rev. Arthur S. Lloyd, John R. Mott, Rev. Frank Mason North, Rev. Cornelius H. Patton, Mrs. Henry W. Peabody, George Wharton Pepper, Rev. Paul de Schweinitz, Rev. T. B. Ray, Rev. Egbert W. Smith, Rev. Charles R. Watson, Rev. L. B. Wolf, James Wood.

William Henry Grant, Rev. George Heber Jones, and Alfred E. Marling, *ex-officio.*

For statistics of the various boards, see pages 189-203.

FEDERATION OF THE WOMAN'S BOARDS OF FOREIGN MISSIONS OF THE UNITED STATES

Purpose: To promote unity, Christian fellowship and co-operation among Woman's Boards; to encourage and disseminate the best methods of work and to plead unitedly for the outpouring of the Spirit of God upon the Church of Christ.

Officers: *Chairman,* Mrs. DeWitt C. Knox, 1748 Broadway, New York City; *Vice-Chairman,* Mrs. O. R. Williamson, 3828 Adams Street, Chicago, Ill.; *Secretary,* Miss Mabel Cratty, 600 Lexington Avenue, New York City; *Treasurer,* Mrs. William I. Haven, 25 Fernwood Road, Summit, N. J.

AMERICAN BIBLE SOCIETY

Purpose: To secure the translation, publication, and circulation of the Holy Scriptures, without note or comment, in all languages and in all lands.

Office: Bible House, New York City.

Officers: *President,* Mr. James Wood; *Corresponding Secretaries,* Rev. John Fox and Rev. William Ingraham Haven; *Treasurer,* Mr. William Foulke.

COMMITTEE ON COOPERATION IN LATIN AMERICA

Represents American Mission Boards working in Latin America, and serves as the Continuation Committee of the Panama Missionary Congress.

Chairman, Robert E. Speer; *Executive Secretary,* Rev. S. G. Inman, 25 Madison Avenue, New York City; *Treasurer,* James H. Post, 129 Front Street, New York City.

COMMITTEE ON CHRISTIAN WORK IN THE CANAL ZONE

Appointed by the Federal Council

Representative, Rev. Sidney S. Conger, 105 East 22d Street, New York City.

AMERICAN HUGUENOT COMMITTEE

Appointed by the Federal Council

Chairman, William Jay Schieffelein; *Treasurer,* Edmund E. Robert; *Delegate of the Franco-Belgian Committee,* Rev. Henri Anet, 105 East 22d Street, New York City.

LAYMEN'S MISSIONARY MOVEMENT OF THE UNITED STATES AND CANADA

Purpose: The enlistment of laymen for the world-wide extension of Christ's kingdom.

Office: 1 Madison Avenue, New York City.

Officers: *Chairman,* James M. Speers; *Vice-Chairman,* Lt.-Col. E. W. Halford; *Treasurer,*. Eben E. Olcott; *General Secretary,* William B. Millar; *Associate General Secretary,* Fred B. Fisher; *Educational Secretary,* W. E. Doughty.

MISSIONARY EDUCATION MOVEMENT OF THE UNITED STATES AND CANADA

Purpose: The preparation and syndication of missionary literature for all ages in the local church, and the training of leaders to use the literature through institutes and summer conferences.

Office: 156 Fifth Avenue, New York City.

Officers: *Chairman,* Samuel Thorne, Jr.; *Vice-Chairman,* H. Paul Douglass; *Treasurer,* James S. Cushman; *Recording Secretary,* F. C. Stephenson; *General Secretary,* Harry Wade Hicks; *Secretaries,* Harry S. Myers, Susan Mendenhall, John J. DeMott, James B. Mershon, Kenneth M. Gould, H. C. Priest, J. C. Worley, F. H. Means.

STUDENT VOLUNTEER MOVEMENT FOR FOREIGN MISSIONS

Object: To cultivate among students of institutions of higher learning in the United States and Canada intelligent and active interest in foreign missions; to enroll a sufficient number of properly qualified Student Volunteers to meet the successive demands of the various Foreign Mission Boards of North America; to help such intended missionaries to prepare for their life work and to lay an equal burden of responsibility on all students who are to remain at home as ministers and lay workers.

Office: 25 Madison Avenue, New York City.

Chairman, John R. Mott; *General Secretary,* Fennell P. Turner; *Treasurer,* James M. Speers.

Official Organ: Student Volunteer Movement Bulletin (quarterly).

AMERICAN McALL MISSIONARY ASSOCIATION

Corresponding Secretary, Mrs. H. L. Wayland, 511 South Forty-second Street, Philadelphia, Pa.

AMERICAN WALDENSIAN AID SOCIETY

General Secretary, Miss Leonora Kelso, 213 West Seventy-sixth Street, New York City.

AMERICAN AND FOREIGN CHRISTIAN UNION

S. W. Thurber, 104 East Thirty-ninth Street, New York City.

CENTRAL AMERICAN MISSION

Rev. C. I. Scofield, Greyshingles, Douglaston, New York.

CHRISTIAN AND MISSIONARY ALLIANCE

President and General Superintendent, Rev. A. B. Simpson, 690 Eighth Avenue, New York City.

AMERICAN COUNCIL, AFRICA INLAND MISSION

General Director, Rev. Chas. E. Hurlburt, 2244 North 29th Street, Philadelphia, Pa.

CHINA INLAND MISSION

Rev. H. W. Frost, Home Director, 25 Elm Street, Summit, N. J.

YALE FOREIGN MISSIONARY SOCIETY (CHANGSHA, CHINA)

General Secretary, Prof. Harlan P. Beach, D.D., 346 Willow Street, New Haven, Conn.

WOMAN'S UNION MISSIONARY SOCIETY OF AMERICA

Mrs. S. T. Dauchy, *Acting Secretary,* 67 Bible House, New York City.

Miss Alice H. Birdseye, *Recording Secretary,* Bible House, New York City.

MISSION TO LEPERS

W. M. Danner, *Secretary,* 105 Raymond Street, Cambridge, Mass.

FRANCO-AMERICAN COMMITTEE ON EVANGELIZATION

Treasurer, Harvey Patterson, 301 West One Hundred and Sixth Street, New York City.

HOME MISSIONS COUNCIL

Purpose: to promote fellowship, conference, and cooperation among Christian organizations doing missionary work in the United States and its dependencies.

Officers: *Chairman,* Rev. Charles L. Thompson, 156 Fifth Avenue, New York City; *Secretary,* Mr. William T. Demarest, 25 East Twenty-second Street, New York City; *Treasurer,* Mr. Charles H. Baker, 287 Fourth Avenue, New York City.

COUNCIL OF WOMEN FOR HOME MISSIONS

Purpose: An organization through which National Women's Home Missionary Boards and Societies may consult as to wider plans, and cooperatively do more efficient work for the homeland. These cooperating agencies are divided into two classes, Constituent and Corresponding, according to the number of representatives and the financial obligation assumed.

The Council prepares senior and junior Home Mission study books for interdenominational use, prepares a program for a nation-wide interdenominational Day of Prayer for Home Missions, cooperates with the Home Missions Council, the Foreign Missions Conference, and the Federation of the Woman's Boards of Foreign Missions of the United States.

Office: 600 Lexington Avenue, New York City.

Officers: *President,* Mrs. Fred S. Bennett; *Corresponding Secretary,* Mrs. F. W. Wilcox; *Recording Secretary,* Miss P. M. Rossman; *Treasurer,* Mrs. P. F. Jerome.

AMERICAN TRACT SOCIETY

Purpose: To diffuse a knowledge of our Lord Jesus Christ as the Redeemer of sinners by printing and circulating the Gospel Message in many languages, dialects, and characters throughout the world.

Office: Park Avenue and Fortieth Street, New York City.

Officers: *President*, William Phillips Hall; *General Secretary*, Rev. Judson Swift; *Treasurer*, Louis Tag.

CHICAGO TRACT SOCIETY

Does missionary work among immigrants in eleven States.

Officers: *President*, Rev. E. F. Williams; *Secretary*, Ernest M. Brooks, 440 South Dearborn Street, Chicago, Ill.; *Treasurer*, Wm. T. Vickery, Continental and Commercial Bank, Chicago.

WORLD CONFERENCE ON FAITH AND ORDER

Suggested by the General Convention of the Protestant Episcopal Church.

Fifty-nine denominations in various countries have appointed commissions to represent them in this world movement.

Officers: *President*, Rt. Rev. Charles P. Anderson, Bishop of Chicago, Chicago, Ill.; *Treasurer*, Mr. George Zabriskie, 49 Wall Street, New York City; *Secretary*, Mr. Robert H. Gardiner, Gardiner, Me.

RELIGIOUS WELFARE LEAGUE FOR THE ARMY AND NAVY

Cooperating with the Federal Council

Office: 1114 Woodward Building, Washington, D. C.

Officers: *Chairman*, Bishop Earl Cranston; *Secretary*, H. K. Carroll; *Treasurer*, Wm. Knowles Cooper.

RELIGIOUS EDUCATION ASSOCIATION

To promote moral and religious training in existing educational agencies, in homes and through the press.

Officers: *President*, Bishop Francis J. McConnell, Denver, Colo.; *Secretary*, Henry F. Cope, 332 Michigan Avenue, Chicago, Ill.

COUNCIL OF CHURCH BOARDS OF EDUCATION

This is an organization of Church Boards of Education of eighteen leading Protestant bodies and is composed of representatives of Boards of Education of the Northern Baptist Convention, American Christian Convention, Congregational, Disciples of Christ, United Evangelical, Friends, Lutheran General Council, Lutheran General Synod, Lutheran United Synod, Methodist Episcopal, Methodist Episcopal, South, Presbyterian, Northern, Presbyterian, Southern, Protestant Episcopal, Reformed in America, Reformed in United States, United Brethren, and United Presbyterian.

The Council is conducting a "Forward Movement for Christian Education," a nation-wide interdenominational campaign in the interests of religious education and the denominational college.

Office: 19 South La Salle Street, Chicago, Ill.
Executive Secretary, Rev. R. Watson Cooper.

WORLD'S SUNDAY SCHOOL ASSOCIATION

An outgrowth of the International Sunday School Association. It is primarily a missionary organization and since January, 1916, is directly representative of the Mission and Sunday School Boards through the appointment of representatives of the Foreign Missions Conference of North America and the Sunday School Council of Evangelical Denominations to the extent of one half of the membership of the Executive Committee of the American Section.

Office: American Section, 1 Madison Avenue, New York City. *General Secretary*, Frank L. Brown; *Treasurer*, A. M. Harris.

INTERNATIONAL SUNDAY SCHOOL ASSOCIATION

Purpose: To promote Sunday-school extension, efficiency, and evangelism.

Office: 5 South Wabash Avenue, Chicago, Ill.
Officers: *President*, Mr. E. K. Warren; *General Secretary*, Mr. Marion Lawrance; *Treasurer*, Mr. E. H. Nichols.

SUNDAY-SCHOOL COUNCIL OF EVANGELICAL DENOMINATIONS

A voluntary organization of evangelical denominations for the extension of religious education through the Sunday-school.

The object of the Council is to advance Sunday-school interests of the cooperating denominations:

1. By conferring together in matters of common interest.

2. By giving expression to common views and decisions.

3. By cooperative action on matters concerning educational, editorial, missionary, and publishing activities.

Office: 1701 Chestnut Street, Philadelphia, Pa.

Officers: *President*, J. Van Ness; *Secretary*, Rev. George T. Webb; *Treasurer*, D. M. Smith.

AMERICAN SUNDAY SCHOOL UNION

Purpose: To establish and maintain Sunday-schools, and to publish and circulate moral and religious publications.

Office: 1816 Chestnut Street, Philadelphia, Pa.

Officers: *President*, Martin L. Finckel; *Recording Secretary*, William H. Hirst; *Treasurer*, John E. Stevenson.

LORD'S DAY ALLIANCE OF THE UNITED STATES

Represents 16 leading Christian denominations.

Purpose: To defend and preserve the Lord's Day as a day of rest and worship and to urge one day of rest in seven for all the toiling masses.

Office: 203 Broadway, New York City.

Officers: *President*, James Yereance, 128 Broadway, New York City; *General Secretary*, Rev. Harry L. Bowlby; *Treasurer*, George M. Thomson.

NEW YORK SABBATH COMMITTEE

Purpose: Concerns itself particularly with Sunday as a civil institution. It seeks to secure freedom from Sunday work for every one from the enslavement of unnecessary work and business, and from the distraction of public amusements and disturbing noise. Its aim is a day of rest with a day of worship.

Office: 31 Bible House, New York City.

Officers: *Chairman*, Theodore Gilman; *General Secretary*, Rev. Duncan J. McMillan; *Treasurer*, E. Francis Hyde, 54 Wall Street, New York City.

WOMAN'S NATIONAL SABBATH ALLIANCE

Object: The promotion of the sanctity of the American Sabbath.

Office: 156 Fifth Avenue, New York City.

Officers: *President,* Mrs. Henry E. Drake; *Corresponding Secretary,* Miss Catherine Murray; *Treasurer,* Miss Anna S. Hallock.

UNITED SOCIETY OF CHRISTIAN ENDEAVOR

Purpose: To provide an earnest Christian life among its members, to increase their mutual acquaintance, and to make them more useful in the service of God.

The first Young People's Society of Christian Endeavor was organized in the Williston Congregational Church, Portland, Me., February 2, 1881, by the pastor, Rev. Francis E. Clark. Beginning with 1882 annual conventions were held for the purpose of promoting fellowship and spreading information regarding the work of the societies.

The United Society of Christian Endeavor was organized in 1885 at the convention held in Old Orchard, Me. Its field includes the societies in the United States, Canada, and Mexico.

In 1895 at the convention held in Boston, Mass., the World's Christian Endeavor Union was organized, and included in its membership all societies in practically every country in the world, and in about eighty evangelical denominations. There are 78,176 societies enrolled with an estimated membership of nearly 4,000,000.

The United Society of Christian Endeavor now holds biennial conventions, and the World's Christian Endeavor Union meets about once in four years in connection with one of the national conventions.

Organizations similar to the United Society are found in all the leading nations of the world.

The four Christian Endeavor fundamental principles are:

Confession of Christ; Service for Christ; Loyalty to Christ's Church; Fellowship with Christ's people.

Office: Christian Endeavor House, Mount Vernon and Hancock Streets, Boston, Mass.

Officers: *President,* Rev. Francis E. Clark; *General Secretary,* William Shaw; *Editorial Secretary,* Amos R. Wells; *Clerk of Corporation,* H. N. Lathrop; *Associate President and National Temperance and Citizenship Superintendent,* Daniel A. Poling; *Treasurer and Publication Manager,* A. J. Shartle; *Southern States Secretary,* Karl Lehmann; *Extension Secretary,* Ira Landrith.

BAPTIST YOUNG PEOPLE'S UNION OF AMERICA

Purpose: A fraternal union of Baptist young people for the enlistment and enlightenment of young people in the great cooperative work of the Kingdom.

The twenty-sixth anniversary convention will be held in Detroit, Michigan, July 5-8, 1917.

Office: 107 South Wabash Avenue, Chicago, Ill.

Officers: *President,* H. B. Osgood; *Recording Secretary,* Mr. George W. Wason; *General Secretary,* Rev. James A. White; *Treasurer,* Orlo O. Montague.

EPWORTH LEAGUE OF THE METHODIST EPISCOPAL CHURCH

Purpose: To promote intelligent and vital piety in the young members and friends of the Church, to aid them in the attainment of purity of heart and in constant growth in grace, and to train them in works of mercy and help.

The League is divided into four departments: first, Spiritual Work, including devotional meetings, personal evangelism and Bible study; second, that of World Evangelism, including the study of Missions, Christian Stewardship and the promotion of some definite missionary enterprise; third, department of Social Service, including studies in Social Service, and Good Citizenship and the promotion of Temperance Reform, social purity and deeds of mercy and help; fourth, department of Recreation and Culture, including the promotion of clean and wholesome athletics, recreation and social life, together with the cultivation of sound literary taste.

The League is divided into two general sections, the Senior League for those young people from sixteen years of age and upward, and the Junior Epworth League for those from eight to sixteen years of age. The present membership of the Epworth League is about 900,000.

Central Office: 740 Rush Street, Chicago, Ill.

Officers: *President,* Bishop Adna W. Leonard, San Francisco, Cal.; *General Secretary and Executive Officer,* Rev. Wilbur F. Sheridan, Chicago, Ill.; *Editor of the Epworth Herald,* Rev. Dan B. Brummitt, Chicago, Ill.

Junior Epworth League, *General Secretary,* Miss Emma A. Robinson, Chicago, Ill.

The League is also organized in Canada and the Methodist Episcopal Church, South. (See Directory, page 68.)

LUTHER LEAGUE OF AMERICA

Its principles are federation and cooperation. Any society of whatever name, connected with a Lutheran congregation or a Lutheran institution of learning, and all district and state organizations, whose admission shall have been in conformity with Article II of the Constitution, which sets forth the basis of the organization, and recommended by the committee on credentials, are entitled to membership. It therefore embraces to-day, upon consistent grounds, all Lutheran Young People's Societies.

Societies are organized in Canada, Porto Rico, India, China, Japan, and British Guiana.

Officers: *President,* C. T. A. Anderson, 35 South Dearborn Street, Chicago, Ill.; *First Vice-President,* O. C. Rhode, 628 Fernwood Avenue, Toledo, O.; *Second Vice-President,* Geo. W. Rapps, 2312 Chestnut Street, Milwaukee, Wis.; *General Secretary,* Harry Hodges, P. O. Box 2027, Philadelphia, Pa.; *Literature Secretary,* Rev. Luther M. Kuhns, 440 Paxton Block, Omaha, Neb.; *Treasurer,* P. Walter Banker, 126 Wyoming Street, Wilkes-Barre, Pa.

Executive Committee: Hon. E. F. Eilert, *chairman,* 318 West Thirty-ninth Street, New York City; William C. Stoever, Lit. D., Philadelphia, Pa.; Rev. E. A. Trabert, Lima, O.; O. C. C. Fetta, Indianapolis, Ind.; I. S. Runyon, New York City; Rev. G. F. Gehr, Wilkinsburg, Pa.; James M. Reynolds, Valatie, N. Y.; Rev. M. J. Bieber, D.D., Toronto, Canada; and the President, Vice-Presidents, General Secretary, Literature Secretary and Treasurer.

Periodicals. *Luther League Review* and *Luther League Topics,* Rev. Luther M. Kuhns, Editor.

INTERNATIONAL COMMITTEE OF YOUNG MEN'S CHRISTIAN ASSOCIATIONS

Purpose: Establishing and assisting Young Men's Christian Associations in any country and generally to promote the spiritual, intellectual, physical and social well-being of young men in accordance with the aims and methods of the Young Men's Christian Associations.

Character of the Organization: Religious, Physical, Educational and Social work for young men and boys.

Office: 124 East Twenty-eighth Street, New York City.

Officers: *Chairman,* Alfred E. Marling; *Vice-Chairman,* William Sloane; *General Secretary,* John R. Mott; *Associate General Secretary,* F. S. Brockman; *Treasurer,* B. H. Fancher.

NATIONAL BOARD OF THE YOUNG WOMEN'S CHRISTIAN ASSOCIATIONS OF THE UNITED STATES OF AMERICA

Purpose: To unite in one body The Young Women's Christian Associations of the United States; to establish, develop and unify such Associations; to participate in the work of the World's Young Women's Christian Association; to advance the physical, social, intellectual, moral and spiritual interests of young women. The ultimate purpose of all its efforts shall be to seek to bring young women to such a knowledge of Jesus Christ as Savior and Lord as shall mean for the individual young woman fulness of life and development of character, and shall make the organization as a whole an effective agency in the bringing in of the Kingdom of God among young women.

Office: 600 Lexington Avenue, New York City.
Officers: *President,* Mrs. Robert E. Speer; *Chairman Executive Committee,* Mrs. John French; *First Vice-President,* Mrs. James S. Cushman; *Second Vice-President,* Mrs. William W. Rossiter; *Secretary,* Mrs. Thomas S. Gladding; *Treasurer,* Mrs. Samuel J. Broadwell; *General Secretary,* Miss Mabel Cratty.

INTERNATIONAL COUNCIL BROTHERHOOD OF ANDREW AND PHILIP*

An interdenominational, international organization for men, seeking to bring all the men together in a given church in one organization, affiliating their activities, rounding all up in the spiritual and aiming to federate them denominationally, interdenominationally, and give them a world-wide vision.

Office: Widener Building, Philadelphia, Pa.
Officers: *President,* Joseph M. Steele; *General Secretary,* Rev. Norman J. Smith; *Treasurer,* William R. Nicholson.

---

*For other Brotherhoods see Directory of various denominations. Brotherhood of Methodist Episcopal Church transferred to Board of Sunday Schools, 58 East Washington St., Chicago, Ill.

BROTHERHOOD OF ST. ANDREW IN THE UNITED STATES OF AMERICA

This is an organization of laymen in the Anglican Communion under two rules, the rule of prayer and the rule of service.

Office: Church House, Twelfth and Walnut Streets, Philadelphia, Pa.

Officers: *President,* Edward H. Bonsall; *General Secretary,* Franklin S. Edmonds; *Executive Secretary,* George Herbert Randall; *Corresponding Secretary,* Walter Miller Kalmey; *Treasurer,* Carl N. Martin.

THE DAUGHTERS OF THE KING

"For His Sake"

President, Mrs. Adam Dunmead, Baltimore, Md.; *General Secretary,* Emma E. Behlendorff, 281 Fourth Avenue, New York City.

THE KING'S DAUGHTERS AND SONS

"In His Name"

Headquarters, 280 Madison Avenue, New York City. *President,* Mrs. Anthony H. Evans, 336 West Eighty-sixth Street, New York City; *General Secretary,* Miss Clara Morehouse; *Treasurer,* Mrs. K. M. Farnsworth.

Periodical. *Silver Cross,* New York City, Editor, Delta McLaurin.

BOY SCOUTS OF AMERICA

Purpose: To develop character, initiative, and resourcefulness in boys by cultivating their interest in activities of practical every-day value through their interest in the fascinating outdoor activities of the Scout program, under carefully selected leadership.

Office: 200 Fifth Avenue, New York City.

Officers: *Chief Scout Executive* James E. West, New York City; *Treasurer,* George D. Pratt, Brooklyn, N. Y.

CAMP FIRE GIRLS

An organization similar to the Boy Scouts. The law of the

Camp Fire: Seek beauty, give service, pursue knowledge, be trustworthy, hold on to health, glorify work, be happy.

Headquarters: 461 Fourth Avenue, New York City.

Officers: *President,* Luther H. Gulick; *Treasurer,* John H. Potter.

ANTI-SALOON LEAGUE

An interdenominational movement, designed to federate the churches and temperance forces of the United States in an organized opposition to the beverage liquor traffic.

Offices: Westerville, O., and Washington, D. C.

Officers: *President,* Bishop Luther B. Wilson, New York City; *General Superintendent,* Rev. P. A. Baker, Westerville, O.; *General Secretary,* S. E. Nicholson, Richmond, Ind.; *Legislative Superintendent,* Rev. Edwin C. Dinwiddie, Washington, D. C.; *Treasurer,* Foster Copeland, Columbus, O.

WOMAN'S CHRISTIAN TEMPERANCE UNION

Organized for the protection of the home, the abolition of the liquor traffic, and the triumph of Christ's Golden Rule in custom and in law.

Office: Evanston, Ill.

Officers: *President,* Miss Anna A. Gordon; *Corresponding Secretary,* Mrs. Frances P. Parks; *Treasurer,* Mrs. Margaret C. Munns.

The World's Woman's Christian Temperance Union is organized in over fifty countries.

NATIONAL TEMPERANCE SOCIETY AND PUBLICATION HOUSE

(Merged with Commission on Temperance of the Federal Council)

Organized to promote the world-wide cause of the temperance educational propaganda.

Office: 105 East Twenty-second Street, New York City.

Officers: *President,* Rev. D. Stuart Dodge; *Acting Secretary,* Rev. Charles S. Macfarland; *Business Manager,* Frederick Gates.

INDIAN RIGHTS ASSOCIATION

A non-political, non-sectarian body organized to secure to

the Indians of the United States the political and civil rights already guaranteed to them by treaty and statutes of the United States, and such as their civilization and circumstances may justify.

Office: 995 Drexel Building, Philadelphia, Pa.

Officers: *President,* Rev. Carl E. Grammer; *Corresponding Secretary,* Herbert Welsh; *General Secretary,* Matthew K. Sniffen; *Treasurer,* Charles J. Rhoads; *Agent,* S. M. Brosius, McGill Building, Washington, D. C.

AMERICAN INSTITUTE OF SOCIAL SERVICE

Purpose: To promote social betterment in all fields of human activity at home and abroad by (1) serving as a depository of the world's funded experience of social interest and value; (2) collecting social facts and information in all parts of the world, and studying and interpreting them in their relation to social betterment; (3) disseminating social knowledge for the education of public opinion, and in so far as practicable aiding in the promotion and guidance of social activities and constructive social movements.

Office: Bible House, New York City.

Officers: *Acting President,* Mornay Williams; *General Secretary,* Rev. Nathaniel M. Pratt; *Acting Treasurer,* M. J. Whitty.

PEACE SOCIETIES AND ORGANIZATIONS IN THE UNITED STATES AND CANADA

THE CHURCH PEACE UNION

The Church Peace Union consists of a Board of Trustees administering a fund of two million dollars, given by Andrew Carnegie for the purpose of work among the churches in the interest of international peace and arbitration.

Trustees of the Church Peace Union

Office: 70 Fifth Avenue, New York City.
Officers: *President,* Rt. Rev. David H. Greer; *Secretary,* Rev. Frederick Lynch.
Other Members: Rev. Peter Ainslie, Rev. Arthur J. Brown, Rev. Francis E. Clark, President W. H. P. Faunce, His Eminence, James Cardinal Gibbons, Archbishop J. J. Glennon, Rev. Frank O. Hall, Bishop E. R. Hendrix, Rabbi Emil G. Hirsch, Hamilton Holt, Prof. William I. Hull, Rev. Charles E. Jefferson, Rev. Jenkin Lloyd Jones, Rt. Rev. William Lawrence, Rev. Charles S. Macfarland, Marcus M. Marks, Dean Shailer Mathews, Edwin D. Mead, Rev. William Pierson Merrill, John R. Mott, George A. Plimpton, Rev. Junius B. Remensnyder, Judge Henry Wade Rogers, Robert E. Speer, Francis Lynde Stetson, James J. Walsh, and Bishop Luther B. Wilson.

WORLD ALLIANCE FOR PROMOTING INTERNATIONAL FRIENDSHIP THROUGH THE CHURCHES

INTERNATIONAL COMMITTEE

Officers

Chairman, J. Allen Baker, M.P.; *Vice-Chairman,* Rev. William P. Merrill; *Secretaries,* Rt. Hon. W. H. Dickinson, M. P., M. Jacques Dumas, Pastor Dr. F. Siegmund-Schultze, Rev. Frederick Lynch; *Organizing Secretary for Europe,* Prof. Benjamin F. Battin.

The World Alliance was established by the Conference held August 25, 1914, in Constance and London.

Ten National Councils have been established, one each in Great Britain, France, Germany, Denmark, Holland, Italy, Norway, Sweden, Switzerland and the United States.

The British National Council has secured individual supporting members to the number of more than 5,000.

AMERICAN SECTION OF INTERNATIONAL COMMITTEE

AMERICAN COUNCIL

Officers

President, Rev. William P. Merrill; *Vice-President,* John R. Mott; *Treasurer,* George A. Plimpton; *Secretaries,* Rev. Frederick Lynch, Rev. Sidney L. Gulick.

Executive Committee

Rev. William P. Merrill, *Chairman*

Rev. Peter Ainslie	Rev. Sidney L. Gulick
Hon. Simeon E. Baldwin	Bishop E. R. Hendrix
Prof. Benjamin F. Battin	Hamilton Holt
James Bertram	Rev. Frederick Lynch
Rev. Nehemiah Boynton	Rev. Charles S. Macfarland
Rev. Arthur J. Brown	Prof. Shailer Mathews
Rev. Francis E. Clark	John R. Mott
Rev. George William Douglas	George A. Plimpton
Pres. W. H. P. Faunce	Rev. J. B. Remensnyder
Bishop David H. Greer	Bishop Luther B. Wilson

The American National Council held its first Conference at Garden City, N. Y., April 25, 1916. It is composed of 260 of the leading Christian citizens of the United States who come from forty-one different communions, whose combined church membership exceeds 23,000,000. The American Council in dealing with the constituent bodies of the Federal Council of the Churches of Christ in America, works in co-operation with its Commission on International Justice and Good-will. This world movement is entirely free from questions concerning church organization and doctrine. All Christians may and should unite in establishing a Christian world order.

The American Council and the Commission on International Justice and Good-will of the Federal Council of

Churches invite every local congregation to establish its own Peacemakers' Committee to cooperate with them in Christianizing America's international relations and in helping them to establish a Christian world order.

The Purpose and Work of the Peacemakers' Committee is to connect the local congregation with the world movement of the churches and to promote study in the local community of the principles of Christian internationalism, to develop the intelligent convictions of church-members in regard to their international responsibilities and duties, and to render possible the collective action of Christian citizens in making America's international relations Christian.

Every Communion in the United States is invited to establish a Peacemakers' Commission while State and City Federations of Churches are also invited to establish suitable committees which may be called Peacemakers' Federations and Leagues. The special work of these general committees is to further the establishment of Peacemakers' Committees by their local congregations and to promote a nation-wide campaign of education in Christian internationalism.

A Manual of Suggestions for Peacemakers' Committees describes in detail the available literature and the methods of work which such committees may undertake.

Every Peacemakers' Committee should enroll promptly at the national office, 105 East 22d St., New York City, in order to render its best service both locally and nationally.

AMERICAN ASSOCIATION FOR INTERNATIONAL CONCILIATION. *Secretary,* Frederick P. Keppel, 407 West 117th Street, New York City.

AMERICAN LEAGUE TO LIMIT ARMAMENTS. Practically merged with American Union Against Militarism. (See below.) *Secretary,* L. Hollingsworth Wood, 43 Cedar Street, New York City.

AMERICAN NEUTRAL CONFERENCE COMMITTEE. *Secretary,* Rebecca Shelley, 70 Fifth Avenue, New York City.

AMERICAN PEACE AND ARBITRATION LEAGUE. *Secretary,* Andrew B. Humphrey, 31 Nassau Street, New York City.

AMERICAN PEACE SOCIETY. *Secretary,* Arthur D. Call, Colorado Building, Washington, D. C.

Departments:

CENTRAL WEST,
116 South Michigan Avenue, Chicago, Ill.

NEW ENGLAND,
6 Beacon Street, Boston, Mass.

NEW YORK-NEW JERSEY,
70 Fifth Avenue, New York City.

PACIFIC COAST,
1119 Hobart Building, San Francisco, Cal.

SOUTH ATLANTIC STATES,
321 North Boulevard, Atlanta, Ga.

Divisions:

BUFFALO PEACE AND ARBITRATION SOCIETY,
Buffalo, N. Y.

CALIFORNIA PEACE SOCIETY,
1119 Hobart Building, San Francisco, Cal.

CONNECTICUT PEACE SOCIETY,
Hartford, Conn.

DELAWARE PEACE SOCIETY,
108 Franklin Street, Wilmington, Del.

FLORIDA PEACE SOCIETY,
Orlando, Fla.

GEORGIA PEACE SOCIETY,
321 North Boulevard, Atlanta, Ga.

INDIANA PEACE SOCIETY,
Indianapolis, Ind.

IOWA PEACE SOCIETY,
Grinnell, Ia.

MAINE PEACE SOCIETY,
95 Exchange Street, Portland, Me.

MARYLAND PEACE SOCIETY,
Baltimore, Md.

MASSACHUSETTS PEACE SOCIETY,
31 Beacon Street, Boston, Mass.

MINNESOTA PEACE SOCIETY,
15 North Sixth Street, Minneapolis, Minn.

MISSOURI PEACE SOCIETY,
Columbia, Mo.

NEBRASKA PEACE SOCIETY,
1834 South Twenty-fifth Street, Lincoln, Neb.

NEW HAMPSHIRE PEACE SOCIETY,
Andover, N. H.

NEW YORK PEACE SOCIETY,
70 Fifth Avenue, New York City.
NORTH CAROLINA PEACE SOCIETY,
Raleigh, N. C.
OREGON PEACE SOCIETY,
Oregonian Building, Portland, Ore.
PENNSYLVANIA ARBITRATION AND PEACE SOCIETY,
Witherspoon Building, Philadelphia, Pa.
RHODE ISLAND PEACE SOCIETY,
Providence, R. I.
TENNESSEE PEACE SOCIETY,
Chattanooga, Tenn.
TEXAS PEACE SOCIETY,
Dallas, Texas.
UTAH PEACE SOCIETY,
Salt Lake City, Utah.
VERMONT PEACE SOCIETY,
Brattleboro, Vt.
WASHINGTON PEACE SOCIETY,
4706 Fourteenth Avenue, N. E., Seattle, Wash.
WASHINGTON (D. C.) PEACE SOCIETY,
1736 G Street, Washington, D. C.
WISCONSIN PEACE SOCIETY,
Madison, Wis.

Sections:

AUBURN PEACE SOCIETY,
Auburn, N. Y.
CHICAGO PEACE SOCIETY,
116 South Michigan Avenue, Chicago, Ill.
CINCINNATI ARBITRATION AND PEACE SOCIETY,
Cincinnati, Ohio.
CLEVELAND PEACE SOCIETY,
Cleveland, Ohio.
CUMBERLAND VALLEY PEACE SOCIETY,
Mechanicsburg, Pa.
DERRY PEACE SOCIETY,
Derry, N. H.
DULUTH PEACE SOCIETY,
Duluth, Minn.
FALL RIVER PEACE SOCIETY,
Fall River, Mass.
GERMAN-AMERICAN PEACE SOCIETY OF NEW YORK,
107 East 112th Street, New York City.
HUDSON AND MOHAWK RIVERS PEACE SOCIETY,
37 Tweedle Building, Albany, N. Y.

HUDSON PEACE SOCIETY,
Hudson, N. Y.

ITALIAN PEACE SOCIETY OF NEW YORK,
2046 First Avenue, New York City.

MINNEAPOLIS PEACE SOCIETY,
1770 Knox Avenue, Minneapolis, Minn.

NEW BEDFORD PEACE SOCIETY,
New Bedford, Mass.

NIAGARA PEACE SOCIETY,
North Tonawanda, N. Y.

NORFOLK PEACE SOCIETY,
Norfolk, Va.

NORTHERN CALIFORNIA PEACE SOCIETY,
1119 Hobart Building, San Francisco, Cal.

NORTHFIELD PEACE SOCIETY,
Northfield, Minn.

PITTSBURGH PEACE SOCIETY,
Pittsburgh, Pa.

POUGHKEEPSIE PEACE SOCIETY,
Poughkeepsie, N. Y.

ST. PAUL PEACE SOCIETY,
573 Ottawa Avenue, St. Paul, Minn.

SOUTHERN CALIFORNIA PEACE SOCIETY,
1119 Hobart Building, San Francisco, Cal.

SPRINGFIELD PEACE SOCIETY,
Springfield, Mass.

TITUSVILLE PEACE SOCIETY,
Titusville, Pa.

WILLIAM LADD PEACE SOCIETY,
Exeter, N. H.

YOUNGSTOWN PEACE SOCIETY,
Youngstown, Ohio.

AMERICAN SCHOOL PEACE LEAGUE, 405 Marlboro Street, Boston, Mass. Mrs. Fannie Fern Andrews.

AMERICAN SOCIETY FOR JUDICIAL SETTLEMENT OF INTERNATIONAL DISPUTES. *Assistant Secretary,* Tunstall Smith, The Preston, Baltimore, Md.

AMERICAN SOCIETY, Woolworth Building, Suite 2560, New York City.

AMERICAN UNION AGAINST MILITARISM, *Secretary,* Crystal Eastman, Munsey Building, Washington, D. C.

ANTI-IMPERIALIST LEAGUE, 3 Spruce Street, Boston, Mass.

ASSOCIATION OF COSMOPOLITAN CLUBS, 40 Mt. Vernon Street, Boston, Mass.

ASSOCIATION TO ABOLISH WAR, 12 Hazelwood Street, Roxbury, Mass.

CANADIAN PEACE SOCIETY. *Secretary,* S. W. Michener, Lambton Mills, Ontario, Canada.

CARNEGIE ENDOWMENT FOR INTERNATIONAL PEACE, 2 Jackson Place, Washington, D. C.

COMMISSION ON INTERNATIONAL JUSTICE AND GOOD-WILL, 105 East Twenty-second Street, New York City. Rev. Charles S. Macfarland and Rev. Sidney L. Gulick.

FEDERATION OF INTERNATIONAL POLITY CLUBS, Fred B. Foulk, 40 Mt. Vernon Street, Boston, Mass.

FELLOWSHIP OF RECONCILIATION, INTERNATIONAL. Edward W. Evans, 125 East Twenty-seventh Street, New York City.

FRIENDS WASHINGTON PEACE HEADQUARTERS, 1811 I Street, Washington, D. C.

GERMAN-AMERICAN PEACE SOCIETY. *Secretary,* Rev. Henry Rexroth, 107 East 112th Street, New York City.

GREAT LAKES INTERNATIONAL ARBITRATION SOCIETY, 174 Euclid Avenue, Detroit, Mich.

INTERCOLLEGIATE PEACE ASSOCIATION. *Secretary,* Prof. S. F. Weston, Antioch College, Yellow Springs, Ohio.

INTERNATIONAL COMMITTEE OF WOMEN FOR PERMANENT PEACE. AMERICAN DELEGATION, 1140 South Michigan Avenue, Chicago, Ill.

INTERNATIONAL WOMAN'S FRIENDSHIP LEAGUE. *Corresponding Secretary,* Miss Josephine C. Locke, 2388 Champlain Street, Washington, D. C.

INTERPARLIAMENTARY UNION, AMERICAN GROUP, Washington, D. C.

LAKE MOHONK CONFERENCE ON INTERNA-TIONAL ARBITRATION, Mohonk Lake, N. Y.

LEAGUE FOR WORLD PEACE. *President,* George H. Shibley, Woodward Building, Washington, D. C.

LEAGUE TO ENFORCE PEACE. *President,* Hon. William Howard Taft, 70 Fifth Avenue, New York City.

MORAL RESISTANCE LEAGUE. Rev. John Haynes Holmes, Church of the Messiah, Thirty-fourth Street and Park Avenue, New York City.

NEBRASKA WESLEYAN UNIVERSITY PEACE AS-SOCIATION, 324 East Twenty-third Street, University Place, Neb.

PEACE ASSOCIATION OF FRIENDS, 20 South Twelfth Street, Philadelphia, Pa.

PEACE ASSOCIATION OF FRIENDS IN AMERICA. *Secretary,* Isaac Wilson, Second National Bank, Richmond, Ind.

PEACE COMMITTEE OF PHILADELPHIA YEARLY MEETING OF FRIENDS. *Secretary,* Arabella Carter, 1305 Arch Street, Philadelphia, Pa.

REDLANDS PEACE SOCIETY. *Secretary,* Mrs. C. H. Covelle, 231 Grant Street, Redlands, Cal.

WOMAN'S CHRISTIAN TEMPERANCE UNION PEACE DEPARTMENT. *National Superintendent,* Mrs. Hannah J. Bailey, Winthrop Center, Me.

WOMAN'S PEACE PARTY. Mrs. Lucia Mead Ames, 19 Euston Street, Brookline, Mass., Mrs. Eleanor G. Carsten, 116 South Michigan Avenue, Chicago, Ill.
> Massachusetts Branch, Sarah Wambaugh, 12 Otis Place, Boston, Mass.
> New York Branch, Margaret Lane, 70 Fifth Avenue, New York City.
> Pennsylvania Branch, Mrs. H. H. Donaldson, 111 South Thirteenth Street, Philadelphia, Pa.
> St. Louis Branch, Mrs. F. J. Taussig, Railway Exchange Building, St. Louis, Mo.

WORLD PEACE ASSOCIATION. *Secretary-Treasurer,* C. A. Ryan, Northfield, Minn.

WORLD PEACE FOUNDATION. Charles H. Levermore, 40 Mt. Vernon Street, Boston, Mass.

WORLD'S COURT LEAGUE. Dr. Samuel T. Dutton, Equitable Building, New York City.

MISSIONARY STATISTICS

HOME MISSIONS STATISTICS FOR THE UNITED STATES FOR THE YEAR 1916

As Reported to the Home Missions Council, January, 1917

NAME OF DENOMINATION AND ORGANIZATION

1 *Adventist*—American Advent Missionary Society......................................
2 *Baptist*—American Baptist Home Mission Society......................................
3   American Baptist Publication Society........................
4   Woman's American Baptist Home Mission Society......................
5   Home Mission Board, Southern Baptist Convention......................
6   Scandinavian Independent Baptist..........
7 *Brethren*—General Mission Board, Church of the Brethren......................
8 *Christian*—American Christian Missionary Society......................
9   Board of Church Extension, Disciples of Christ......................
10   Christian Women's Board of Missions......................
11   Mission Board of the Christian Church......................
12 *Congregational*—American Missionary Association......................
13   Congregational Church Building Society......................
14   Congregational Home Missionary Society......................
15   Congregational Sunday School and Publishing Society......................
16 *Evangelical*—Missionary Society, Evangelical Association......................
17   Woman's Missionary Society, Evangelical Association......................
18   Home and Foreign Mission Society, United Evangelical Church......................
19 *Friends*—Five Years Meeting, Friends in America......................
20 *German Evangelical*—Home Mission Board, German Evangelical Synod of N. A....
21 *Lutheran* (Evangelical)—Evan. Luth. Joint Synod of Ohio and Other States......
22   Porto Rican Mission Board, Gen. Council, Evangelical Luth. Ch. of N. A....
23   Woman's Miss. Soc. Augustana Synod, Evan. Luth. Ch. of N. A...........
24   Woman's Miss. Soc., Ministerium of Pennsylvania and Adjacent States......
25   United Norwegian Lutheran Church of America......................
26 *Methodist*—Freedmen's Aid Society, Methodist Episcopal Church......................
27   Home and Foreign Miss. Dept., African M. E. Church......................
28   Woman's Home Missionary Society, M. E. Church......................
29   Woman's Parent Mite Miss. Society, African M. E. Church......................
30   Board of Church Extension, M. E. Church South......................
31   Board of Missions, M. E. Church South, Home Dept......................
32   Gen. Mission Board, Free Methodist Church......................
33   Board of Home Missions, Methodist Protestant Church......................
34   Missionary Society, Wesleyan Methodist Connection of America......................
35 *Moravian*—Board of Church Extension, American Moravian Church......................
36 *Presbyterian*—Board of Home Missions, Presbyterian Church, U. S. A......................
37   Board of Missions for Freedmen, Presbyterian Church, U. S. A......................
38   Presbyterian Board of Publication and Sabbath School Work......................
39   Board of Church Erection Fund, Gen. Assembly, Presbyterian Ch., U. S. A...
40   Woman's Board of Home Missions, Presbyterian Ch., U. S. A......................
41   Executive Committee of Home Missions, Presbyterian Ch. in U. S...........
42   Presbyterian Committee of Publication, Southern Presbyterian Church......
43   Board of Home Missions, United Presbyterian Ch. of N. A......................
44   Board of Church Extension, United Presbyterian Ch. of N. A......................
45   Associate Reformed Presbyterian Synod of the South......................
46   Central Board of Missions, Reformed Presbyterian Church......................
47 *Protestant Episcopal*—Domestic and Foreign Missionary Society......................
48 *Reformed*—Board of Domestic Missions, Reformed Church in America......................
49   Board of Home Missions, Reformed Church in U. S......................
50   Boards of Missions, Christian Reformed Church......................
51 *Swedish Evangelical*—Swedish Evan. Mission Covenant of America......................
52 *United Brethren*—Home Miss. Soc., United Brethren in Christ......................
53 *Universalist*—Universalist General Convention......................
54   Women's National Missionary Association Universalist Church......................
55   Women's Universalist Missionary Society of Massachusetts......................
56 *Miscellaneous*—American Bible Society......................
57   American Seamen's Friend Society......................
58   American Tract Society......................
59   Church of the New Jerusalem, Board of Home and Foreign Missions.........

[1] Including work among Mexicans in Texas. [2] Including some work for constituent State Societies and city. [3] Including expenses for Foreign Missionary Societies. [4] Estimated from last year's report. [5] In conjunction with General Council, Evangelical Lutheran Church in N. A. [6] This number includes all missionaries fully and partly supported. [7] Report covers 13 months.

	Year Ending Report.	Total Appropriation.	Raised and Appropriated Outside Board.	Missionaries Fully Supported by Board.	Missionaries Partly Supported by Board.	Native Workers Supported by Board.	Church Sustentation (Support of Churches).	Church and Parsonage
1..	Sept. 30, 1916	....	$5,000.00	....	20	....	$1,579.31	....
2..	1916	$625,901.17	....	268	962	79	197,384.23	32,16
3..	Mar. 31, 1916	267,697.78	....	74	117	....	....	....
4..	Apr. 1, 1916	236,054.10	....	245	62	23	....	....
5..	May 1, 1916	404,048.00	....	280	1,129	....	....	37,11
6..	1916	5,900.00	....	6	6	....	....	....
7..	Feb. 29, 1916	....	80,000.00	....	....	....	2,195.00	3,63
8..	Sept. 30, 1916	153,228.54	208,649.82	....	193	....	....	....
9..	Sept. 30, 1916	173,039.43	....	....	....	....	....	152,15
10..	Sept. 30, 1916	263,382.39	....	123	69	32	....	....
11..	Oct. 1, 1916	13,887.62	12,000.00	4	30	....	9,662.37	56
12..	1916	510,635.40	....	607	130	....	....	....
13..	1915	223,122.43	....	....	....	....	223,122.43	....
14..	Mar. 31, 1916	290,325.76	347,681.41	....	1,729	....	186,052.71	....
15..	Feb. 29, 1916	78,000.05	....	19	38	....	....	....
16..	Aug. 31, 1916	115,274.19	....	....	603	....	....	2,17
17..	June, 1916	5,600.00	....	6	....	3	....	....
18..	Oct. 1, 1916	99,815.00	27,373.00	....	307	....	8,205.00	10,20
19..	1916	15,950.00	....	14	1	....	....	....
20..	1916	53,118.70	....	7	96	....	....	18,00
21..	July, 1916	86,000.00	....	....	112	3	....	20,000
22..	1916	[4]14,512.13	....	....	....	....	....	....
23..	June, 1916	6,009.10	....	....	....	....	....	....
24..	May 1, 1916	6,115.55	....	....	....	....	....	650
25..	May 1, 1916	65,000.00	....	8	110	....	49,000.00	5,000
26..	1916	148,453.71	7,377.15	....	317	....	....	....
27..	Mar. 31, 1916	27,492.65	....	....	842	....	....	....
28..	July, 1916	688,375.00	....	....	295	11	125,824.54	....
29..	1916	23,473.09	14,951.09	....	57	....	....	....
30..	Mar. 31, 1916	571,107.79	....	....	....	....	....	571,107
31..	1916	[4]120,470.00	[4]494,485.00	[4]10	[4]240	[4]65	[4]61,000.00	[4]4,794
32..	Oct., 1916	10,705.00	....	....	6	2	4,547.00	2,550
33..	Apr. 30, 1916	26,189.94	30,000.00	1	19	....	9,717.71	2,865
34..	1916	14,300.00	....	15	....	12	....	....
35..	Aug. 31, 1916	8,575.00	13,049.56	[6]9	30	11	....	2,575
36..	Mar. 31, 1916	1,000,048.96	603,398.51	1,854	....	91	510,076.65	....
37..	Apr., 1916	210,872.65	....	[6]663	....	....	....	....
38..	Mar. 31, 1916	240,292.32	....	151	....	....	....	....
39..	1916	332,578.00	....	....	....	....	....	332,578
40..	1916	240,291.92	....	....	....	....	....	....
41..	Mar. 31, 1916	181,162.00	443,618.00	82	362	22	76,666.00	9,543
42..	1916	68,000.00	10,000.00	24	10	....	....	....
43..	June 30, 1916	179,417.00	....	70	229	....	....	....
44..	Dec. 30, 1916	107,332.00	....	....	....	....	....	92,379
45..	1916	38,500.00	6,500.00	3	37	....	8,000.00	....
46..	1915	26,166.00	....	30	....	10	8,902.00	7,660
47..	Oct. 1, 1916	732,639.44	....	....	....	....	258,144.37	....
48..	Apr. 30, 1916	196,091.15	....	35	187	....	76,165.82	30,240
49..	July 1, 1916	206.500.00	....	5	160	75	81,700.00	86,700
50..	1916	90,400.00	....	20	....	5	13,500.00	3,700
51..	1916	7,270.00	....	36	80	....	....	....
52..	1916	42,353.00	56,256.63	....	135	....	....	....
53..	Oct, 1916	8,949.68	14,000.00	....	12	....	3,000.00	....
54..	Oct. 1, 1916	13,553.68	....	1	6	....	100.00	2,175
55..	1916	4,212.53	....	3	3	....	957.00	....
56..	1915	796,934.57	....	9	....	657	....	....
57..	Mar. 31, 1916	....	....	2	4	....	....	....
58..	Apr. 1, 1916	29,999.04	....	....	....	....	....	....
59..	May, 1916	9,000.00	....	3	9	1	....	....
		10,114,323.46	2,374,340.17	4,687	8,754	1,102	1,915,501.83	1,430,523

	General Evangelism.	American Indians.	Immigrants.	Mountaineers.	Negroes.	Orientals in America.
1..						
2..	9,178.27	15,017.94				
3..	88,083.94		21,238.16		6,021.00	1,559.00
4..	6,651.00	14,904.00	56,291.00		44,192.00	7,623.00
5..	187,234.00	7,000.00	15,000.00	47,494.00	15,000.00	
6..						
7..	5,150.00					
8..	57,146.07		5,390.00			
9..						
10..	22,925,30	2,435.00	6,942.26	41,443.20	66,817.65	19,108.96
11..	100.00				582.73	
12..		29,673.32		68,271.12	320,061.62	15,944.35
13..						
14..			41,073.33			
15..						
16..	104,096.45		5,332.50			
17..						
18..	74,950.00					
19..		4,000,00			8,000.00	1,000.00
20..		1,700.00				
21..						
22..						
23..	1,051.86					
24..						
25..						
26..						
27..					27,492.65	
28..		10,890.00	10,188.00	40,305.00	54,795.00	38,850.00
29..					23,473.09	
30..						
31..		3,980.00	3,500.00	5,500.00	1,000.00	
32..	1,520.80			40.00		1,012.50
33..						
34..				400.00	8,900.00	
35..	1,500.00	3,133.44				
36..		86,318.23	82,702.99	16,119.32	1,417.10	
37..					210,872.65	
38..	164,959.57		26,705.06	6,000.00	11,000.00	
39..						
40..		52,982.51	1,032.11	119,806.60		
41..	6,944.00	3,811.00	21,816.00	43,714.00	16,348.00	1,000.00
42..						
43..	500.00		11,358.00	22,170.00		
44..				4,000.00		6,320.00
45..	2,000.00			2,000.00		
46..		3,479.00			3,501.00	
47..		61,170.47			111,652.73	2,870.00
48..		24,152.62	6,253.95	27,706.78	1,000.00	3,593.33
49..	800.00	1,000.00	32,600.00		700.00	3,000.00
50..	13,500.00	41,400.00	2,000.00			
51..						
52..						
53..	10,708.49				50.00	100.00
54..	3,968.00				12,647.96	
55..						75.00
56..						
57..						
58..						
59..						
	762,967.75	367,047.53	380,923.36	444,970.02	945,524.68	101,556.14

	Other Dependent People.	Alaska.	Cuba.	Hawaii.	Mexico.	Philippines.
1..						
2..	4,953.54		27,308.93		38,682.08	
3..						
4..	1,464.00	6,600.00	5,510.00		16,009.00	
5..						
6..						
7..						
8..		2,000.00				
9..						
10..					[1]17,224.69	
11..						
12..		1,712.75		4,854.04		
13..						
14..		1,705.10				
15..				48.04		
16..						
17..						
18..						
19..		2,950.00				
20..						
21..						
22..						
23..						
24..	2,503.74					
25..						
26..						
27..						
28..		14,730.00		9,200.00		
29..						
30..						
31..	[4]1,500.00					
32..						
33..						
34..						
35..		8,030.73				
36..	22,224.56	30,633.21	34,497.67			
37..						
38..						
39..						
40..		39,849.98	10,504.42			
41..	1,320.00					
42..						
43..						
44..						
45..					2,000.00	
46..	2,624.00					
47..	4,406.11	68,825.19		26,685.85		82,203.52
48..						
49..						
50..						
51..		7,270.00				
52..	3,040.00					
53..	1,200.00					
54..	321.42					
55..						
56..						
57..	879.60					
58..						
59..						
	46,436.97	184,306.96	77,821.02	40,787.93	73,915.72	82,203.52

	Porto Rico.	Sunday Schools.	Education (Maintenance of Mission Schools).	Publication and Information (Periodicals, etc.).	Administration (Salaries, Rent, etc.).	For Specials (Not Otherwise Accounted for).	Miscellaneous.
1..							
2..	26,424.09		146,727.99	7,508.91	25,277.52	27,399.73	67,875.02
3..		71,857.91		27,630.95	17,347.20	33,959.62	
4..	4,584.00		52,328.22	5,815.72	13,082.16		
5..				12,000.00	22,000.00	12,638.00	
6..					1,000.00	100.00	
7..							
8..		25,595.40		15,466.29	34,702.33	10,875.32	4,053.13
9..					20,889.43		
10..	10,239.83			25,718.99	16,336.49	34,190.12	
11..	4,441.39		520.00	192.56	2,222.48	42.82	
12..	14,719.28			6,849.17	48,549.75		
13..							
14..				²4,599.03	²42,585.07	14,310.52	
15..	62.02	65,412.95		1,577.28	8,700.75	2,199.01	
16..				1,602.25		³2,071.03	
17..							
18..				1,200.00	1,775.00	3,479.00	
19..							
20..							
21..				1,300.00	2,100.00		
22..							
23..	⁵834.19					671.03	
24..	651.89		282.52	410.00	133.10	1,201.54	282.74
25..					9,100.00		
26..			118,156.79	3,196.43	21,646.45	10,454.04	
27..				8,237.96	6,078.04		
28..	13,997.00		31,510.00	29,529.96	36,980.00	339,000.00	
29..							
30..							
31..				⁴991.00	⁴7,005.00		
32..					424.00		
33..				1,198.82	3,274.11	9,433.74	
34..					5,000.00		
35..					50.00		
36..	53,248.65			22,724.89	55,986.78	56,319.14	27,749.77
37..							
38..				21,944.79	9,682.50		
39..							
40..	34,999.78						
41..				4,000.00	14,018.00		
42..		40,000.00		18,000.00	20,000.00		
43..				2,500.00	11,547.00		
44..				538.66	3,427.62		
45..		1,000.00	30,000.00				
46..							
47..	29,847.44	5,460.00		49,849.75	32,324.01	111,283.64	
48..				5,481.35	12,833.10	8,663.45	
49..		5,000.00		5,600.00	13,900.00		
50..					1,100.00	15,200.00	
51..							
52..				1,053.89	6,329.12		
53..			900.00	1,000.00	6,141.15	800.00	
54..		100.00	420.00	941.11	3,480.45	1,977.70	
55..			165.00	263.10			
56..				13,010.60	48,321.65		
57..				29,119.04			
58..					700.00		
59..					320.70		
	194,049.56	214,426.26	376,010.52	326,052.50	586,370.46	695,769.45	99,960.66

FOREIGN MISSIONS STATISTICS OF NORTH AMERICA, 1916

PREPARED BY THE SPECIAL SUBCOMMITTEE ON STATISTICS OF
THE COMMITTEE OF REFERENCE AND COUNSEL OF THE
FOREIGN MISSIONS CONFERENCE

The following tables include an abbreviated statistical statement of the income, staff, and mission work, so far as these are known, of all Protestant organizations of Canada and the United States directing or aiding the missionary enterprise in Alaska, Hawaii, Latin America, Europe, and the non-Christian world, excepting those "Home Mission" Boards working in one or more of these fields. A total of the expenditure of the latter organizations in these areas will be found in the table of summation.

In addition to those listed; mention is made of certain societies whose purpose is such that attention should be called to them:

The Federation of Women's Boards of Foreign Missions of North America, as an organization, is not responsible for the conduct of foreign mission work. Like the Foreign Missions Conference, it is a consulting body only. It has no income other than dues for running expenses from its constituency.

The China Medical Board of the Rockefeller Foundation, while not a direct missionary agency, has entered the field of cooperation with mission boards at work in China, that medical missions may be strengthened and materially helped. It is in process of establishing at Peking and Shanghai medical schools of the first rank, besides lending its assistance to existing institutions in other parts of China.

The World's Student Christian Federation is not technically a missionary society. Its work in mission lands is missionary in character, serving the students of all institutions, whether denominational or otherwise.

The Mandingo Association is a recently formed organiza-

189

tion to develop a distinctive Christian African civilization, adapted to the needs of the people.. It is to be promoted in the country itself and through the people themselves, and all permeated by the teachings of Jesus Christ.

The Laymen's Missionary Movement, working in the interest of both home and foreign missions, is one of the very effective "home base" organizations.

Three additional educational institutions, with American boards of trustees, should regularly be reported: Iconium College, which has had its work interrupted by the war; Peking University, which is being reorganized as the union institution for higher education in North China; and Cairo University, which has not yet begun its work.

Formerly these statistics were prepared by the "Home Base Committee," under the direction of the Rev. Fred P. Haggard, D.D., whose faithful work made the presentation possible. A few slight changes in the typographical form have been made, but no essential change in the plan of gathering or presenting the information has been adopted. Owing to the departure of Dr. Haggard for Russia, it was necessary that the work be placed in new hands at a late date. Charity with respect to minor errors will therefore not be amiss. The unavoidable delay in doing the preliminary work also explains the failure of many organizations to send returns for use in these tables.

The committee is especially grateful for the ready cooperation on the part of those societies and organizations which are not affiliated with the Foreign Missions Conference. The response from these has been as general and as cordial as it has been from those directly related to the Conference.

FOREIGN MISSIONS STATISTICS OF NORTH AMERICA

SUMMARY

Note:—This table includes data for those areas only which are included in this survey. Incomes for the "Home Mission" Societies amounting to $576,931 were reported through the Home Missions Council. Allowance has been made for duplication of entries.

Certain organizations are here recorded which raise money for missions and which have their own identity in home base activities, but whose incomes at home and whose work abroad are reported fully by other organizations. The totals under each heading in the detailed tables are the totals for the 146 Societies in column 1 of this table. The 49 Societies here indicated in column 2 represent those organizations whose names in each case are indented in the list of Societies which are further indicated by the double asterisk (**) foot notes.

	Societies Having Independent Entries	Societies Whose Data are Included in Those of Other Organizations	Home Mission Societies Working in Areas Included in This Survey	Total Income for the Missionary Enterprise in Areas Included in This Survey	Home Income "For Work"	Home Income "For Investment"	Home Income "For Outside Philanthropy"	Field Income
	1	2	3	4	5	6	7	8
Totals.................	146	49	7	$26,214,137	$20,982,424	$381,261	110,311	$4,740,141
Canada.................	16	7	......	1,273,636	1,140,516	60,222	....	72,898
United States...........	130	42	7	24,940,501	19,841,908	321,039	110,311	4,667,243

Societies	Income		Foreign Staff				
	Home	Field	Total (a)	Ordained	Unordained	Wives	Unmarried Women, Including Widows
	1	2	3	4	5	6	7
Grand Totals, Canada and U. S. (b)........	$20,405,493	$4,740,141	10,778	2,995	1,337	3,394	2,953
CANADA							
Totals, Canada (b)......................	1,140,516	72,898	730	202	72	237	218
BAPTIST							
Canadian Baptist For. Miss. Board*.......	114,467	10,102	103	33	1	30	39
Un. Bapt. Wom. Miss. U., Maritime**...	26,970	......	...	...	...	...	...
Wom. Bapt. For. Miss. Soc. Ont., W.**§..	13,046	......	...	...	...	...	...
Wom. Bapt. For. Miss. Soc., O. and Q.**..	3,986	......	...	...	...	...	...
CHURCH OF ENGLAND							
Miss. Soc., Church of England*§§..........	133,135	1,808	68	21	3	19	25
Wom. Aux. Miss. Soc., Ch. of Eng.**....	37,359	......	23	...	...	...	23
CONGREGATIONAL							
Canadian Cong. For. Miss. Soc.**(c).......	7,392	......	...	...	...	...	...
Canadian Cong. Wom. Bd. of Miss.**(c)....	4,021	......	...	...	...	...	...
HOLINESS							
Holiness Movement Church‡(d)............	8,000	......	7	2	...	2	3
MENNONITE							
Mennonite Miss. Soc., Ontario Conf.(e).....	4,703	......	10	6	...	4	...
METHODIST							
Miss. Soc. Methodist Ch., Canada*.......	402,574	27,065	175	62	21	83	65
Wom. Miss. Soc., Meth. Ch. Can.**§§(f) .	112,465	14,302	56	...	...	...	56
PRESBYTERIAN							
Bd. For. Miss., Presbyterian Ch.*(g).......	389,245	33,673	263	72	28	88	75
Wom. Miss. Soc., Pres. Ch., East**......	27,158	......	...	...	...	...	...
Wom. Miss. Soc., Pres. Ch., West**......	91,998	7,062	...	...	...	...	...
Gwalior Presbyterian Miss.‡..............	8,457	......	3	2	...	...	1
MISCELLANEOUS							
Canadian McAll Association...............	3,117	......	...	...	...	...	...
China Inland Miss., Canadian Br.†(h)......	27,764	......	(i) 57	§	§	§	§
Evang. Union of So. Am., N. A. Br.†(h)....	7,927	......	...	...	...	...	...
For. Dept. Y. W. C. A., Canada†..........	1,882	......	3	...	...	...	3
Lebanon Hospital, Canadian Com.‡(h).....	63	......	...	...	...	...	...
Mission to Lepers, Canadian Br.(h)........	7,769	......	...	...	...	...	...
Sudan Interior Mission...................	20,000	250	41	4	19	11	7
UNITED STATES							
Totals, United States(b).................	$19,264,977	$4,667,243	10,048	2,793	1,265	3,157	2,735
ADVENTIST							
American Advent Mission Society*.........	34,837	2,912	17	5	1	5	6
Wom. H. and F. Miss. Soc., Ad. Ch.**§§ .	13,125	......	7	2	...	2	3
Seventh-Day Adventist Denom.§§..........	872,667	261,120	735	136	252	287	60

* Data include those of one or more other organizations.   In totals, allowance is made for duplication of data.
** Data included in those of related organizations.   In totals, allowance is made for duplication of data.
† Data from "Home Base Statistics" for 1915.   ‡ Data from "World Statistics of Christian Missions."
§ Data incomplete or not available.   §§ Data for those areas only which are included in this survey.

(a) This total is greater than the sum of the subsidiary columns.   Some Societies were unable fully to distribute the staff under the several headings.
(b) Allowance is made for duplication of data.

Native Staff				Stations	Church					Educational	Medical		
Total (a)	Ordained	Unordained	Women	Out-stations, Having Regular Services	Organized Churches	Communicants	Communicants Added During the Year	Sunday Schools	Teachers and Pupils	Total Under Instruction in All Grades	Men Physicians	Women Physicians	Hospitals and Dispensaries
8	9	10	11	12	13	14	15	16	17	18	19	20	21
48,677	3,807	26,209	11,522	19,046	11,816	1,177,746	83,854	24,194	1,219,428	672,717	385	179	900
1,972	55	833	305	1,891	191	24,514	2,212	991	35,786	37,336	36	21	86
656	6	550	100	1,184	73	10,181	§605	461	10,910	12,616	2	5	11
...	...	...	...	...	...	...	...	...	...	...	..	..	...
...	...	...	...	...	...	...	...	...	...	...	..	..	...
50	5	§	§	1	19	724	§	49	2,875	736	3	3	7
...	...	...	...	...	...	...	...	...	...	...	..	1	...
...	...	...	...	...	...	...	...	...	...	...	..	..	...
...	...	...	...	...	...	...	...	...	...	...	..	..	...
8	...	7	1	2	...	...	...	3	200	71	..	.	...
...	...	...	...	...	...	...	...	...	...	...	..	..	...
486	6	276	204	189	§	1,633	157	80	4,902	7,891	13	3	18
164	...	...	164	151	...	...	...	...	...	2,970	..	3	2
771	37	§	§	504	85	11,076	1,225	398	16,899	15,962	17	9	36
...	...	...	...	...	...	...	...	...	...	...	..	..	...
...	...	...	...	...	...	...	...	...	...	...	..	..	...
1	1	...	...	1	...	...	...	...	...	...	..	..	...
...	...	...	...	...	...	...	...	...	...	...	..	..	...
...	...	...	...	...	...	...	...	...	...	...	..	..	...
...	...	...	...	...	...	...	...	...	...	...	..	..	...
...	...	...	...	10	14	900	225	...	...	60	1	1	14
46,705	3,752	25,376	11,217	17,155	11,625	1,153,232	81,642	23,203	1,183,642	635,381	349	158	814
77	14	50	13	14	11	1,000	100	16	1,400	1,000	1	..	3
65	3	50	12	14	2	440	14	16	1,400	1,000	..	..	3
1,168	60	§	§	353	842	24,902	j)3,752	1,255	30,608	10,928	15	6	§ 33

(c) This Society works under the American Board of Commissioners for Foreign Missions. The income is deducted from the income reported by that Society.

(d) The income is an estimate. The remaining data are for China only.

(e) The field report is for work in Africa. The Society also supports work in China and in India under the Christian Missionary Alliance. The income may include some funds used for the latter purpose.   (f) Administrative expenses are not included.

(g) Includes data for work among Chinese in Canada.

(h) The main headquarters are in Great Britain.

(i) Missionaries from Canada.   (j) Baptisms during the year.

Societies	Home	Field	Total	Ordained	Unordained	Wives	Unmarried Women, Including Widows
	1	2	3	4	5	6	7
BAPTIST							
American Baptist For. Miss. Soc.*	$1,700,200	$1,176,556	713	221	49	253	182
Wom. Amer. Bapt. For. Miss. Soc.**	(*l*) 680,290	......	162	...	...	...	...
For. Miss. Bd., Nat'l Bapt. Conv.	32,891	......	6	2	...	1	3
For. Miss. Bd., So. Baptist Conv.*	517,223	129,054	315	133	...	131	51
Wom. Miss. Union, So. Bapt. Conv.**§§	181,849	......	...	...	...	...	...
For. Miss. Soc., General Baptists	2,500	......	3	1	...	1	1
Free Baptist Wom. Miss. Soc.**‡(*m*)	10,175	......	...	...	...	...	...
General Miss. Bd., Ch. of Brethren	77,184	549	66	23	...	22	21
Seventh-Day Baptist Miss. Soc.*	12,966	2,164	9	3	...	2	4
Wom. Ex. Bd., Seventh-Day Bapt.**	3,600	......	...	...	...	...	...
Scandinavian Independent Baptist	5,680	100	10	4	1	4	1
BRETHREN							
For. Miss. Bd., Brethren in Christ	8,488	1,200	28	10	...	9	9
For. Miss. Soc., Brethren Church‡	4,357	......	5	2	1	2	1
Hephzibah Faith Miss. Asso.‡	§	322	14	6	...	4	4
CHRISTIAN AND DISCIPLES							
Christian Woman's Board of Miss.§§	121,414	12,775	85	21	3	19	34
Foreign Christian Miss. Society	458,614	50,536	187	91	...	69	27
For. Miss. Bd., Christian Church*	23,990	1,173	12	5	...	5	2
Wom. Bd. For. Miss., Christian Ch.**	4,213	......	...	...	...	...	...
CHURCHES OF GOD							
Bd. Miss., Gen. Eld., Ch. of God*	7,838	......	4	2	...	1	1
Wom. Gen. Miss. Soc., Ch. of God.**	4,465	......	...	...	...	...	...
CONGREGATIONAL							
Am. Bd. of Com. for For. Miss.*	(*n*) 1,265,737	371,809	663	178	52	220	213
Wom. Bd. of Missions**	215,423	45	...	...	...	...	...
Wom. Bd. of Miss., Interior**	130,265	713	85	...	...	...	85
Wom. Bd. of Miss., Pacific**	19,553	......	...	...	...	...	...
American College, Madura**(*o*)	80	......	...	...	...	...	...
Central Turkey College**(*o*)	3,031	......	...	...	...	...	...
Euphrates College**(*o*)	5,474	......	...	...	...	...	...
Jaffna College**(*o*)	22,141	......	...	...	...	...	...
St. Paul's Institute**(*o*)	2,500	......	...	...	...	...	...
Bd. Hawaiian Evangelical Asso.	52,042	......	122	42	12	36	32
EVANGELICAL							
H. and F. Miss. Soc., U. Evan. Ch.*	41,421	§1,083	30	12	3	9	6
Wom. H. and F. Miss., U. Ev. Ch.**‡	18,920	......	...	...	...	...	...
Miss. Soc. Evangelical Asso.*	39,256	3,548	28	9	...	8	11
Wom. Miss. Soc., Evan. Asso.**	15,316	2,347	19	...	...	8	11
EVANGELISTIC ASSOCIATIONS							
National Asso., Holiness	4,800	65	10	3	...	3	4
Peniel Missionary Society§§	(*p*) 3,583	......	6	...	1	1	4
Pentecost Bands of the World(*q*)	5,834	36	21	8	...	5	8
FRIENDS							
American Friends' Bd. of For. Miss.*	44,395	9,804	49	(*r*) 8	5	12	19
Wom. For. Miss. Union of Friends**(*s*)	20,500	......	...	...	...	...	...
Bd. For. Miss., Friends, New Eng.(*t*)	4,725	2,350	4	1	...	1	2

* Data include those of one or more other organizations. In totals, allowance is made for duplication of data.

** Data included in those of related organizations. In totals, allowance is made for duplication of data.

† Data from "Home Base Statistics" for 1915.

‡ Data from "World Statistics of Christian Missions."

§ Data incomplete or not available.

§§ Data for those areas only which are included in this survey.

(*l*) Includes a legacy of $300,000.

m) This Society supports work in India under other Baptist Societies.

Total	Ordained	Unordained	Women		Organized Churches	Communicants	Communicants Added During the Year	Sunday Schools	Teachers and Pupils		Men Physicians	Women Physicians	Hospitals and Dispensaries
8	9	10	11	12	13	14	15	16	17	18	19	20	21
8,884	407	6,870	1,607	4,856	2,895	320,759	13,333	4,738	219,825	80,569	37	18	79
1,785	...	§	§ 297	...	...	...	...	...	...	40,722	..	8	15
35	25	8	2	25	23	40,049	64	25	463	403	..	..	....
697	166	402	129	910	459	42,630	6,473	609	27,561	13,531	13	2	19
1	...	1	...	...	2	60	30	2	50	....	..	..	
158	...	111	47	63	16	1,486	123	54	1,878	1,664	3	2	5
15	...	...	...	...	3	122	...	4	158	134	..	2	1
11	4	2	5	5	6	450	50	8	400	300	..	..	....
19	...	19	...	9	4	350	51	1	......	620	..	..	....
16	...	§8	§	10	8	§ 249	...	23	627	....	..	..	....
214	§	§	§	62	53	4,941	447	83	5,161	2,861	2	5	10
803	§	§	41	217	186	16,884	1,691	365	20,560	6,013	§	§	§ 25
23	14	4	5	25	19	1,338	194	42	3,696	......	..	..	....
...	...	...	...	...	...	...	...	...	......	....	..	..	....
18	...	14	4	...	...	...	...	...	......	270	..	..	....
...	...	...	...	...	...	...	...	...	......	....	..	..	....
5,263	335	352	1,490	1,461	701	83,135	6,233	1,475	86,198	86,581	32	17	78
...	...	...	...	...	...	...	...	...	......	....	..	2	6
...	...	...	...	...	...	...	...	...	......	....	..	..	....
...	...	...	...	...	...	...	...	...	......	....	..	..	....
...	...	...	...	...	...	...	...	...	......	....	..	..	....
...	...	...	...	...	...	...	...	...	......	....	..	..	....
...	...	...	...	...	...	...	...	...	......	....	..	..	....
55	45	...	10	...	110	9,236	...	110	10,005	78,216	..	..	....
42	2	31	9	16	12	436	75	16	840	367	1	..	2
65	23	12	30	25	19	1,395	133	64	4,049	601	1	..	2
30	...	...	30	...	...	......	...	...	......	§	..	..	..
39	...	18	21	3	1	64	...	1	135	64	..	..	1
6	1	...	5	...	...	......	...	...	......	....	1	..	....
48	9	5	4	10	4	150	50	20	750	305	..	..	....
63	4	28	31	60	21	2,406	176	51	4,110	5,094	2	..	....
15	1	3	11	2	1	68	...	5	300	289	..	..	....

(n) The amount contributed by the Canadian Congregational Societies is deducted from the income The independent incomes of the five colleges reported below are included in this income; though these amounts are not regularly so reported.

(o) This college regularly reports through the American Board of Commissioners for Foreign Missions, though it has an independent Board of Trustees and certain independent funds.

(p) Amount spent in 1916.

(q) The work in Egypt is suspended on account of the war.

(r) There are also six women who are recorded ministers.

(s) This Society contributes to the several Friends' Boards conductin foreign mission work.

(t) Work suspended on account of the war.

Societies	Home	Field	Total	Ordained	Unof a ne	W ves	
	1	2	3	4	5	6	7
FRIENDS (Continued)							
Bd. of Miss., Friends, California‡§§......	$13,429	$......	17	6	...	4	7
For. Miss. Asso., Friends, Phila..........	12,142	226	11	2	2	3	4
Friends' For. Miss. Soc., Ohio...........	15,779	3,092	10	2	...	2	6
GERMAN EVANGELICAL							
For. Miss. Bd., German Evangelical......	46,691	5,905	24	12	...	6	6
LUTHERAN							
Bd. China Miss., Hauge Lutheran........	31,177	1,307	21	5	2	7	7
Bd. For. Miss., Evan. Lutheran Soc.‡.....	28,236	730	12	5	...	5	2
Bd. For. Miss., Gen. Council, Luth.......	107,676	1,504	39	15	1	11	12
Bd. For. Miss., Gen. Synod, Luth.*.....	114,002	30,209	58	21	1	17	19
Wom. H. and F. Miss., Gen. Syn.**.....	38,054	......	18	...	...	...	18
Bd. For. Miss., Synod of Missouri........	51,958	613	26	15	...	10	1
Bd. Miss., Latin. Am., Gen. Council(v)....	30,857	380	7	2	...	2	3
Bd. Miss., Lutheran Brethren§§..........	8,000	600	13	6	...	4	3
China Miss. Soc., Augustana Synod......	40,115	......	34	11	4	14	5
Inter-Synod. Orient Miss. Soc.(u)........	5,404	......	8	2	1	3	2
Lutheran Bd. Miss., (Free Church).......	24,634	565	18	7	...	6	5
Lutheran Joint Synod, Ohio, etc.(w)......	17,132	......	3	2	...	1	...
Lutheran Synod, Iowa, etc................	(x) 18,726	......	....	...	...	...	...
Miss. Bd., United Danish Lutheran......	10,277	200	9	3	...	3	3
Norwegian Evan. Lutheran Church......	45,212	......	20	5	2	7	6
Pan Lutheran Miss. Soc., Latin Am......	3,575	200	2	2	...	2	...
Santal Miss., American Com.(y).........	7,093	......	2	1	...	1	...
Scandinavian Alliance Mission...........	49,069	......	108	108	§	§	§
Swedish Evangelical Free Church‡........	§	638	2	...	...	...	2
Swedish Evangelical Miss. Covenant......	31,716	370	27	10	...	10	7
United Norwegian Lutheran Church......	108,572	1,592	78	26	4	28	20
MENNONITE							
Bd. For. Miss., Gen. Conf. Menn.‡........	27,550	......	16	7	...	7	2
China Mennonite Miss. Society..........	11,074	4,971	31	6	6	9	10
For. Miss. Conf., Mennonite Brethren.....	15,216	103	11	4	...	3	4
Bd. For. Miss., Menn. Brethren**(z)....	7,219	......	15	8	...	5	2
Mennonite Bd. Miss. and Charities§§......	26,244	4,055	20	5	2	7	6
United Orphanage and Miss. Soc.(u).....	23,400	175	10	3	...	3	4
METHODIST							
Bd. For. Miss., Methodist Episcopal*.....	2,957,866	1,035,260	1,455	371	93	402	589
Wom. For. Miss. Soc., M. E. Ch.**.....	1,024,610	147,126	528	...	...	...	528
Bd. For. Miss., Meth. Protestant........	26,518	⊦7,940	⊦12	3	...	3	6
Bd. Miss., Methodist Episcopal, So.§§.....	862,969	56,655	374	121	...	108	145
Gen. Miss. Bd., Free Methodist*........	74,412	3,275	87	20	9	28	30
Wom. For. Miss. Soc., Free Meth.**.....	56,289	2,723	....	...	...	...	...
H. and F. Miss. Dept., African M. E.*§§...	51,816	......	75	⊦70	...	2	3
Wom., Mite Miss. Soc., A. M. E.**§§...	4,002	......	...	...	...	...	...
Wom. H. and F. Miss., A. M. E.**§§...	8,825	......	...	...	...	...	...
Miss. Soc., African Methodist Zion*§§.....	5,300	......	23	7	12	⊦ 4	...
Wom. H. and F. Miss., A. M. E. Z.**§§.	2,500	......	...	...	...	...	...
Mis. Soc., Wesleyan Methodist‡..........	13,033	250	21	6	2	7	6
Prim. Meth. For. Miss., Am. Aux........	661	......	...	...	...	...	...
Wom. For. Miss. Soc., Meth. Prot.......	20,000	1,000	11	2	...	2	7
MORAVIAN							
Moravian Church(a).................	42,704	§353	117	44	13	54	6

* Data include those of one or more other organizations. In totals, allowance is made for duplication of data.
** Data included in those of related organizations In totals, allowance is made for duplication of data.
† Data from "Home Base Statistics" for 1915.
‡ Data from "World Statistics of Christian Missions."
§ Data incomplete or not available.
§§ Data for those areas only which are included in this survey.

(u) Work suspended on account of war.   (v) Formerly the Porto Rican Mission Board.

	Native Staff			Sta-tions	Church					Educa-tional	Medical		
Total	Ordained	Unordained	Women	Out-stations Having Regular Services	Organized Churches	Communicants	Communicants Added During the Year	Sunday Schools	Teachers and Pupils	Total Under Instruction in All Grades	Men Physicians	Women Physicians	Hospitals and Dispensaries
8	9	10	11	12	13	14	15	16	17	18	19	20	21
22	...	15	7	17	8	884	...	5	.....	232	..	..	....
9	4	2	3	10	6	883	50	35	2,533	107	..	..	....
17	1	9	7	4	3	425	29	9	710	491	1	2	6
277	74	160	43	68	8	2,207	...	§	2,472	3,517	..	..	4
128	3	87	38	39	16	1,241	390	12	1,594	911	2	..	2
16	1	7	8	6	3	325	...	9	730	267	..	..	..
484	3	...	...	350	...	12,686	792	§	7,335	8,760	..	..	4
987	4	820	163	833	606	17,209	1,803	365	23,652	7,434	..	3	5
163	...	...	163	...	...	......	...	...	......	1,490	..	..	5
95	...	95	...	48	6	210	...	42	1,687	.....	..	...	1
10	1	6	3	12	8	353	...	15	1,400	70	..	..	..
28	...	27	1	18	3	400	50	2	99	600	..	..	1
37	...	33	4	9	6	228	67	9	79	110	2	..	3
...	...	...	...	...	1	......	...	...	......	.....	..	..	..
57	4	53	...	24	14	427	68	19	525	200	1	..	2
...	...	...	...	...	...	......	...	...	......	.....	..	..	..
14	1	10	3	10	1	100	...	17	600	30	..	..	..
9	...	6	3	...	4	358	...	5	42	56	2	..	1
...	...	...	...	1	1	45	...	2	60	60	..	..	..
§	§	§	§	§	§	§	§	§	§	§	§	§	§
9	1	5	3	4	5	529	...	4	173	114	..	..	....
80	§	§	§	33	6	1,744	240	...	.....	662	2	..	2
221	6	193	22	72	23	3,027	...	38	2,250	1,037	3	..	3
42	...	25	17	3	4	225	...	9	466	441	..	..	1
52	1	30	21	17	5	127	...	4	527	772	..	..	....
127	2	83	42	10	6	1,900	...	8	300	345	..	1	2
4	4	...	...	...	...	......	...	...	......	.....	..	..	....
56	...	30	26	9	...	525	47	...	......	.....	1	1	2
23	...	10	13	...	...	......	...	3	450	285	..	..	....
11,482	1,265	7,013	3,204	§ 205	2,463	203,479	9,098	7,424	352,578	135,436	39	30	101
3,204	...	...	3,204	...	...	......	...	...	......	42,382	..	25	65
101	15	86	...	66	17	1,628	236	72	4,375	1,103	..	..	....
416	283	...	133	...	604	33,553	3,039	663	39,328	13,430	10	3	16
230	9	143	78	108	32	2,841	388	71	3,483	1,800	2	..	3
...	...	...	...	...	...	......	...	...	......	.....	..	..	....
552	60	457	35	...	146	17,426	...	120	1,226	547	..	..	....
...	...	...	...	...	...	......	...	...	......	.....	..	..	....
6	4	...	2	...	...	5,590	550	15	.....	.....	..	..	....
20	...	12	8	2	4	100	...	5	300	.....	..	1	2
51	...	13	38	4	4	300	21	2	95	600	..	..	2
168	16	152	...	65	...	11,952	108	63	8,731	.....	6	..	....

(w) This Society has taken over part of the work of the Hermannsburg Mission in India. On account of the war, its missionaries have not been permitted to enter India. The work is being supervised by other agencies. (x) Expended through missionary Societies in Germany.

(y) The main headquarters are in India. (z) All work under other Societies.

(a) This is an international Society with its main headquarters in Germany. The report, except for home income, is an arbitrary division indicating the approximate proportion for which the American Moravians are responsible.

Societies	Home	Field	Total	Ordained	Unordained	Wives	Unmarried Women, Including Widows
	1	2	3	4	5	6	7
PENTECOSTAL CHURCH OF NAZARENE							
Gen. For. Miss. Bd., Pentecostal Church§§..	$50,309	$......	35	10	1	10	14
PRESBYTERIAN AND REFORMED							
Associate Pres. Church†	505		...	...	...	...	...
Bd. For. Miss., Asso. Ref. Presby.‡	19,478	3,795	22	6	...	4	12
Bd. For. Miss., Presbyterian Ch.*	2,328,026	713,073	1,331	374	159	461	309
Wom. Bd. For. Miss., Pres. N. Y.**	140,740	......	169	...	...	89	80
Wom. For. Miss. Soc., Pres.**	222,747	......	283	14	2	159	108
Wom. N. Pacific, Pres. Bd. Miss.**	10,732	......	18	1	...	1	16
Wom. Occi. Bd. For. Miss., Pres.**	26,094	......	29	...	...	...	29
Wom. Presbyterian Bd., Northwest** ...	137,042	......	....	...	...	...	...
Wom. Pres. Bd. For. Miss., So. W.**	63,431	......	26	2	...	...	24
Bd. For. Miss., Reformed Ch. (Dutch)* ...	369,819	26,259	127	31	17	41	38
Wo. Bd. For. Miss., Ref. Ch. (Dutch)** ..	91,295	......	....	...	...	...	...
Bd. For. Miss., Ref. Ch. (German)*	212,974	16,081	60	18	5	22	15
Wom. Miss. Soc., Ref. Ch. (German)**‡..	23,801	......	....	...	...	...	...
Bd. For. Miss., Ref. Pres. (Coven.).......	51,906	1,396	45	11	8	14	12
Bd. For. Miss., United Presby.*	494,276	208,189	278	62	25	71	120
Wom. Gen. Miss. Soc., U. Pres.**	105,365	1,142	87	...	...	...	87
Exec. Com. For. Miss., Pres. (South)......	534,682	116,388	358	109	39	125	85
Miss. Soc. Calvinistic Meth	8,019	......	....	...	...	...	...
PROTESTANT EPISCOPAL							
Dom. and For. Miss. Soc., Prot. Ep.§§.....	962,686	63,147	345	86	55	80	124
REFORMED EPISCOPAL							
Bd. For. Miss., Ref. Episcopal*†..........	4,445	26	4	2	...	2	...
Wom. For. Miss. Soc., Ref. Ep.**	4,445	......	....	...	...	...	...
UNITED BRETHREN							
Dom. Fro. and For. Miss. Soc., U. B.*§§...	3,365	360	5	2	...	1	2
Wom. Miss. Asso., U. B.**	2,776	......	....	...	...	...	...
For. Miss. Soc., United Brethren*	118,086	21,402	60	18	4	19	19
Wom. Miss. Asso., United Breth.**	49,705	......	....	...	...	...	...
UNIVERSALIST							
Universalist General Convention*	22,161	1,458	7	2	...	2	3
Wom. Nat. Miss. Asso., Univ.**	5,646	......	3	...	...	...	3
MISCELLANEOUS							
Africa Inland Miss., Am. Council	43,975	133	133	15	36	38	44
Am. and For. Christian Union...........	2,500	400	2	1	...	1	...
American Bible Society§§	350,913	......	108	24	60	20	4
Am. Christian Hospital, Konia	5,121	4,560	5	1	1	3	1
Am. Col. for Girls, Constantinople	69,480	......	29	...	3	1	25
American Com. Lebanon Hospital‡	1,390	......	....	...	...	...	...
American McAll Association............	72,107	......	80	30	...	30	20
American Ramabai Association‡..........	3,962	......	....	...	...	...	...
American Red Cross§§	808,258	......	....	...	...	...	...
American Tract Society§§	10,568	......	....	...	...	...	...
Armenia and India Relief Asso.‡	42,379	......	....	...	...	...	...
Arthur T. Pierson Mem. Bible Sch.(c) ..... (d)	10,600	......	....	...	...	...	...
Bible Faith Mission.....................	3,547	1,500	....	...	...	...	...
Bd. For. Miss., Internat'l Holiness	21,000	......	....	...	...	...	...
Burning Bush Mission.................. §			13	4	4	2	3
Canton Christian College..............	55,610	52,592	30	...	16	10	4
Central American Mission‡	13,658	1,650	27	1	9	10	7
China Inland Mission, Am. Council......	118,358	...... (e)	53	§	§	§	§
Christian and Missionary Alliance........	199,127	13,689	264	83	17	81	83

* Data include those of one or more other organizations. In totals, allowance is made for duplication of data.
** Data included in those of related organizations. In totals, allowance is made for duplication of data.
† Data from "Home Base Statistics" for 1915.   ‡ Data from "World Statistics of Christian Missions."
§ Data incomplete or not available.   §§ Data for those areas only which are included in this survey.

	Native Staff			Stations	Church					Educational	Medical		
Total	Ordained	Unordained	Women	Out-stations, Having Regular Services	Organized Churches	Communicants	Communicants Added During the Year	Sunday Schools	Teachers and Pupils	Total Under Instruction in All Grades	Men Physicians	Women Physicians	Hospitals and Dispensaries
8	9	10	11	12	13	14	15	16	17	18	19	20	21
87	5	45	37	9	15	543	178	66	2,800	504	..	..	
23	7	10	6	6	12	549	...	7	216	358	..	3	5
6,097	402	3,493	2,202	3,080	914	148,638	16,380	2,793	176,168	74,763	86	28	172
...	...	...	...	...	...	...	...	...	...	...	2	15	....
...	...	...	...	...	...	...	...	...	...	...	..	3	
...	...	...	...	...	...	...	...	...	...	...		2	
781	48	465	268	317	66	6,705	591	315	12,687	14,663	11	8	22
156	17	103	36	107	25	2,784	455	93	5,544	1,258	2	..	4
75	...	50	25	27	6	848	78	25	810	1,068	5	2	10
1,229	112	743	374	554	151	43,925	5,723	425	24,233	27,596	8	4	22
75	...	...	75	10	...	...	...	...	...	200	..	2	11
1,092	55	926	111	1,111	501	33,021	3,768	626	36,993	16,036	22	3	71
...	...	...	...	...	...	...	...	...	...	...	..	..	....
1,216	167	706	343	434	222	16,951	2,041	363	22,520	13,034	15	3	25
17	§	§	§	5	1	62	...	9	147	....	1	..	1
...	...	...	...	...	...	...	...	...	...	...	..	..	....
5	...	4	1	2	2	......	...	2	140	78	1	..	
176	32	103	41	632	102	7,307	1,358	134	8,303	2,034	1	2	5
...	...	...	...	...	...	...	...	...	...	...	..	..	....
13	5	7	1	5	4	317	23	5	466	180	..	..	....
1	...	...	1	...	...	......	...	2	120	80	..	..	....
69	...	67	2	24	11	207	...	9	502	2,692	2	3	26
...	...	...	...	...	...	300	...	1	30	...	..	..	....
494	1	472	21	415	...	......	...	...	......	....	1	..	....
9	1	4	4	...	...	......	...	1	150	(b) 4	2	..	2
19	...	7	12	...	...	......	...	...	......	290	..	..	....
500	§	§	§	...	...	4,000	...	40	1,500	....	..	..	....
...	...	...	...	...	...	...	...	...	...	...	..	..	....
...	...	...	...	...	...	...	...	...	...	...	..	..	....
...	...	...	...	...	...	...	...	...	...	...	..	..	....
64	3	53	8	...	35	2,670	...	36	900	800	..	..	....
...	...	...	...	...	...	...	...	...	...	...	..	..	....
43	...	34	9	...	...	......	...	7	1,051	804	3	..	1
39	...	38	1	16	25	1,598	...	7	419	50	2	..	2
508	19	384	105	209	98	6,940	1,042	138	7,163	4,746	..	..	....

(b) Nurses in training.
(c) The current expenses are met by.the Societies participating in this school.
(d) An average of three years' contributions for equipment.

Societies	Income		Foreign Staff				
	Home	Field	Total	Ordained	Unordained	Wives	Unmarried Women, Including Widows
	1	2	3	4	5	6	7
MISCELLANEOUS (Continued)							
Christian Asso., U. of Penn.............	$3,729	$......	2	...	1	1	...
Christian Col., Women, Madras..........	25,000		....	...	...	...	...
Church of God Mission(e)...............	30,000	1,033	11	4	1	4	2
Comm. on Coop. in Latin America....... (f)	6,700	......	....	...	...	...	...
Federal Council of the Churches......... (g)	131,589	......	....	...	...	...	...
For. Dept. National Bd., Y. W. C. A.....	59,661	......	46	...	...	...	46
Foreign Missions Conference............. (h)	52,000	......	....	...	...	...	...
For. Sunday School Asso................	1,735	......	....	...	...	...	...
Franco-Am. Com. of Evangelization†.....	1,506	......	....	...	...	...	...
Free Kindergarten, Hawaii	18,428	......	35	...	...	...	35
Gospel Missionary Society‡..............	1,458	......	7	3	...	3	1
Gould Mem. Home and Indus. School(i) ..	486	......	....	...	...	...	...
Harvard Mission‡.......................	322	......	....	...	...	...	...
For. Dept., Inter. Com., Y. M. C. A.*....	814,143	......	317	(j) 1	172	144	...
Princeton Mission**(k).................	12,000	......	13	1	9	3	...
International Medical Miss. Soc..........	3,000	......	....	...	...	...	...
International Reform Bureau(l)..........	3,015	......	2	1	...	1	...
James M. Taylor Miss. Work**‡(m)....	21,201	......	....	...	...	...	...
Mackenzie College, Sao Paulo........... (n)	9,850	100,000	18	1	11	5	1
Mission to Lepers, American Com.(o).....	27,998	......	....	...	...	...	...
Missionary Education Movement§§.......	90,924	......	....	...	...	...	...
Robert College........................	147,439	......	50	3	43	...	4
South China Boat Mission..............	1,000	655	2	...	1	...	1
Stearns' Church and Bible Classes........	44,958	......	7	2	...	2	3
Student Volunteer Movement............	52,816	......	....	...	...	...	...
Sudan United Mission, Am. Council......	7,461	......	6	2	...	2	2
Syrian Protestant College..............	137,236	73,019	48	8	15	19	6
Union Medical Col., Women, So. India(p)..	752	......	....	...	...	...	...
University of Nanking†................. (q)	45,256	24,807	51	9	14	22	6
Waldensian Aid Society.................	46,838	......	....	...	...	...	...
Wom. Bd. Miss., Pacific Islands**(m)...	3,008	......	....	...	...	...	...
Woman's Union Missionary Society.......	67,947	15,807	38	...	...	...	38
World's Christian Endeavor Union.......	8,007	......	....	...	...	...	...
World's Faith Missionary Asso.**‡(m)...	500	......	....	...	...	...	...
World's Sunday School Asso............. (r)	38,517	......	7	3	1	3	...
Yale Foreign Missionary Society.........	49,039	16,500	26	3	13	8	2

* Data include those of one or more other organizations. In totals, allowance is made for duplication of data.

** Data included in those of related organizations. In totals, allowance is made for duplication of data.

† Data from "Home Base Statistics" for 1915.

‡ Data from "World Statistics of Christian Missions."

§ Data incomplete or not available.

§§ Data for those areas only which are included in this survey.

(e) Report for China and India only.

(f) Income for eight months, not including contributions from Mission Boards.

(g) The total contributed income.

(h) Income in addition to contributions from Mission Boards.

Native Staff				Sta-tions	Church					Educational	Medical		
Total	Ordained	Unordained	Women	Out-stations, Having Regular Services	Organized Churches	Communicants	Communicants Added During the Year	Sunday Schools	Teachers and Pupils	Total Under Instruction in All Grades	Men Physicians	Women Physicians	Hospitals and Dispensaries
8	9	10	11	12	13	14	15	16	17	18	19	20	21
...	...	...	...	...	...	......	...	...	......	....	1	..	....
46	7	32	7	23	18	364	...	14	445	157	..	..	....
...	...	...	...	...	...	......	...	...	......	....	..	..	....
...	...	...	...	...	...	......	...	...	......	....	..	..	....
...	...	...	...	...	...	......	...	...	......	....	..	..	....
...	...	...	...	...	...	......	...	...	......	....	..	..	....
9	...	1	8	...	...	......	...	...	......	1,059	..	..	....
...	...	...	...	1	3	100	50	3	175	75	1	..	4
...	...	...	...	...	...	......	...	...	......	60	..	..	....
...	...	...	...	...	...	......	...	...	......	....	..	..	....
...	...	...	...	...	...	......	...	...	......	....	..	..	....
...	...	...	...	...	...	......	...	...	......	....	..	..	....
2	...	2	...	...	...	......	...	...	......	....	..	..	....
38	3	12	23	...	...	......	...	...	......	846	..	..	....
...	...	...	...	...	...	......	...	...	......	....	..	..	....
27	...	27	...	...	...	......	...	...	......	479	1	..	....
5	...	2	2	1	...	14	...	...	......	8	1	..	1
...	...	...	...	...	...	......	...	...	......	....	..	..	....
8	...	6	2	2	2	60	4	4	250	150	..	..	....
40	...	39	1	...	...	......	...	...	......	976	..	..	4
58	...	...	...	...	...	......	...	...	......	....	..	..	....
...	...	...	...	...	...	......	...	...	......	....	..	..	....
140	...	5	135	2	2	292	...	66	3,456	1,148	..	8	8
1	...	1	...	...	...	......	...	...	......	....	..	..	....
58	...	15	43	...	...	......	...	...	......	238	4	1	4

(i) Work interrupted by the war.
(j) Reported by the Princeton Mission. Doubtless there are other ordained men.
(k) This is the Peking (China) work of the Foreign Department of the International Committee of the
     young Men's Christian Association.
(l) This Society works on the mission fields for moral and social reforms in cooperation with the mis-
     sionary Societies.
(m) This organization contributes through regularly organized missionary Societies.
(n) This is in addition to the annual grant from the Board of Foreign Missions of the Presbyterian Church.
(o) The headquarters are in Great Britain.
(p) This college has not yet begun work.
(q) Income raised in America in addition to the contributions of the missionary Societies participating.
(r) Contributions from the United States.

YEAR	Home Income, not Including Amount Received for Investment	Total Native Contributions	Missionaries							
			Ordained Men (not Physicians)	Unordained Men (not Physicians)	Men Physicians	Wives (not Physicians)	Other (not Men Physicians)	Men Physicians	Special, Short Term and st.	Total Missionaries
Totals for 1916....	$20,804,087 00	$4,750,681 00	*3,071	*1,277	391	*3,322	*2,922	186	287	10,601
Totals for 1915....	18,793,990 98	4,541,982 36	3,016	887	396	3,175	2,689	183	151	10,497
Totals for 1914 (1).	17,168,611 18	4,235,991 44	3,168	639	403	2,970	2,546	185	...	9,969
Totals for 1913....	16,043,630 76	3,855,286 32		3,803	397	2,807	2,607	171	...	9,785
Totals for 1912 (2).	17,317,366 55	....							...	9,919
Totals for 1911 (m).	12,290,005 00	2,035,247 00		3,148		2,361	2,072		...	7,593
Totals for 1910 (m).	11,908,671 00	1,688,075 00		3,137		2,448	1,850		...	7,267
Totals for 1909 (m).	11,317,405 00	1,375,308 00		3,558		2,270	1,848		...	7,677
Totals for 1908 (m).	10,061,433 00	1,623,562 00		2,710		2,169	1,754		...	6,611
Totals for 1907 (m).	9,458,633 00	1,153,874 00		2,446		1,951	1,527		...	5,909
Totals for 1906 (m).	8,980,448 00	1,311,679 00		2,426		1,806	1,536		...	5,768
Totals for 1905 (m).	8,120,725 00	1,282,500 00		2,209		1,612	1,312		...	5,145
Totals for 1904 (m).	7,807,992 00	1,011,824 00		2,415		1,700	1,370		...	5,489
Totals for 1903 (m).	6,964,976 00	611,245 00		2,484		1,758	1,492		...	5,740
Totals for 1902 (m).	6,727,903 00	580,227 00		1,962		1,602	1,286		...	4,850
Totals for 1901 (m).	6,228,173 00	....		1,968		1,458	1,219		...	4,304

* Physicians included.

Total Native Workers	Stations with Resident Missionaries	Out-stations	Organized Congregations	Total Persons in full Membership	Communicants Added During Year	Sunday-schools	Number Enrolled (teachers and pupils)	Colleges, Universities, Theo. Sem. and Training Schools	Number Enrolled (teachers and pupils)	Other Schools	Number Enrolled (teachers and pupils)	Hospitals and Dispensaries
49,305	2,241	20,160	11,683	1,170,539	84,078	24,438	1,212,287	625,016				903
50,001	2,318	17,198	11,203	1,175,010	119,942	23,259	1,161,234	615	26,282	14,103	557,493	748
50,743	2,219	16,105	9,946	1,439,857	159,286	22,269	1,166,518	606	55,412	12,969	492,318	737
48,454	1,999	15,729	9,436	1,366,551	121,811	21,345	1,044,039	419	34,462	12,525	477,980	688
......	......		9,937	1,163,419	2	21,489	1,035,046	354	28,303	29,546	403,436	263
32,236	13,550		.....	876,292	87,067					11,129	429,974	......
29,193	13,558		.....	835,103	82,085					10,632	515,108	......
30,476	13,144		.....	789,576	70,992					9,949	437,138	......
29,115	12,852		.....	736,978	87,075					9,315	360,233	......
26,760	12,817		.....	545,180	63,916					8,855	344,213	......
25,493	12,074		.....	624,869	74,594					8,932	308,870	......
22,047	9,448		.....	569,720	57,476					8,638	303,835	......
22,593	9,936		.....	399,983	56,306					8,066	301,170	......
15,842	9,598		.....	432,765	37,487					7,136	267,007	......
19,698	10,328		.....	560,960	48,419					6,616	255,281	......
19,493	7,958		.....	397,340	34,308					6,509	266,995	......

CHURCH AND SUNDAY SCHOOL STATISTICS

STATISTICS OF THE CHURCHES OF THE UNITED STATES FOR 1916

Gathered and Arranged by

H. K. CARROLL, LL.D.

These statistics cover the territory of the United States and its possessions exclusively. Ministers, churches, and communicants of various denominations in foreign countries are deducted from the denominational totals.

Where official denominational returns are to be had, they are used. Where such returns are not available, the best denominational sources of information are sought for approximate figures. In some cases the census returns of 1906 are the latest and only ones available. It is chiefly the very small bodies which report no statistics.

Estimates, generally by denominational statisticians, are given in a few cases for the increase of the year, where denominational reports are not ready.

The order of arrangement follows the alphabet, and classification is according to name or to historical relation. The non-Christian bodies are few and easily separable from the Christian. A great body of evangelical churches, embracing nearly eighteen million communicants, is found in the Table of the constituent bodies of the Federal Council of the Churches of Christ in America. There are, of course, evangelical bodies not included in the Council, for example, the Southern Baptist Convention.

It is necessary to give again a word of explanation concerning the figures for the Roman Catholic Church in the column of communicants. The "Official Catholic Directory" reports only "population," which includes with communicants the unconfirmed baptized; that is, children who have not been admitted to their first communion. The rule adopted in the census of 1890, and followed in that of 1906, deducts 15 per cent from Catholic population and sets down the remaining 85 per cent as communicants. Representatives of that church object to the process, but as the rule to report only members or communicants is applied to all other denominations, there is obviously no convenient way of making an exception in this case. It should be said that the figures for "population" in "The Official Catholic Directory" are, for a large number of dioceses and archdioceses, estimates, given in round numbers; as, for example, Baltimore, 261,000; Boston, 900,000; Cincinnati, 200,000.

The figures for Jewish members are misleading. The denomination furnishes no statistics, and nothing later than the figures gathered directly by circular from congregations by the Government in its census of 1906 is obtainable. The census gives an even smaller number of members than this table, counting only heads of families, according to the Jewish rule. The number of adults connected with Jewish congregations must be 700,000 or more.

The Christian Catholic Church (Dowie) has for years refused to give statistical information. So also have the Catholic Apostolic branches. The Church of Christ, Scientist, has furnished no returns for *members* since 1907.

Changes in the totals for 1915 have been made. In not a few cases the statistics officially given for that year proved to be incorrect and were revised a year later by the denominational authorities. In other instances, estimates given in advance of regular returns needed to be slightly increased or decreased. For 1915 the Disciples of Christ were represented by the figures given for the previous year, those for 1915 having been delayed by the process of revision. When the returns for 1915 appeared they showed an apparent decrease of about 229,000 members which, the denominational statistician explained, was "due to the substitution of actual data for random guesses." The number given for 1916 indicates a gain over the revised figures for 1915 of about 44,000. There is an apparent heavy loss of churches of that denomination this year due, we are told, to the same cause. Fortunately, such immense changes are rare, most of the revisions being of minor importance.

THE GAINS OF THE CHURCHES IN 1916

The churches of the United States have not suffered serious financial losses from the European war and the increased cost of living the past year; as to church-membership there has been an encouraging increase over the year 1915. The churches have given freely toward the millions of money sent to the war-afflicted populations of Europe and Asia, and yet maintained their own regular work, evangelistic, missionary, benevolent, and educational, with undiminished force. It appears from the full statistical tables which follow that the religious bodies, Catholic, Protestant, Eastern Orthodox, and non-Christian, had in 1916 an aggregate of over 40,000,000 communicants or members, crossing the forty million mark by about 17,000. The net increase of the year was 747,000, or 204,000 more than the increase for 1915. In 1890 the total religious strength was 20,618,000, so that in twenty-six years following the net increase has been 19,398,000 or 94 per cent., while the gain in the population of the country for the same period has been about 39,000,000 or 61 per cent. The churches therefore gained faster than the population during this period. Of the gains in 1916 about 216,000 were of the Roman Catholic Church, and some 500,000 of the Protestant bodies. Among the latter, 136,000 are credited to the Methodist, 132,-000 to the Baptist, and upward of 79,000 to the Presbyterian and Reformed group. The Disciples of Christ had a gain of 44,000 on the basis of their revised returns for 1915, the Episcopal Church of 27,000, and the Lutheran bodies of 20,000.

It quite clearly appears that what are known as evangelical churches are still enjoying a healthy growth, although their percentage of gains may on the average be slightly declining. The group of thirty churches constituting the Federal Council report a net increase of 254,000 members over last year, though four of the bodies, aggregating more than 1,600,000 communicants, do not count at all in the gains for 1916, not having reported any later figures than for 1913 or 1914 except in one case. The totals of the group are 17,996,435 members, 139,083 churches, and 103,622 ministers.

The gain in 1916 in number of churches of all denominations was small, only 117. In the previous year, however, there was a net loss. The smallness of the increase this year is due to decreases reported by several denominations and denominational groups. The Disciples of Christ sustain an apparent loss of 769 churches caused by faulty method of counting in previous years; the Methodist Episcopal Church loses 68, the Northern Baptist 33, the Northern Presbyterian 97, the Episcopal 7. These and other losses reduce the considerable gains of the Roman Catholics, 199, the United Brethren, 70, the Lutheran Synodical Conference, 105, etc. It is quite evident that rural churches in particular are being closed or merged for the sake of economy and efficiency.

The gain in ministers is 2,643, which is nearly double that of 1915. The largest gain, 478, is reported by the Roman Catholic Church; the Baptists added 365, the Lutherans 159, and other bodies smaller numbers.

TABLE I

DENOMINATIONS	Statistics of the Churches in 1916 — In the United States Only			Gains of the Churches in 1916 — In the United States Only		
	Ministers	Churches	Communicants	Ministers	Churches	Communicants
Adventists:						
1. Evangelical......................	c 8	c 18	c 481	...	...	......
2. Advent Christians................	828	640	30,316	262	3	1,326
3. Seventh-Day.....................	558	2,036	77,724	6	49	4,381
4. Church of God...................	34	22	800	...	...	......
5. Life and Advent Union...........	c 12	c 12	c 509	...	...	......
6. Church of God in Jesus Christ......	61	66	2,224	...	...	......
Total Adventists..............	1,501	2,794	112,054	268	52	5,707
Baptists:						
1. Baptist Churches (North)..........	e 8,572	e 9,542	e1,289,909	282	d 33	37,276
2. Baptist Churches (South)..........	e 15,588	e 24,564	e 2,779,546	69	113	93,994
3. Baptist Churches (Colored)........	f13,806	f16,842	f2,133,635	...	...	......
4. Six-Principle....................	9	13	731	...	...	......
5. Seventh-Day.....................	98	82	8,255	...	6	109
6. Free............................	805	1,110	65,440	...		
7. Freewill........................	914	834	57,231	...	...	......
8. General.........................	570	560	34,100	14	15	500
9. Separate........................	c 100	c 76	c 5,180	...	...	......
10. United.........................	c 260	c 196	c 13,698	...	...	......
11. Baptist Church of Christ..........	c 99	c 93	c 6,416	...	...	......
12. Primitive......................	c 1,500	c 2,922	c 102,311	...	...	......
13. Primitive (Colored)...............	c 1,480	c 797	c 35,076	...	...	......
14. Old Two-Seed-in-the-Spirit Predesti- narian......................	c 35	c 55	c 781	...	...	......
15. Church of God and Saints of Christ..	c 75	c 48	c 1,823	...	...	......
Total Baptists...............	43,911	57,734	6,534,132	365	101	131,879
Brethren (Dunkards):						
1. Conservative.....................	3,106	980	100,000	74	15	3,000
2. Old Order.......................	219	70	3,500	3	...	......
3. Progressive......................	314	230	24,794	14	20	1,750
4. Seventh-Day (German).............	6	15	300	...	...	......
Total Dunkard Brethren........	3,645	1,295	128,594	91	35	4,750
Brethren (Plymouth):						
1. Brethren I.......................	.....	c 134	c 2,933	...	...	......
2. Brethren II......................	.....	c 128	c 4,752	...	...	......
3. Brethren III.....................	.....	c 81	c 1,724	...	...	......
4. Brethren IV......................	.....	c 60	c 1,157	...	...	......
Total Plymouth Brethren.......	.....	403	10,566	...	...	......
Brethren (River):						
1. Brethren in Christ.................	178	68	3,731	...	...	......
2. Old Order or Yorker...............	c 24	c 9	c 423	...	...	......
3. United Zion's Children.............	c 22	c 28	c 749	...	...	......
Total River Brethren..........	224	105	4,903	...	...	......

c. Census of 1906.
d. Decrease.
e. Estimates; returns for 1916 not yet ready.
f. From American Baptist Year Book for 1915.

TABLE I—Continued

DENOMINATIONS	STATISTICS OF THE CHURCHES IN 1916 IN THE UNITED STATES ONLY			GAINS OF THE CHURCHES IN 1916 IN THE UNITED STATES ONLY		
	Ministers	Churches	Communicants	Ministers	Churches	Communicants
Buddhists:						
1. Chinese Temples.................	c 1	c 62	....	...	...	.....
2. Japanese Temples.................	c 14	c 12	c 3,165	...	...	.....
Total Buddhists...............	15	74	3,165	...	...	.....
Catholic Apostolic:						
1. Catholic Apostolic...............	c 14	c 11	c 2,907	...	...	.....
2. New Apostolic....................	c 19	c 13	c 2,020	...	...	.....
Total Catholic Apostolic........	33	24	4,927	...	...	.....
Catholic (Eastern Orthodox):						
1. Armenian Apostolic..............	20	57	65,000	...	4	.....
2. Russian Orthodox.................	225	260	100,000	46	33	5,000
3. Greek Orthodox..................	80	70	175,000	...	...	.....
4. Syrian Orthodox.................	32	34	45,000	2	4	.....
5. Serbian Orthodox.................	39	45	76,000	18	14	12,000
6. Roumanian Orthodox.............	5	5	20,000	...	...	.....
7. Bulgarian Orthodox..............	3	4	4,500	...	1	1,000
Total Eastern Catholics........	404	475	485,500	66	56	18,000
Catholics (Western):						
1. Roman Catholic *f*.................	e20,050	e15,362	e14,295,225	478	199	215,732
2. Polish Catholic...................	37	45	20,145	...	...	.....
3. American Old Catholic............	42	40	15,000	14	20	5,000
Total Western Catholics........	20,129	15,447	14,330,370	492	219	220,732
Christadelphians...........................	.....	70	1,500	...	...	.....
Christians.............................	1,066	1,360	106,159	...	25	d 2,329
Christian Catholic (Dowie)...............	c 35	c 17	c 5,865	...	...	.....
Christian Union........................	365	330	16,825	5	10	525
Church of Christ Scientist.................	2,998	1,499	85,096	170	85	.....
Churches of God (Winebrennarian)........	434	484	28,033	d 6	d 9	d 617
Churches of the Living God (Colored):						
1. Christian Workers for Friendship.....	c 51	c 44	c 2,676	...	...	.....
2. Apostolic......................	c 30	c 15	c 752	...	...	.....
3. Church of Christ in God...........	c 20	c 9	c 858	...	...	.....
Total Churches of the Living God.	101	68	4,286	...	...	.....
Churches of the New Jerusalem:						
1. General Convention...............	102	128	8,500	d 7	d 1	.....
2. General Church..................	38	22	1,272	...	...	59
Total New Jerusalem Churches...	140	150	9,772	d 7	d 1	59

c. Census of 1906.
d. Decrease.
e. Estimates; returns for 1916 not yet ready.
f. The figures in the third column are 85 per cent. of the Catholic population.

TABLE I—Continued

DENOMINATIONS	STATISTICS OF THE CHURCHES IN 1916 IN THE UNITED STATES ONLY			GAINS OF THE CHURCHES IN 1916 IN THE UNITED STATES ONLY		
	Ministers	Churches	Communicants	Ministers	Churches	Communicants
Church Transcendent.....................	2	3	148	...	...	4
Communistic Societies:						
1. Shakers.............................	.....	6	233	...	d 9	d 283
2. Amana.............................	.....	c 7	c 1,756	...		.....
Total Communistic Societies.....	.....	13	1,989	...	d 9	d 283
Congregationalists........................	e 5,974	e 6,106	e 790,488	d 23	3	10,074
Disciples of Christ:						
1. Disciples of Christ.................	6,324	8,533	1,177,792	386	d 769	44,053
2. Churches of Christ.................	c 2,100	c 2,649	159,658	...	...	.....
Total Disciples of Christ........	8,424	11,182	1,337,450	386	d 769	44,053
Evangelical Bodies:						
1. Evangelical Association.............	1,056	1,625	120,387	20	d 1	1,767
2. United Evangelical Church.........	516	948	89,530	d 12	d 27	2,895
Total Evangelical Bodies........	1,572	2,573	209,917	8	d 28	4,662
Faith Associations:						
1. Apostolic Faith Movement..........	.....	c 6	c 538	...	...	.....
2. Peniel Missions.....................	c 30	c 11	c 703	...	...	.....
3. Metropolitan Church Association.....	c 29	c 6	c 466	...	...	.....
4. Hephzibah Faith Association........	c 36	c 10	c 293	...	...	.....
5. Missionary Church Association......	c 35	c 32	c 1,256	...	...	.....
6. Heavenly Recruit Church...........	c 55	c 27	c 938	...	...	.....
7. Apostolic Christian Church.........	c 19	c 42	c 4,558	...	...	.....
8. Christian Congregation.............	c 26	c 9	c 395	...	...	.....
9. Voluntary Missionary Soc'y (Colored)	c 11	c 3	c 425	...	...	.....
Total Faith Associations........	241	146	9,572	...		.....
Free Christian Zion Church..............	c 20	c 15	c 1,835	...	...	.....
Friends:						
1. Orthodox...........................	1,287	748	97,514	d 28	d 27	d 842
2. "Hicksite".........................	35	160	17,806	d 64	d 7	76
3. "Wilburite"........................	c 47	c 48	c 3,880	...	...	.....
4. Primitive..........................	c 10	c 8	c 171	...	...	.....
Total Friends..................	1,379	964	119,371	d 92	d 34	d 766
Friends of the Temple....................	c 3	c 3	c 376	...	...	.....
German Evangelical Protestant............	c 59	c 66	c 34,704	...	...	.....
German Evangelical Synod................	1,089	1,389	274,787	4	11	10,690
Jewish Congregations....................	1,084	1,769	a 143,000	...	...	.....
Latter-Day Saints:						
1. Utah Branch........................	2,460	913	345,000	25	8	15,000
2. Reorganized Branch................	1,800	800	70,000	100	25	3,000
Total Latter-Day Saints........	4,260	1,713	415,000	125	33	18,000

a. See explanation on page 205.
c. Census of 1906.
d. Decrease.
e. Estimates; returns for 1916 not yet ready.

TABLE I—Continued

DENOMINATIONS	STATISTICS OF THE CHURCHES IN 1916 IN THE UNITED STATES ONLY			GAINS OF THE CHURCHES IN 1916 IN THE UNITED STATES ONLY		
	Ministers	Churches	Communicants	Ministers	Churches	Communicants
Lutherans:						
1. General Synod...................	1,425	1,847	360,749	d 1	17	4,677
2. United Synod, South..............	261	1,494	54,662	d 10	4	957
3. General Council.................,	1,664	2,427	494,989	24	8	24,218
4. Synodical Conference.............	3,268	3,901	827,056	136	105	5,670
5. United Norwegian...............	650	1,650	173,534	d 24	20	1,877
(Independent Synods)						
6. Ohio...........................	669	912	137,190	d 6	d 173	d 5,165
7. Buffalo.........................	35	44	5,530	....	....	......
8. Hauge's........................	160	290	22,906	d 12	d 64	d16,842
9. Eilsen's........................	5	26	1,100	1	...	d 1,400
10. Iowa..........................	600	1,201	123,197	15	166	769
11. Norwegian.....................	447	986	97,586	15	d 64	d 602
12. Danish in America..............	71	108	14,263	...	d 7	917
13. Icelandic......................	15	50	4,179	...	...	240
14. Immanuel......................	23	26	19,000	...	...	......
15. Suomi (Finnish)................	36	147	15,020	2	9	1,101
16. Finnish Apostolic *a*...........	70	309	22,000	...	...	......
17. Finnish National *a*............	22	72	8,000	...	...	......
18. Norwegian Free................	185	391	28,712	9	11	2,662
19. Danish United.................	141	190	15,161	10	d 12	1,071
20. Church of the Lutheran Brethren *a*...	13	18	2,000	...	...	......
Independent Congregations........	87	200	27,500	...	...	......
Total Lutherans...............	9,847	15,289	2,454,334	159	20	20,150
Scandinavian Evangelical Bodies:						
1. Swedish Evangelical Miss. Covenant..	436	270	40,000	34	d 80	.....
2. Swedish Evangelical Free Mission....	152	154	18,500	...	...	.....
3. Norwegian Evangelical Free........	75	153	4,400	...	...	.....
Total Swedish Evangelical.......	663	577	62,900	34	d 80	.....
Mennonites:						
1. Mennonite......................	560	257	14,148	...	...	.....
2. Bruederhoef....................	32	20	1,033	...	...	.....
3. Amish..........................	128	64	9,888	...	...	.....
4. Amish (Old Order)..............	161	60	5,496	...	5	d 844
5. Amish (Conservative)............	60	23	2,619	d 1	1	1,419
6. Reformed......................	32	14	1,029	...	...	.....
7. General Conference.............	180	116	15,451	8	4	2,654
8. Church of God in Christ...........	11	9	300	...	...	.....
9. Old Order (Wisler).............	20	21	1,421	d 1	1	d 267
10. Bundes Conference.............	46	27	2,425	...	...	.....
11. Defenceless...................	12	14	824	...	d 1	.....
12. Mennonite Brethren in Christ.......	155	140	5,516	6	43	503
Miscellaneous....................	91	48	4,646	...	...	.....
Total Mennonites..............	1,488	813	64,796	12	53	3,465

a Not embraced in list of *Lutheran Church Year Book,*
c. Census of 1906.
d. Decrease.
e. Estimated; returns for 1916 not yet ready.

TABLE I—Continued

DENOMINATIONS	STATISTICS OF THE CHURCHES IN 1916 IN THE UNITED STATES ONLY			GAINS OF THE CHURCHES IN 1916 IN THE UNITED STATES ONLY		
	Ministers	Churches	Communicants	Ministers	Churches	Communicants
Methodists:						
1. Methodist Episcopal..............	18,763	28,360	3,743,031	*d* 50	*d* 68	85,437
2. Union American Methodist Episcopal.	170	225	20,000	...	...	.....
3. African Methodist Episcopal.......	5,000	6,000	620,000	...	...	.....
4. African Union Methodist Episcopal..	200	125	4,000	...	...	.....
5. African Methodist Episcopal Zion....	3,552	3,180	568,608	...	...	.....
6. Methodist Protestant..............	1,410	2,400	*f* 201,110	...	...	.....
7. Wesleyan Methodist..............	590	600	20,500	...	*d* 75	.....
8. Methodist Episcopal, South.........	7,320	16,993	2,123,785	117	206	51,750
9. Congregational Methodist..........	337	333	15,529	...	...	.....
10. New Congregational Methodist......	*c* 59	*c* 35	*c* 1,782	...	...	.....
11. Zion Union Apostolic..............	*c* 33	*c* 45	*c* 3,059	...	...	.....
12. Colored Methodist Episcopal........	3,072	3,196	240,798	...	...	.....
13. Primitive.......................	74	94	8,600	...	...	200
14. Free Methodist...................	1,193	1,165	35,149	...	*d* 6	117
15. Reformed Methodist Union Episcopal	25	30	1,172	*d* 5	*d* 2	*d* 1,328
16. Independent Methodist.............	2	2	1,161	...	...	.....
Total Methodists..............	41,800	62,783	7,608,284	62	55	136,176
Moravians:						
1. Moravians......................	144	126	20,859	*d* 1	...	713
2. Union Bohemians and Moravians....	4	21	1,000	...	...	.....
Total Moravians..............	148	147	21,859	*d* 1	...	713
Nonsectarian Bible Faith Churches.........	*c* 50	*c* 204	*c* 6,396	...	...	.....
Pentecostal Bodies:						
1. Pentecostal Church of the Nazarene..	780	941	33,419	5	99	1,280
2. Apostolic Holiness Church.........	231	72	2,700	116	36	1,430
Total Pentecostal Bodies........	1,011	1,013	36,119	121	135	2,710
Presbyterians:						
1. Northern.......................	9,585	9,784	1,543,027	25	*d* 97	47,870
2. Cumberland.....................	736	1,446	63,735	8	7	1,441
3. Cumberland (Colored).............	*c* 375	*c* 196	*c* 18,066	...	...	.....
4. Welsh Calvinistic.................	91	142	14,668	10	1	*d* 209
5. United........................	973	992	156,954	*d* 8	2	3,303
6. Southern.......................	1,861	3,437	348,223	11	*d* 1	15,884
7. Associate......................	7	13	500	*d* 2	*d* 1	.....
8. Associate Reformed, South..........	112	156	14,282	*d* 1	1	*d* 539
9. Reformed (Synod).................	128	113	8,481	...	2	*d* 153
10. Reformed (General Synod)..........	16	17	3,300	...	...	.....
11. Reformed Covenanted.............	.....	1	40	...	...	.....
12. Reformed in the United States and Canada.......................	1	1	325	...	...	*d* 35
Total Presbyterians............	13,885	16,298	2,171,601	43	*d* 86	67,562

c. Census.
d. Decrease.
e. Estimates; returns for 1916 not yet ready.
f. Revised statistics are promised soon.

TABLE I—Continued

DENOMINATIONS	STATISTICS OF THE CHURCHES IN 1916 IN THE UNITED STATES ONLY			GAINS OF THE CHURCHES IN 1916 IN THE UNITED STATES ONLY		
	Ministers	Churches	Communicants	Ministers	Churches	Communicants
Protestant Episcopal:						
1. Protestant Episcopal..............	5,598	8,054	1,066,970	60	*d* 7	26,074
2. Reformed Episcopal...............	82	80	11,465	*d* 1	...	665
Total Protestant Episcopal......	5,680	8,134	1,078,435	59	*d* 7	26,739
Reformed:						
1. Reformed (Dutch)................	775	724	131,724	25	6	4,877
2. Reformed (German)..............	1,245	1,773	326,112	32	14	5,653
3. Christian Reformed.............	172	237	37,207	11	6	911
4. Hungarian Reformed.............	31	74	19,500	...	...	500
Total Reformed...............	2,223	2,808	514,543	68	26	11,941
Reformed Catholic........................	7	6	3,250	...	...	......
Salvation Army..........................	3,225	967	28,203	264	26	539
Schwenkfelders..........................	6	6	1,072	...	...	29
Social Brethren..........................	15	17	1,262	...	...	......
Society for Ethical Culture...............	7	6	2,450	...	...	......
Spiritualists.............................	.....	1,500	200,000	...	...	......
Theosophical Society.....................	.....	174	5,861	...	20	1,147
Unitarians..............................	504	472	*e* 71,110	*d* 8	3	568
United Brethren:						
1. United Brethren.................	1,937	3,577	345,705	62	70	6,490
2. United Brethren (Old Constitution)..	310	515	21,172	...	...	......
Total United Brethren..........	2,247	4,092	366,877	62	70	6,490
Universalists...........................	662	865	58,300	6	102	3,300
Independent Congregations................	267	879	48,673	...	...	......
Grand Total in 1916............	182,843	225,321	40,016,709	2,643	117	746,669
Grand Total in 1915............	180,200	225,204	39,270,040	1,312	*d* 289	542,962

c . Census of 1906.
d. Decrease.
e. Estimated.

TABLE II—Summary

DENOMINATIONS	SUMMARY FOR 1916			NET GAINS FOR 1916		
	Ministers	Churches	Communicants	Ministers	Churches	Communicants
Adventists (6 bodies)...................	1,501	2,794	112,054	268	52	5,707
Baptists (15 bodies).....................	43,911	57,734	6,534,132	365	101	131,879
Brethren (Dunkard) (4 bodies)...........	3,645	1,295	128,594	91	35	4,750
Brethren (Plymouth) (4 bodies)...........	.....	403	10,566	...	...	.....
Brethren (River) (3 bodies)..............	224	105	4,903	...	...	.....
Buddhists (2 bodies)....................	15	74	3,165	...	...	.....
Catholic Apostolic (2 bodies)...........	33	24	4,927	...	...	.....
Catholic (Eastern Orthodox) (7 bodies).....	404	475	485,500	66	56	18,000
Catholic (Western) (3 bodies)............	20,129	15,447	14,330,370	492	219	220,732
Christadelphians.......................	.....	70	1,500	...	...	.....
Christians..........	1,066	1,360	106,159	d 90	25	d 2,329
Christian Catholic (Dowie)..............	35	17	5,865	...	...	.....
Christian Union.......................	365	330	16,825	5	10	525
Church of Christ Scientist...............	2,998	1,499	85,096	170	85	.....
Churches of God (Winebrennarian)........	434	484	28,033	d 6	d 9	d 617
Churches of the Living God (Colored) (3 bodies).............................	101	68	4,286	...	...	.....
Churches of the New Jerusalem (2 bodies)..	140	150	9,772	d 7	d 1	59
Church Transcendent....................	2	3	148	...	...	4
Communistic Societies (2 bodies).........	.....	13	1,989	...	d 9	d 283
Congregationalists.....................	5,974	6,106	790,488	d 23	3	10,074
Disciples of Christ (2 bodies)............	8,424	11,182	1,337,450	386	d 769	44,053
Evangelical (2 bodies)..................	1,572	2,573	209,917	8	d 28	4,662
Faith Associations (9 bodies)............	241	146	9,572	...	...	.....
Free Christian Zion Church.............	20	15	1,835	...	...	.....
Friends (4 bodies).....................	1,379	964	119,371	d 92	d 34	d 766
Friends of the Temple..................	3	3	376	...	...	.....
German Evangelical Protestant..........	59	66	34,704	...	...	.....
German Evangelical Synod..............	1,089	1,389	274,787	4	11	10,690
Jewish Congregations...................	1,084	1,769	143,000	...	...	.....
Latter-Day Saints (2 bodies)............	4,260	1,713	415,000	125	33	18,000
Lutherans (21 bodies)...................	9,847	15,289	2,454,334	159	20	20,150
Scandinavian Evangelical (3 bodies).......	663	577	62,900	34	d 80	.....
Mennonites (12 bodies).................	1,488	863	64,796	12	53	3,456
Methodists (16 bodies)..................	41,800	62,783	7,608,284	62	55	136,176
Moravians (2 bodies)...................	148	147	21,859	d 1	...	713
Nonsectarian Bible Faith Churches.......	50	204	6,396	...	...	.....
Pentecostal (2 bodies)..................	1,011	1,013	36,119	121	135	2,710
Presbyterians (12 bodies)...............	13,885	16,298	2,171,601	43	d 86	67,562
Protestant Episcopal (2 bodies)..........	5,680	8,134	1,078,435	59	d 7	26,739
Reformed (4 bodies)....................	2,223	2,808	514,543	68	26	11,941
Reformed Catholic.....................	7	6	3,250	...	...	.....
Salvation Army.......................	3,225	967	28,203	264	26	539
Schwenkfelders.......................	6	6	1,072	...	...	29
Social Brethren.......................	15	17	1,262	...	...	.....
Society for Ethical Culture..............	7	6	2,450	...	...	.....
Spiritualists..........................	.....	1,500	200,000	...	...	.....
Theosophical Society...................	.....	174	5,861	...	20	1,147
Unitarians............................	504	472	71,110	d 8	3	568
United Brethren (2 bodies)..............	2,247	4,092	366,877	62	70	6,490
Universalists.........................	662	865	58,300	6	102	3,300
Independent Congregations..............	267	879	48,673	...	...	.....
Grand Total in 1916............	182,843	225,321	40,016,709	2,643	117	746,669
Grand Total in 1915............	180,200	225,204	39,270,040	1,312	d 289	542,962

d. Decrease.

TABLE III

NET GAINS IN COMMUNICANTS OF RELIGIOUS BODIES IN THE TWENTY-FIVE
YEARS, 1890–1915

Religious Bodies of Upward of 300,000 Communicants	Returns for 1915	Returns for 1890	Net Gains in 25 years	Percentage of Gain
Roman Catholic...................	14,079,493	6,231,417	7,848,076	126—
Methodist Episcopal..............	3,657,594	2,240,354	1,417,240	63+
Southern Baptist................	2,685,552	1,280,066	1,405,486	109+
Methodist Episcopal South........	2,072,035	1,209,976	862,059	71+
Baptist (Colored)................	2,133,635	1,348,989	784,646	58+
Presbyterian, Northern...........	1,495,157	788,224	706,933	90—
Disciples of Christ..............	1,133,739	641,051	492,688	77—
Baptist, North..................	1,252,633	800,450	452,183	56+
Protestant Episcopal............	1,040,896	532,054	508,842	96—
Lutheran Synodical Conference....	821,386	357,153	464,233	130—
Congregationalist...............	780,418	512,771	267,647	52+
African Methodist Episcopal......	620,000	452,725	167,275	37—
African Methodist Episcopal Zion.	568,608	349,788	218,820	63—
Lutheran General Council.........	470,771	324,846	145,925	45—
Lutheran General Synod..........	356,072	164,640	191,432	116—
United Brethren.................	339,215	202,474	136,741	68—
Presbyterian (South)............	332,339	179,721	152,618	118—
Latter-Day Saints, Utah.........	330,000	144,352	185,648	77+
Reformed (German)...............	320,459	204,018	116,441	57+
Totals......................	34,490,002	17,965,069	16,524,933	92—
All other bodies...............	4,780,038	2,653,238	2,126,800	80+
Grand Total.................	39,270,040	20,618,307	18,651,733	90+

TABLE IV.

NET GAINS IN COMMUNICANTS OF GROUPS OF RELIGIOUS BODIES IN
TWENTY-FIVE YEARS

Denominational Groups or Families	1915	1890	in 25 Years
Catholics (3 bodies)......................	14,109,638	6,240,602	7,869,036
Methodists (16 bodies).....................	7,472,108	4,589,284	2,882,824
Baptists (15 bodies).......................	6,402,253	3,717,969	2,684,284
Lutherans (20 bodies)......................	2,434,184	1,231,072	1,203,112
Presbyterians (12 bodies)..................	2,104,039	1,278,332	825,707
Disciples of Christ (2 bodies).............	1,293,397	641,051	652,346
Episcopal, Protestant (2 bodies)...........	1,051,696	540,509	511,187
Reformed (4 bodies)........................	502,602	309,458	193,144
Eastern Orthodox (7 bodies)................	467,500	13,939	453,561
Latter-Day Saints (2 bodies)...............	397,000	166,125	230,875
United Brethren (2 bodies).................	360,387	225,281	135,106
Evangelican (2 bodies).....................	205,255	133,313	71,942
Friends (4 bodies).........................	120,712	107,208	13,504
Brethren, (Dunkards) (4 bodies)............	123,844	73,795	50,049
Adventists (6 bodies)......................	106,347	60,491	45,856
Totals................................	37,150,962	19,328,429	17,822,533

DISTRIBUTION OF CHURCH-MEMBERS BY STATES

For Denominations Embracing Four Fifths of the Total Membership in the United States

This table includes all those denominations which were able to furnish statistics of their members by states, and it represents only Continental United States, excluding Alaska, Hawaii, and the colonial possessions.

Not many of the churches observe state lines in reporting their statistics. The Baptists, the Congregationalists, and the Disciples of Christ do, but they are exceptions to the rule.

Presbyteries, conferences, classes, synods, etc., often cross state lines, and, indeed, include parts of several states.

The New York classis, of the Reformed Church in America, for example, not only has churches, ministers, and members in New York City, but also in Maine, Kentucky, Nebraska, Oklahoma, and New Mexico.

The Synod of Appalachia of the Southern Presbyterian Church, has churches in the states of Virginia, North Carolina, and Tennessee.

Conferences of the Methodist Episcopal Church lap and overlap one another in a quite bewildering way. For example, the Delaware Conference, (colored) covers territory embraced in a dozen white conferences, having churches not only in Delaware, but also in Maryland, Virginia, Pennsylvania, New Jersey, and New York. Then the East German and East Swedish Conferences occupy also part of the same territory.

The dioceses of the Protestant Episcopal Church generally do not cross state lines, but there are some notable exceptions.

The dioceses of the Roman Catholic Church, in a number of cases, ignore state lines.

The compilations, with half a dozen exceptions, were made or revised by denominational statisticians. Those for the

Lutherans, made by Dr. Kopenhaver, include the various bodies of that name, but are incomplete. For most of the denominations the figures, where not strictly accurate, are at least approximate.

All the denominations represented, with one exception—the Roman Catholic—belong to the Evangelical list. Three large colored Methodist bodies, having, perhaps, a million and a half of members, furnish no statistics of any kind; the Evangelical Association and the United Evangelical Church, the Mennonites, the Christian Church and other bodies give no indication of state lines in their reports.

The total of members or communicants of the bodies represented in the table is 33,299,142, which is more than four fifths of the grand total of all religious bodies in the United States, Christian and Non-Christian. Any comparison that may be attempted with the population of the states must take this fact into account.

Considering Protestants only, the states show preferences as follows:

Alabama, two thirds Baptist.

Arkansas, more than half Baptist.

Delaware, nearly half Methodist.

Georgia, Baptist largely.

Indiana, Methodist largely.

Iowa, Methodist largely.

Kansas, a Methodist state.

Kentucky, a Baptist state.

Maine, Baptist, first; Methodist, second; and Congregationalist, third.

Maryland, a Methodist state.

Massachusetts, a Congregationalist state.

Michigan, a Methodist state.

Minnesota, Lutheran.

Mississippi, Baptist.

Missouri, Baptist.

Nebraska, Methodists lead.

New Hampshire, Congregationalists lead.

New Jersey, Methodists lead, 121,832.

New York, more Methodists, 376,285.

North Carolina, more Baptists, 420,428.

North Dakota, more Lutherans.

Ohio, Methodists predominate, 393,000.

Oklahoma: Methodists, 99,846; Baptists, 99,340; there are other Baptist bodies, but there are also other Methodist bodies to be heard from.

Pennsylvania: first, Presbyterians, 398,034; second, Lutherans, 388,157; third, Methodists, 376,223.

Rhode Island is an Episcopal state; with Baptists a close second.

South Carolina is a Baptist state.

South Dakota is a Lutheran state.

Tennessee, the Baptists are first.

Texas: the Baptists are first, 500,698; the Methodists second, 357,812; the Roman Catholics third, 346,962.

Utah is Mormon.

Vermont, the Congregationalists lead.

Virginia, Baptists first, Methodists second.

Washington is strongly Methodist.

West Virginia is strongly Methodist.

Wisconsin is strongly Lutheran.

As to the Roman Catholic Church, it is first in all New England, in New York, New Jersey, Pennsylvania, Maryland, Illinois, Iowa, Louisiana, Michigan, Minnesota, Missouri, Montana, Nebraska, Arizona, New Mexico, North Dakota, Ohio, Oregon, South Dakota, Washington, Wisconsin, and Wyoming.

The states indicating a high proportion of communicants to population are Connecticut, Massachusetts, Rhode Island, and Louisiana, with one communicant to every two and a fraction of the population.

These states have one communicant in every 3, or a little less of the population: Alabama, Delaware, Georgia, Illinois, Kentucky, Maryland, Michigan, Minnesota, Missouri, New York, New Jersey, North Carolina, Ohio, Pennsylvania, South Carolina, Virginia, and Wisconsin.

Arkansas, California, Florida, Maine, Nebraska, North Dakota, Tennessee, and West Virginia have one in four or a little less.

Arizona and Colorado have one in five or a little less; Washington one in six; Oklahoma one in seven; and Nevada one in eleven. Doubtless returns of the Mormons would reduce this number.

The average of the total of communicants, 33,299,142, given in this table to the total population, 102,017,312, is as one to three plus.

MEMBERS OR COMMUNICANTS BY STATES

REPRESENTING FOUR FIFTHS OF GRAND TOTAL IN UNITED STATES

		Baptist Northern, 1916	Baptist Southern, 1915	Baptist, Colored, 1915	Congregational, 1915	Disciples of Christ, 1916	Lutheran All bodies, 1916
1	Alabama		204,283	261,868	4,728	4,749	1,200
2	Arizona	2,721			448	1,487	95
3	Arkansas		111,185	96,070	638	13,117	2,225
4	California	39,632			32,668	33,082	14,890
5	Colorado	16,605			11,198	11,344	7,745
6	Connecticut	26,872			70,175	530	6,654
7	Delaware	3,800		599		202	783
8	District of Columbia		9,121	24,056	3,246		4,046
9	Florida		51,741	51,045	2,862	3,277	624
10	Georgia		293,244	309,142	6,056	16,432	3,836
11	Idaho	6,494			2,588	4,578	2,058
12	Illinois	105,180	62,046		57,391	116,172	192,470
13	Indiana	72,601			5,534	131,456	60,405
14	Iowa	48,251			38,381	65,075	81,232
15	Kansas	61,096			16,871	65,042	30,286
16	Kentucky		241,513	79,079	769	130,377	4,810
17	Louisiana		65,669	123,573	1,768	3,228	6,806
18	Maine	34,253			21,248	637	1,010
19	Maryland		12,623	18,884	851	[1] 8,206	39,258
20	Massachusetts	84,097			130,380	1,267	11,797
21	Michigan	50,350			34,358	13,048	92,658
22	Minnesota	27,884			22,863	4,757	212,516
23	Mississippi		159,187	227,037	286	4,043	595
24	Missouri		195,907	30,492	10,099	139,889	70,420
25	Montana	4,025			3,475	3,470	6,728
26	Nebraska	17,382			18,203	23,325	56,382
27	Nevada	555			257		323
28	New Hampshire	15,282			19,614		833
29	New Jersey	76,592			10,523	455	34,226
30	New Mexico		5,337		338	2,960	253
31	New York	174,178			61,555	10,572	130,023
32	North Carolina		255,574	164,854	3,126	18,379	21,202
33	North Dakota	5,703			8,256	280	47,581
34	Ohio	103,683			44,977	102,633	125,106
35	Oklahoma		82,412	16,928	3,456	34,023	4,279
36	Oregon	15,899			6,124	17,495	6,979
37	Pennsylvania	157,493			17,101	38,293	388,157
38	Rhode Island	19,346			10,046	79	3,517
39	South Carolina		143,944	203,491	526	2,308	14,314
40	South Dakota	8,708			10,982	1,598	36,431
41	Tennessee		194,229	95,924	2,159	21,201	2,436
42	Texas		336,679	164,019	2,418	48,459	30,179
43	Utah	1,375			1,656	267	326
44	Vermont	9,652			22,979	348	419
45	Virginia		163,939	254,193	348	33,348	15,622
46	Washington	17,934			14,983	18,359	19,977
47	West Virginia	59,577		12,381	307	17,848	5,862
48	Wisconsin	20,839			29,280	2,227	264,890
49	Wyoming	1,850			1,955	730	585
		1,289,909	2,588,633	2,133,635	770,050	1,170,652	[2] 2,065,049

[1] Includes District of Columbia.   [2] Incomplete.

MEMBERS OR COMMUNICANTS BY STATES
Representing Four Fifths of Grand Total in United States

	Methodist Episcopal, 1915	Methodist Episcopal, South, 1916	Presbyterian Northern, 1916	Presbyter an South ern, 96	Presbyterian United, 1916	Presbyterian Cumberland, 1916	Protestant Episcopal, 1916	Reformed in America, 1916	Reformed in United States, 1916
1	26,274	170,683	4,533	19,805	....	3,027	10,568	.....	.....
2	3,047	1,541	4,268	....	....	....	2,379	.....	.....
3	12,709	109,478	6,775	10,699	40	5,020	4,578	.....	104
4	83,005	12,945	50,235	....	3,572	234	28,484	....	140
5	33,879	1,922	21,915	....	2,674	....	8,098	13	200
6	35,805	....	3,405	....	219	....	46,307	.....	1,020
7	27,604	....	6,046	....	....	....	4,187	.....	.....
8	3	2,647	9,384	583	170	....	18,947	.....	775
9	10,780	51,524	2,475	9,818	....	125	9,638	.....	.....
10	31,364	221,834	1,994	24,744	....	186	10,748	.....	.....
11	12,162	....	4,253	....	393	....	2,689	.....	34
12	271,869	7,361	109,021	....	9,567	3,062	38,138	5,804	1,805
13	249,580	....	55,859	....	2,488	1,288	8,556	267	10,007
14	176,035	....	57,563	....	9,400	79	7,691	6,878	5,047
15	141,628	918	42,231	....	4,554	....	6,551	298	1,353
16	32,032	107,329	13,704	21,835	....	11,143	9,635	119	2,442
17	22,402	39,026	987	9,368	....	457	10,013	.....	.....
18	22,604	....	410	....	....	....	5,762	55	.....
19	129,750	12,454	17,532	1,552	....	....	36,753	.....	15,231
20	69,890	....	6,745	....	2,905	....	70,758	.....	108
21	129,291	....	45,335	....	985	....	31,322	13,973	1,636
22	54,198	....	31,013	....	....	....	20,152	1,052	783
23	44,598	117,031	2,499	19,178	....	1,877	5,956	.....	.....
24	91,191	135,269	47,413	16,397	1,766	5,194	14,490	....	1,021
25	10,332	1,356	6,521	....	....	....	4,783	133	.....
26	71,895	....	24,436	....	2,460	....	7,739	684	1,939
27	1,129	....	469	....	....	....	1,016	.....	.....
28	12,625	....	826	....	....	....	6,480	.....	.....
29	121,832	....	98,217	....	1,882	....	65,775	33,197	616
30	4,373	6,349	3,729	236	....	36	1,666	192	.....
31	376,285	....	213,925	....	11,253	....	219,796	61,441	7,128
32	25,357	201,453	11,341	56,369	....	....	17,197	.....	6,061
33	11,567	....	8,531	....	....	....	2,307	247	1,005
34	393,004	....	134,593	....	21,936	20	49,086	287	52,173
35	39,709	60,137	17,912	3,269	367	1,408	3,677	490	.....
36	25,487	995	15,480	....	951	....	6,024	.....	655
37	376,223	....	325,713	....	72,321	....	119,260	1,556	199,900
38	7,201	....	1,108	....	884	....	20,413	....	.....
39	59,381	106,233	7,936	29,677	....	....	10,867	43	.....
40	20,144	....	9,047	....	....	....	7,910	1,130	1,900
41	57,514	144,173	16,221	26,102	....	25,720	10,799	.....	265
42	43,051	314,761	28,743	36,587	432	5,167	18,206	.....	.....
43	1,640	....	1,915	....	....	....	1,145	.....	.....
44	16,889	....	62	....	571	....	6,198	.....	.....
45	7,005	199,025	2,381	47,998	....	....	33,211	.....	2,438
46	39,357	3,207	28,551	....	1,994	....	10,312	248	68
47	81,354	49,349	11,223	14,006	1,130	....	6,803	.....	920
48	59,697	....	22,449	....	574	....	17,372	2,879	9,003
49	3,442	....	2,430	....	142	....	2,808	.....	.....
	3,578,190	2,079,000	1,539,354	348,223	4 155,630	64,043	1,063,250	130,984	325,777

3 Included in adjoining States.   4 Not including 1,324 colored members.

MEMBERS OR COMMUNICANTS BY STATES

REPRESENTING FOUR FIFTHS OF GRAND TOTAL IN UNITED STATES

		Roman Catholic 1915	United Brethren in Christ 1916	Grand Total by States	Population of States in 1916— Federal Estimate
1	Alabama	34,000	....	745,718	2,332,608
2	Arizona	34,000	....	49,986	255,544
3	Arkansas	19,550	....	392,188	1,739,723
4	California	437,043	2,374	738,304	2,938,654
5	Colorado	93,826	1,269	210,688	962,060
6	Connecticut	399,246	....	590,233	1,244,479
7	Delaware	24,650	....	67,871	213,380
8	District of Columbia	5	....	72,975	363,980
9	Florida	48,450	225	242,584	893,493
10	Georgia	16,476	179	936,235	2,856,065
11	Idaho	13,600	....	48,849	438,586
12	Illinois	1,257,397	22,036	2,259,319	6,152,257
13	Indiana	212,012	57,093	867,146	2,816,817
14	Iowa	218,790	11,521	725,943	2,224,771
15	Kansas	107,933	18,815	497,574	1,829,545
16	Kentucky	146,090	1,003	801,880	2,379,639
17	Louisiana	498,440	419	782,156	1,829,130
18	Maine	111,892	....	197,871	772,489
19	Maryland	229,500	7 11,473	534,067	1,362,807
20	Massachusetts	1,190,709	....	1,568,656	3,719,156
21	Michigan	507,450	3,441	923,847	3,054,854
22	Minnesota	399,807	1,583	776,608	2,279,603
23	Mississippi	23,803	....	606,090	1,951,674
24	Missouri	416,500	3,869	1,179,917	3,410,692
25	Montana	83,895	428	125,146	459,494
26	Nebraska	102,647	7,337	334,429	1,271,375
27	Nevada	5,525	....	9,274	106,734
28	New Hampshire	113,900	....	169,560	442,506
29	New Jersey	504,050	....	947,365	2,948,017
30	New Mexico	122,887	257	148,613	410,283
31	New York	2,464,340	4,125	3,734,621	10,273,375
32	North Carolina	6,197	....	787,110	2,402,738
33	North Dakota	87,950	....	173,427	739,201
34	Ohio	682,637	76,595	1,786,730	5,150,356
35	Oklahoma	34,538	3,992	306,597	2,202,081
36	Oregon	56,922	2,168	155,179	835,741
37	Pennsylvania	1,532,530	68,016	3,296,563	8,522,017
38	Rhode Island	233,750	....	296,344	614,315
39	South Carolina	7,905	....	586,625	1,625,475
40	South Dakota	64,555	....	162,405	698,509
41	Tennessee	16,150	2,924	615,817	2,288,004
42	Texas	346,962	....	1,375,663	4,429,566
43	Utah	8,925	....	17,249	434,083
44	Vermont	72,207	....	129,325	363,699
45	Virginia	36,890	14,986	811,384	2,192,019
46	Washington	79,900	909	235,799	1,534,221
47	West Virginia	46,718	21,469	328,947	1,386,038
48	Wisconsin	491,150	2,913	923,273	2,500,350
49	Wyoming	11,050	....	24,992	179,559
		6 13,655,344	341,419	33,299,142	102,017,312

5 Included in Maryland.
6 85% of Catholic population. Total *does not* include 500,000 Ruthenian population scattered over half of the States.
7 Including District of Columbia.

STATISTICS OF SUNDAY SCHOOLS

The larger and many of the smaller denominations make returns for Sunday-schools in their annual statistics; but a considerable number, including the Roman Catholic and the Eastern Orthodox bodies, do not. The United States Census of Religious Bodies of 1906 gathered information under this head from these and other denominations; in fact from all that have Sunday-schools. Quite a number of churches, such as the Primitive Baptists, the Old Order Brethren, and other small bodies, have no Sunday-schools.

Most of the returns given in the accompanying tables are for the year 1916, some are for 1915, others are for 1914 and the rest go back to the census of 1906. Those for 1914 are taken from the full statistical tables in the *Encyclopaedia of Sunday Schools*.

The statistics for what are known as the evangelical churches are probably quite accurate, though those given for the African Methodist Episcopal, African Methodist Episcopal Zion, and Colored Methodist Episcopal ·Churches are not very recent. These bodies have reported no figures of any kind for two or three years. The grand totals may be reasonably regarded as approximate, not exact, but rather under than over the real figures.

The gains in the ten years since the United States Census of Sunday-schools in 1906 are very large, reaching far beyond six million scholars, or a percentage of 40—. The net increase in membership of all the churches in the same period has been 4,756,433 or a percentage of 13+. That there has been an actual net increase of 6,116,622 scholars in the Sunday-schools does not seem easy to explain, without impeaching the fulness of the returns of 1906 or the accuracy of those of 1916; but the distribution of gains among denominational groups and denominations appears to confirm it.

The larger increases in the item of scholars are as follows:

	GAIN IN TEN YEARS Scholars	TOTAL IN 1916 Scholars
Baptist group	486,923	3,385,837
Congregational	51,404	689,493
Disciple group	306,236	940,767
Brethren (Dunkards)	65,630	144,205
Evangelical bodies	64,771	279,769
Friends group	16,038	69,799
German Evangelical	18,585	134,691
Lutheran group	230,798	1,013,584
Mennonite group	8,297	53,219
Methodist group	2,745,533	7,218,463
Presbyterian group	419,796	1,930,971
Reformed group	93,457	455,005
Protestant Episcopal	18,646	482,997
United Brethren group	127,481	428,801
Roman Catholic	1,368,465	2,850,000

The Roman Catholic gain is over 89 per cent.; the Disciple, 50—; the United Brethren 42+; the Methodist 61+; the Lutheran 30—; the Reformed 29+; the Presbyterian 27+.

The Methodist Episcopal Church shows an increase of 1,543,799, or 57+ per cent.; the Methodist Episcopal Church, South, 707,720, or 68+ per cent.

The increase in the number of schools, 15,500, is at the rate of 1,550 a year; and the increase of officers and teachers, 307,271, is at the rate of more than 30,000 a year.

TABLE I

STATISTICS OF SUNDAY SCHOOLS BY DENOMINATIONS IN THE UNITED STATES

Denominations	Sunday Schools	Officers and Teachers	Scholars
Adventists:			
1. Evangelical............................	a 9	a 57	a 264
2. Advent Christians......................	345	2,476	17,557
3. Seventh Day...........................	2,740	11,603	81,225
4. Church of God..........................	a 16	a 30	a 200
5. Life and Advent Union..................	a 7	a 45	a 259
6. Churches of God in Jesus Christ...........	a 80	a 240	a 1,140
Total Adventists......................	3,197	14,451	100,645
Baptists:			
1. Baptists (North) ⎫			
2. Baptists (South) ⎬	m 42,869	m 325,475	m 3,288,992
3. Baptists (Colored) ⎭			
4. Six-Principle.......................	a 9	a 74	a 414
5. Seventh Day........................	74	599	5,796
6. Free.................................	793	9,023	56,817
7. Freewill.............................	a 263	a 1,440	a 12,720
8. General..............................	275	1,375	11,000
9. Separate.............................	a 45	a 312	a 1,962
10. United..............................	a 23	a 168	a 1,360
11. Baptist Church of Christ..................	a 9	a 37	a 402
12. Primitive (c)........................	c......	c......	c......
13. Primitive (Colored)......................	a 166	a 911	a 6,224
14. Old Two-Seed-in-the-Spirit Predestinarian....	....	....	....
15. Church of God and Saints of Christ.........	a 1	a 6	a 150
Total Baptists.......................	44,527	339,440	3,385,837
Brethren (Dunkards):			
1. Conservative............................	1,277	12,320	126,745
2. Old Order (c)...........................	c........	c........	c........
3. Progressive............................	179	2,418	17,322
4. Seventh-Day German.....................	b 3	b 12	b 138
Total Dunkard Brethren................	1,459	14,750	144,205
Brethren (Plymouth):			
1. Brethren I..............................	80	306	2,716
2. Brethren II.............................	102	514	5,745
3. Brethren III............................	28	72	720
4. Brethren IV (c).........................	c........	c........	c........
Total Plymouth Brethren...............	210	892	9,181
Brethren (River):			
1. Brethren in Christ.......................	a 49	a 455	a 2,695
2. Old Order or Yorker (c)....................	c........	c........	c........
3. United Zion's Children..................	a 2	a 18	a 117
Total River Brethren...................	51	473	2,812
Buddhists:			
1. Chinese Temples........................	....	....	....
2. Japanese Temples.......................	a 19	a 48	a 913
Total Buddhists......................	19	48	913

a. Census of 1906.
b. 1914.
c. Reports no Sunday Schools
m. 1915.

TABLE I—Continued

STATISTICS OF SUNDAY SCHOOLS BY DENOMINATIONS IN THE UNITED STATES

Denominations	Sunday Schools	Officers and Teachers	Scholars
Catholic Apostolic:			
1. Catholic Apostolic..........................	*a* 6	*a* 10	*a* 420
2. New Apostolic.............................	*a* 3	*a* 10	*a* 250
Total Catholic Apostolic...............	9	20	670
Catholic (Eastern Orthodox):			
1. Armenian Apostolic.......................	*a* 4	*a* 9	*a* 340
2. Russian Orthodox.........................	100	100	10,000
3. Greek Orthodox...........................	*a* 4	*a* 6	*a* 371
4. Syrian Orthodox..........................	*a* 1	*a*1	*a* 50
5. Serbian Orthodox.........................	6	6	88
6. Roumanian Orthodox......................	....	....	....
7. Bulgarian Orthodox.......................	....	....	....
Total Eastern Catholics................	115	122	10,849
Christadelphians..............................	*b* 22	*b* 78	*b* 480
Christians....................................	956	*a* 10,510	72,673
Christian Catholic (Dowie)...................	*c*........	*c*........	*c*........
Christian Union.............................	350	*a* 1,514	*a* 9,234
Church of Christ Scientist...................	1,499	*a* 3,155	*a* 16,116
Churches of God (Winebrennarian)...........	422	3,897	36,596
Churches of the Living God (Colored): (*a*)			
1. Christian Workers for Friendship...........	43	122	886
2. Apostolic...............................	13	67	585
3. Church of Christ in God..................	6	21	289
Total Churches of the Living God........	*a* 62	*a* 210	*a* 1,760
Churches of the New Jerusalem:			
1. General Convention.......................	61	349	3,280
2. General Church...........................	10	29	207
Total New Jerusalem Churches..........	71	369	3,487
Church Transcendent..........................	2	9	53
Communistic Societies:			
1. Shakers.................................	*a* 6	*a* 17	*a* 103
2. Amana..................................	....	....	....
Total Communistic Societies............	6	17	103
Congregationalists.............................	*m* 18,282	*d* 76,610	*m* 689,493
Disciples of Christ:			
1. Disciples of Christ........................	9,300	*d* 95,169	884,681
2. Churches of Christ.......................	*a* 1,260	*a* 5,112	*a* 56,086
Total Disciples of Christ...............	8,772	100,281	940,767
Evangelical Bodies:			
1. Evangelical Association....................	1,595	30,103	139,978
2. United Evangelical Church................	936	14,002	139,791
Total Evangelical Bodies...............	2,531	44,105	279,769

a. Census of 1906.
b. 1914.
c. Reports no Sunday Schools.
d. Estimated.
m. 1915.

TABLE I—Continued

STATISTICS OF SUNDAY SCHOOLS BY DENOMINATIONS IN THE UNITED STATES

DENOMINATIONS	Sunday Schools	Officers and Teachers	Scholars
Faith Associations: (a)			
1. Apostolic Faith Movement.................	6	30	245
2. Peniel Missions..........................	7	40	308
3. Metropolitan Church Association...........	4	29	360
4. Hephzibah Faith Association..............	9	75	402
5. Missionary Church Association.............	34	271	1,916
6. Heavenly Recruit Church.................	14	116	527
7. Apostolic Christian Church...............	32	130	1,932
8. Christian Congregation...................	7	73	332
9. Voluntary Missionary Society (Colored)......	3	21	390
Total Faith Associations...............	a 116	a 785	a 6,412
Free Christian Zion Church....................	a 7	s 63	a 340
Friends:			
1. Orthodox..............................	b 850	b 7,143	b 63,171
2. "Hicksite"............................	a 110	a 795	a 6,423
3. "Wilburite"...........................	a 7	a 33	a 205
4. Primitive c............................	c........	c........	c........
Total Friends.........................	967	7,971	69,799
Friends of the Temple......................	a 3	a 21	a 168
German Evangelical Protestant..............	a 61	a 1,225	a 11,362
German Evangelical Synod......................	1,302	13,382	134,691
Jewish Congregations.........................	a 600	a 2,239	a 49,514
Latter-Day Saints:			
1. Utah Branch...........................	a 865	a 17,784	a 143,461
2. Reorganized branch.....................	746	4,705	44,714
Total Latter-Day Saints...............	1,611	22,489	188,175
Lutherans:			
1. General Synod.........................	1,757	29,504	291,900
2. United Synod, South.....................	402	4,105	38,196
3. General Council........................	2,418	30,448	292,828
4. Synodical Conference....................	690	3,014	181,414
5. United Norwegian......................	664	4,497	37,269
(Independent Synods):			
6. Ohio.................................	691	4,328	62,036
7. Buffalo...............................	b 25	b 79	b 1,050
8. Hauge's..............................	200	580	4,022
9. Eilsen's..............................	b 8	b 24	b 900
10. Iowa.................................	712	1,076	29,156
11. Norwegian............................	350	3,200	28,000
12. Danish in America.....................	63	268	2,596
13. Icelandic............................	31	180	1,810
14. Immanuel............................	56	325	2,830
15. Suomi (Finnish).......................	180	1,002	8,123
16. Finnish Apostolic......................	b 309	b 500	b 4,500
17. Finnish National......................	b 72	b 276	b 1,724
18. Norwegian Free.......................	255	1,100	10,250
19. Danish United........................	161	946	7,079
20. Church of the Lutheran Brethren..........	b 18	b 100	b 1,400
Independent Congregations.................	b 210	b 829	b 6,501
Total Lutherans.....................	9,272	86,381	1,013,584

a. Census of 1916.
b. 1914.
c. Reports no Sunday schools.

TABLE I—Continued

STATISTICS OF SUNDAY SCHOOLS BY DENOMINATIONS IN THE UNITED STATES

DENOMINATIONS	Sunday Schools	Officers and Teachers	Scholars
Scandinavian Evangelical Bodies:			
1. Swedish Evangelical Mission Covenant.......	b 300	b 3,500	b 29,000
2. Swedish Evangelical Free Mission...........	b 104	b 300	b 5,700
3. Norwegian Evangelical Free................	b 35	b 325	b 2,500
Total Scandinavian Evangelical.........	439	4,125	37,200
Mennonites:			
1. Mennonite..............................	a 170	a 1,967	a 15,798
2. Bruederhoef (c).........................	c........	c........	c........
3. Amish..................................	a 57	a 798	a 6,367
4. Amish (Old Order).......................	a 6	a 66	a 493
5. Amish (Conservative)....................	....	....	....
6. Reformed (c)............................	c........	c........	c........
7. General Conference......................	101	a 1,148	16,889
8. Church of God in Christ (c)..............	c........	c........	c........
9. Old Order (Wisler) (c)..................	c........	c........	c........
10. Bundes Conference.......................	a 22	a 181	a 3,230
11. Defenceless.............................	a 13	a 142	a 1,102
12. Mennonite Brethren in Christ.............	110	1,217	7,600
Miscellaneous.............................	a 22	a 161	a 1,740
Total Mennonites.....................	501	5,680	53,219
Methodist:			
1. Methodist Episcopal.....................	29,165	392,049	4,244,541
2. Union American Methodist Episcopal.......	175	200	15,000
3. African Methodist Episcopal..............	b 5,700	b 152,305	b 351,828
4. African Union Methodist Protestant........	a 66	a 441	a 5,266
5. African Methodist Episcopal Zion.........	b 3,220	b 15,520	b 251,730
6. Methodist Protestant.....................	b 2,180	a 18,970	b 144,666
7. Wesleyan Methodist......................	605	3,337	28,364
8. Methodist Episcopal, South................	16,711	147,699	1,747,880
9. Congregational Methodist.................	a 182	a 1,146	a 8,785
10. New Congregational Methodist.............	a 27	a 143	a 1,298
11. Zion Union Apostolic.....................	a 36	a 212	a 1,508
12. Colored Methodist Episcopal..............	b 3,019	b 11,117	b 348,292
13. Primitive...............................	84	1,566	14,621
14. Free Methodist..........................	1,261	8,528	53,464
15. Reformed Methodist Union Episcopal.......	30	50	500
16. Independent Methodist....................	2	45	720
Total Methodists.....................	52,463	753,328	7,218,463
Moravian Bodies:			
1. Moravians..............................	122	1,610	16,362
2. Union Bohemians and Moravians...........	a 2	a 6	a 97
Total Moravians.....................	124	1,616	16,459
Nonsectarian Bible Faith Churches.............	a 33	a 158	a 1,976
Pentecostal Bodies:			
1. Pentecostal Church of the Nazarene........	902	5,752	39,594
2. Apostolic Holiness Church................	....	....	....
Total Pentecostal Bodies..............	902	5,752	39,594

a. Census of 1906.
b. 1914.
c. Reports no Sunday schools.

TABLE I—Continued

STATISTICS OF SUNDAY SCHOOLS BY DENOMINATIONS IN THE UNITED STATES

Denominations	Sunday Schools	Officers and Teachers	Scholars
Presbyterians:			
1. Northern..........................	9,511	141,033	1,261,883
2. Cumberland........................	751	e 2,100	44,085
3. Cumberland (Colored).................	a 192	a 933	a 6,952
4. Welsh Calvinistic...................	b 156	a 1,705	11,062
5. United...........................	b 1,015	b 14,203	b 141,280
6. Southern..........................	2,848	29,005	285,739
7. Associate.........................	995	15,415	154,646
8. Associate Reformed, South.............	160	1,329	12,417
9. Reformed (Synod)...................	123	b723	10,649
10. Reformed (General Synod)..............	a 23	a 255	a 2,013
11. Reformed (Covenanted)................	a 1	a 20	a 132
12. Reformed in the United States and Canada...	30	17	113
Total Presbyterians....................	15,805	206,738	1,930,971
Protestant Episcopal:			
1. Protestant Episcopal..................	a 7,585	53,389	473,030
2. Reformed Episcopal..................	85	882	9,967
Total Protestant Episcopal.............	7,670	54,271	482,997
Reformed:			
1. Reformed (Dutch)....................	807	13,000	118,890
2. Reformed (German)..................	1,727	29,825	316,832
3. Christian Reformed..................	124	1,600	17,733
4. Hungarian Reformed..................	28	44	1,550
Total Reformed.....................	2,686	44,469	455,005
Reformed Catholic....................	....	....	....
Roman Catholic......................	a 10,875	a 62,470	k2,850,000
Polish Catholic......................	a 22	a 26	a 1,289
American Old Catholic..................	40	200	3,000
Salvation Army......................	700	12,113	45,141
Schwenkfelders......................	6	54	1,638
Social Brethren......................	a 6	a 23	a 180
Society for Ethical Culture...............	b 5	b 64	b 466
Spiritualists........................	b 150	b 750	b 2,256
Theosophical Society..................	b 28	b 30	....
Unitarians.........................	348	3,150	15,900
United Brethren:			
1. United Brethren.....................	3,453	43,617	406,715
2. United Brethren (Old Constitution)........	b 437	b 4,219	b 22,086
Total United Brethren.................	3,890	47,836	428,801
Universalists.......................	520	b 7,575	38,382
Union and Undenominational Schools...........	a 14,508	a 97,410	a 651,814
Grand Total in 1916..................	208,222	†2,053,345	*21,454,433
Grand Total in 1906, according to U. S. Census..........................	192,722	1,746,074	15,337,811
Net Increase in ten years...............	15,500	307,271	6,116,622

* This grand total includes in some cases officers and teachers with scholars.

† This grand total would be a little larger if some churches reported officers and teachers separately from scholars.

    a. Census of 1906.

    b. 1914.

    e. Incomplete returns.

    k. Estimate of Editor of Catholic Directory for 1913.

TABLE II

SUMMARY OF SUNDAY SCHOOLS IN THE UNITED STATES

Denominations	Sunday Schools	Officers and Teachers	Scholars
Adventists (6 bodies)........................	3,197	14,451	100,645
Baptists (15 bodies)........................	44,527	339,440	3,385,837
Brethren (Dunkards) (4 bodies)................	1,459	14,750	144,205
Brethren (Plymouth) (3 bodies)................	210	892	9,181
Brethren (River) (3 bodies)...................	51	473	2,812
Buddhists (2 bodies).........................	19	48	913
Catholic Apostolic (2 bodies).................	9	20	670
Catholic (Eastern Orthodox) (7 bodies)..........	115	122	10,849
Christadelphians............................	22	78	480
Christians..................................	956	10,510	72,673
Christian Union.............................	350	1,514	9,234
Church of Christ Scientist....................	1,499	3,155	16,116
Churches of God (Winebrennarian).............	422	3,897	36,596
Churches of the Living God (Colored) (3 bodies)....	62	210	1,760
Churches of the New Jerusalem(2 bodies).........	71	369	3,487
Church Transcendent........................	2	9	53
Communistic Societies (2 bodies)...............	6	17	103
Congregationalists..........................	18,282	76,610	689,493
Disciples of Christ (2 bodies).................	8,772	100,281	940,767
Evangelical Bodies (2 bodies).................	2,531	44,105	279,769
Faith Associations (9 bodies).................	116	785	6,412
Free Christian Zion Church...................	7	63	340
Friends (4 bodies)..........................	967	7,971	69,799
Friends of the Temple.......................	3	21	168
German Evangelical Protestant................	61	1,225	11,362
German Evangelical Synod....................	1,302	13,382	134,691
Jewish Congregations........................	600	2,239	49,514
Latter Day Saints (2 bodies).................	1,611	22,489	188,175
Lutherans (20 bodies).......................	9,272	86,381	1,013,584
Swedish Evangelical Bodies (3 bodies)..........	439	4,125	37,200
Mennonites (12 bodies)......................	501	5,680	53,219
Methodists (16 bodies)......................	52,463	753,328	7,218,463
Moravian Bodies (2 bodies)..................	124	1,616	16,459
Nonsectarian Bible Faith Churches............	33	158	1,976
Pentecostal Bodies (2 bodies)................	902	5,752	39,594
Presbyterians (12 bodies)...................	15,805	206,738	1,930,971
Protestant Episcopal (2 bodies)...............	7,670	54,271	482,997
Reformed (4 bodies)........................	2,686	44,469	455,005
Roman Catholic.............................	10,875	62,470	2,850,000
Polish Catholic.............................	22	26	1,289
American Old Catholic.......................	40	200	3,000
Salvation Army.............................	700	12,113	45,141
Schwenkfelders.............................	6	54	1,638
Social Brethren..	6	23	180
Society for Ethical Culture...................	5	64	466
Spiritualists...............................	150	750	2,250
Theosophical Society........................	28	30	....
Unitarians.................................	348	3,150	15,900
United Brethren (2 bodies)...................	3,890	47,836	428,801
Universalists...............................	520	7,575	38,382
Union and Undenominational Schools............	a 14,508	a 97,410	a 651,814
Grand Total in 1916........................	208,222	2,053,345	21,454,433
Grand Total in 1906 according to U. S. Census..	192,722	1,746,074	15,337,811
Net increase in ten years....................	15,500	307,271	6,116,622

a. Census of 1906.

FEDERATION IN ENGLAND AND WALES

Constituted by the Congregational, Baptist, Methodist, Presbyterian, and Free Episcopal Churches and Society of Friends in England and Wales.

Purpose: *a.* To facilitate fraternal intercourse and cooperation among the Evangelical Free Churches; *b.* To assist in the organization of local Councils; *c.* To encourage devotional fellowship and mutual counsel concerning the spiritual life and religious activities of the Churches; *d.* To advocate the New Testament doctrine of the Church, and to defend the rights of the associated Churches; *e.* To promote the application of the law of Christ in every relation of human life.

Office: Memorial Hall, Farringdon Street, London, E. C., England.

Officers: *President,* Rev. Alex. McConnell; *Secretary,* Rev. F. B. Meyer.

Five Methodist bodies, aggregating 976,555 communicants, the Baptists, 392,034 communicants, the Congregationalists, 452,489, the Presbyterians and the Welsh Calvinistic Methodist, 270,495, the Churches of Christ, 14,778, the Disciples of Christ, 1,713, the Friends, 17,466, the Moravians, 3,313, the Free Episcopal, 1,352, the Reformed Episcopal, 1,278 and Lady Huntingdon's Connection, 2,200, are connected with the Federation, representing 2,133,673 communicants and 9,064 ministers, according to returns of 1913.

Plans for a closer federation were under consideration in 1916, under the leadership of the Rev. J. H. Shakespeare, most of the Free Churches participating.

WORLD'S EVANGELICAL ALLIANCE

Office, 19 Russell Square, London, W. C., England. *General Secretary,* H. M. Gooch.

THE WORLD'S RELIGIONS

The sources of the world statistics which follow are indicated. It should be borne in mind that they are not very recent, but date back to near the beginning of the present century. It is certain that the figures given for Protestant population in North America are much too small. The Protestant population for the United States alone can hardly be much short of 75,000,000, to say nothing of the millions in Canada.

FOLLOWERS OF THE VARIOUS CREEDS

(According to Whitaker's Almanac, London, 1916)

Christians	564,510,000
Confucianists and Taoists	300,830,000
Mohammedans	221,825,000
Hindus	210,540,000
Animists	158,270,000
Buddhists	138,031,000
Shintoists	25,000,000
Jews	13,052,846
Unclassified	15,280,000
Grand total	1,647,388,846

DIVISIONS OF CHRISTIANITY

(According to Whitaker's Almanac)

Roman Catholic	272,860,000
Eastern Orthodox	120,000,000
Protestant	171,650,000

CONTINENTAL DISTRIBUTION OF CHRISTIANS AND JEWS

	Roman Catholic	Eastern Orthodox	Protestant	Jews
Europe	183,760,000	98,000,000	93,000,000	9,950,175
Asia	5,500,000	17,200,000	6,000,000	484,359
Africa	2,500,000	3,800,000	2,750,000	404,836
North America	36,700,000	1,000,000	65,000,000	2,144,061
South America	36,200,000	....	400,000	50,000
Oceania	8,200,000	....	4,500,000	19,415
Totals, from Webb-Mulhall	272,860,000	120,000,000	171,650,000	13,052,846

TOTALS BY CONTINENTS

	Christianity	Other Faiths	Totals
Europe....................	374,760,000	14,750,175	389,510,175
Asia......................	28,700,000	863,484,359	892,184,359
Africa....................	9,050,000	149,875,836	158,925,836
North America............	102,700,000	10,379,061	113,079,061
South America............	36,600,000	1,570,000	38,170,000
Oceania..................	12,700,000	42,769,415	55,469,415
Totals................	564,510,000	1,082,828,846	1,647,338,846

NON-CHRISTIAN AND NON-JEWISH FAITHS

	Confucianists and Taoists	Mohammedans	Buddhists	Hindus	Animists
Europe.........		3,800,000			
Asia............	300,000,000	142,000,000	138,000,000	210,000,000	42,000,000
Africa..........	30,000	51,000,000	11,000	300,000	98,000,000
North America..	100,000	15,000		100,000	20,000
South America..		10,000		110,000	1,250,000
Oceania........	700,000	25,000,000	20,000	30,000	17,000,000
Totals.......	300,830,000	221,825,000	138,031,000	210,540,000	158,270,000

(Not included in this table are the Shintoists—25,000,000 —all in Asia; and 15,280,000 unclassified, of whom 8,000,000 are in North America, 6,000,000 in Asia, 1,000,000 in Europe, 150,000 in South America, and 130,000 in Africa.)

ORDER OF THE CHRISTIAN CHURCHES IN THE CONTINENTS

In Europe, the Roman Catholic is first, the Eastern Orthodox second, and the Protestant third.

In Asia, the Eastern Orthodox is first, the Protestant second, the Roman Catholic third.

In Africa, the Eastern Orthodox is first, the Protestant second, the Roman Catholic third.

In North America, the Protestant is first, the Roman Catholic second, the Eastern Orthodox third.

In South America the Roman Catholic is first, the Protestant second.

In Oceania the Roman Catholic is first, the Protestant second.

The Roman Catholic is first in Europe, South America, and Oceania.

The Eastern Orthodox is first in Asia and Africa.

The Protestant is first in North America.

CHIEF DIVISIONS OF PROTESTANTISM

This is simply a first attempt to present statistics of members and adherents of the leading Protestant communions of the world. There are, of course, other bodies which could properly appear in this list. It is very difficult, indeed well-nigh impossible, to secure complete and trustworthy returns, which shall, at the same time, be up to date.

The statement for the Anglican Communion is by no means satisfactory. It is not very late, and it is at best only approximate.

That for the Baptists is taken from the *American Baptist Year Book* for 1915; and that for the Congregationalists from the *Congregational Year Book* for the same year. The population in each case is estimated on the basis of two adherents to each communicant.

The presentation for Methodism may be accepted as fairly accurate, and is, for the most part, of latest date.

The Lutheran figures are those of Prof. J. N. Lenker, except for the United States, and are several years old.

The Presbyterian and Reformed statistics are taken from the *Presbyterian Year Book* for other countries than the United States, and are probably quite conservative. They are in part for 1916 and in part for 1915 and earlier years.

The estimate of population is made on the basis of two adherents for each member in all cases in so far as the United States is concerned, which is probably too low for some denominations but high enough for the general average; it is also applied to Baptist and Congregational communicants in other countries.

Population means the total of communicants or members, and of adherents.

ANGLICAN COMMUNION

The Anglican Communion includes the Church of England in England and Wales, Scotland and Ireland, and the British Colonies, and the Protestant Episcopal Church in the United States. The figures are not very recent except for the Protestant Episcopal Church, which are for 1916. Population includes communicants and adherents.

	Communicants	Population
England and Wales............................	....	16,750,000
Scotland and Ireland.........................	....	750,000
British Colonies, Canada, Australia, etc...........	....	6,000,000
United States and Missions....................	1,086,089	*3,258,267
Total.....................................		26,758,267

BAPTIST COMMUNION

Communicants from *American Baptist Year Book;* adherents estimated on usual basis.

	Communicants	Population
America, United States, Canada, South America...	6,141,768	*18,425,304
Europe.......................................	617,652	*1,852,956
Asia..	196,158	*588,474
Africa..	14,991	*44,973
Australasia...................................	30,168	*90,504
Totals....................................	7,000,737	21,002,211

CONGREGATIONAL COMMUNION

Communicants from *Congregational Year Book;* adherents estimated on usual basis.

	Communicants	Population
United States, Canada, Missions.................	887,488	*2,662,464
Great Britain and Ireland......................	493,378	1,480,134
Australasia...................................	21,229	63,687
Missions in Asia and Africa....................	49,629	148,887
Totals....................................	1,451,724	4,355,172

LUTHERAN COMMUNION

All items from Lenker's statement except United States.

	Communicants	Population
United States (1916)...........................	2,454,334	*†7,363,002
Germany......................................		40,000,000
Scandinavia...................................		10,463,000
Finland and Poland............................		3,460,000
Russia (other parts than Finland and Poland).....		4,590,000
Hungary......................................		1,310,000
Austria, France, Holland, British Isles............		1,042,000
Asia..		412,000
Africa..		431,000
Oceania (Australia, New Zealand, etc.)...........		244,000
South America.................................		770,000
British America...............................		424,396
Total.....................................		70,509,398

* Estimated by compiler on basis of 2 adherents to each communicant.
† Lenker's estimate for Lutherans in U. S. is 13,000,000.

METHODIST COMMUNION

	Communicants	Population
United States, Canada and Missions.............	8,425,895	*25,277,685
Great Britain and Ireland and Missions...........	1,253,521	‡6,267,605
Australasia....................................	174,608	‡873,040
Totals...................................	9,854,024	32,418,330

* Estimated by compiler on basis of 2 adherents to each communicant.
‡ British and Australian Wesleyans estimate 4 adherents to each communicant.

PRESBYTERIAN AND REFORMED COMMUNION

All items except the first are taken from the *Presbyterian Year Book* for 1917.

	Communicants	Population
United States, 1916...........................	2,686,144	*8,058,432
Canada.......................................	343,457	†943,457
England and Wales............................	287,166	887,166
Ireland......................................	110,077	310,077
Scotland.....................................	1,350,722	3,750,722
Germany.....................................		5,000,000
Holland......................................		2,500,000
Hungary.....................................		3,000,000
Switzerland..................................		1,700,000
France.......................................		1,000,000
Other countries in Europe.....................		1,050,000
Africa.......................................		1,000,000
Asia...		600,000
Australasia..................................		900,000
South America...............................		100,000
Total...................................		30,799,854

* Estimated by compiler on basis of 2 adherents to each communicant.
† Evidently too low. The Government census of 1911 returned 1,117,200, including Newfoundland.

SUMMARY

	Population
Anglican Communion..............................	26,758,267
Baptist Communion..............................	21,002,211
Congregational Communion.......................	4,355,172
Lutheran Communion............................	70,509,398
Methodist Communion...........................	32,418,330
Presbyterian and Reformed Communion............	30,799,854
Total.....................................	185,843,232

This total, which does not include a considerable number of minor Protestant bodies in Europe, and some large as well as many small Protestant bodies in the United States, is, nevertheless, much larger than the highest figure given by any of the statisticians of Europe for Protestantism in the world. *Whitaker* gives 171,651,000 as the total, and *Webb-*

Mulhall, 177,300,000. But these estimates are not at all recent; they date back to the beginning or near the beginning of the present century. *Whitaker* allots to North America only 65,000,000 Protestant population; *Webb-Mulhall,* 69,000,000. The former estimate is only large enough to cover the Protestant population in the United States alone in 1900, exclusive of Canada. There were in 1900 about 18,500,000 Protestant communicants in the United States, which, at the ratio of two and one half adherents to each communicant, would yield about 65,000,000 population. The number of Protestant members in the United States in 1916 is upward of 25,000,000, which, on the basis of two adherents to each communicant, perhaps a safer ratio, yields a Protestant population of 75,000,000. It would therefore appear that a revision of the estimates for Protestantism in the world must carry it up to 190,000,000 or 195,000,000, unless, indeed, there has been a large decrease of Protestants in Europe and other countries, of which there is no other evidence at hand than the destruction of life by the war.

ROMAN CATHOLIC CHURCH IN NORTH AMERICA

The figures generally given for the Roman Catholic Church in North America will also have to be revised and brought down to date. According to *Webb-Mulhall* there was in the United States at the beginning of the present century 11,000,-000 Catholic population, and 26,800,000 in the rest of North America, with 37,400,000 in South America, making a total for America of 75,200,000. At the end of 1915 the Catholic population of the United States, not including our insular possessions, was 16,564,000; including the insular possessions, the estimate of the Catholic Directory calls for 24,922,-000. If to this aggregate Canada be added with 3,113,794, Mexico and Central America with Cuba, and other adjacent islands, there will be a total of more than 50,000,000 Catholic population for North America.

PUBLICATIONS OF THE FEDERAL COUNCIL

Books

Christian Unity at Work. Fourth Edition. The Second Council, of 1912. A Record of the Federative Movement for four years. Edited by Charles S. Macfarland, General Secretary of the Federal Council. Published by authority of the Council. $1.00; postpaid, $1.20.

The Origin and History of the Federal Council. By Elias B. Sanford. $1.50.

The Federal Council of the Churches. The Record of the First Council at Philadelphia, 1908. Edited by Elias B. Sanford, Honorary Secretary. $1.25; postpaid, $1.50.

Church Federation. The story of Interchurch Federation at Carnegie Hall, New York, in 1905; an Initial and Preparatory Session of the Federal Council. Edited by Elias B. Sanford. $1.50; postpaid, $1.75.

The Churches of the Federal Council: Their History, Organization, and Distinctive Characteristics. Edited by Charles S. Macfarland. $1.00; postpaid, $1.10.

The Library of Christian Cooperation. (The Reports and Proceedings of the Third Quadrennial Council.) $5.00.

Volume I—*The Churches of Christ in Council.* Edited by Charles S. Macfarland. $1.00.

Volume II—*The Church and International Relations.* Edited by Sidney L. Gulick and Charles S. Macfarland. $1.00.

Volume III—*The Church and International Relations.* Edited by Sidney L. Gulick and Charles S. Macfarland. $1.00.

Volume IV—*The Churches and International Relations—Japan.* Edited by Charles S. Macfarland. $1.00.

Volume V—*Christian Cooperation and World Redemption.* Edited by Charles S. Macfarland. $1.00.

Volume VI—*Cooperation in Christian Education.* Edited by Henry H. Meyer. $1.00.

The Country Church—The Decline of its Influence and the Remedy. The Result of an Investigation, by Charles O. Gill and Gifford Pinchot, of the Commission on The Church and Country Life. $1.25; postpaid, $1.36.

The Church and Country Life. Edited by Prof. Paul L. Vogt. Postpaid, $1.00.

A Yearbook of the Church and Social Service. Compiled by Harry F. Ward, Associate Secretary of the Commission on the Church and Social Service. Paper, 35 cents; cloth, 55 cents; postpaid.

Federal Council Year Book. A Directory of the Federal Council, Its Constituent Bodies and Other Denominations, Interdenominational Societies, etc., with statistics. Compiled by Henry K. Carroll. Postpaid, 50 cents.

Spiritual Culture and Social Service. Fourth Edition. By Charles S. Macfarland. $1.00; postpaid, $1.10.

A Social Survey for Rural Communities. By G. Frederick Wells. Paper, 10 cents.

Motion Pictures in Religious and Educational Work, with Practical Suggestions for their Use. By Edward M. McConoughey. Paper, 10 cents.

The Fight for Peace, an Aggressive Campaign for American Churches. By Sidney L. Gulick, Secretary of the Federal Council Commission on International Justice and Good-Will. Paper, 25 cents; cloth, 50 cents; postpaid.

Selected Quotations on Peace and War. Source Book for the use of Sunday School teachers in connection with the Lessons on International Peace, prepared by the Federal Council Commission on Christian Education. $1.00; postpaid, $1.10.

The Japanese Problem in the United States. Prepared by Professor H. A. Millis for the Commission on Relations with Japan. Illustrated. $1.50; postpaid, $1.60.

Books Specially Recommended

The Social Creed of the Churches. By Harry F. Ward. 50 cents; postpaid, 55 cents.

Christian Service and the Modern World. By Charles S. Macfarland. 75 cents; postpaid, 80 cents.

The Christian Ministry and the Social Order. Edited by Charles S. Macfarland. $1.25; postpaid, $1.35.

The Industrial Situation. By Frank Tracy Carlton. 75 cents; postpaid, 80 cents.

The Gospel of Labor. By Charles Stelzle. 10 cents; postpaid, 12 cents.

America and the Orient, Outline of a Constructive Policy. By Sidney L. Gulick. 25 cents; postpaid, 35 cents.

Orders may be sent to: The Book Department of the Federal Council, 105 East 22d Street, New York City.

Pamphlets

Reports:

Annual Reports for 1914. Postpaid, 20 cents.

Annual Reports for 1915. Postpaid, 20 cents.

Proceedings of the Second Quadrennial Council of 1912, to accompany the volume Christian Unity at Work.

Proceedings of the Third Quadrennial Council of 1916, to accompany the volumes The Library of Christian Progress. Postpaid, 25 cents.

Annual Report of the Home Missions Council, 1914. Postpaid, 20 cents.

Annual Report of the Home Missions Council, 1915. Postpaid, 20 cents.

Annual Report of the Home Missions Council, 1916. Postpaid, 60 cents.

The Federal Council and the Federative Movement:

Price Per Hundred

The Federal Council: Its Plan, Purpose, and Work..... $0.50

Statement of Principles of the Federal Council—Bulletin No. 7.. .50

A Descriptive Directory of State and Local Federations of Churches.. 5.00

Christian Nurture and Religious Education........... 1.00

Commissions on the Church and Social Service and the Church and Country Life:

What Every Church Should Know About Its Community 3.00

Social Service for Young People..................... 5.00

Continuous Toil and Continuous Toilers, or One Day in Seven for Industrial Workers...................... 2.00

The Church and Modern Industry.................... 1.75

The Church's Appeal in Behalf of Labor............. 1.00

A Plan of Social Work for the United Churches....... 1.00

Social Service Catechism........................... .75

The South Bethlehem Industrial Investigation......... 1.75

The Muscatine Industrial Investigation............... 1.75

The Church and Industrial Warfare, being a report on the Colorado and Michigan Strikes................. 5.00

Reading Lists on Social Questions................... .75

Suggestions for Labor Sunday...................... 1.00

Labor Sunday Program............................. 1.00

The Open Forum; by William Horton Foster......... 1.50
Save our Soldiers and Sailors....................... .80

Commission on Interchurch Federations (State and Local):
Christian Conquests Through Interchurch Activities.... 4.00
World Needs a Church Heartily One; by William P.
Merrill .... .60
Suggestions for State and Local Federations.......... 2.00
Kinds and Kindliness of Cooperation; by A. W. An-
thony 1.50
Model Constitution for a County or City Federation.... 1.00
How to Organize a Church Federation................ .50

Commission on International Justice and Good-will: Single
copies Free
Europe's War America's Warning; by Charles S. Macfarland.
The Churches of Christ in America and International Peace;
by Charles S. Macfarland.
A Hundred Years of Peace.
The Churches and International Friendship.
The Delusion of Militarism; by Charles E. Jefferson.
The American Japanese Problem.
A Comprehensive Immigration Policy and Program. (Second
Edition.)
The Appeal of Asia to America. (Second Edition.)
The Pacific Coast and the New Oriental Policy.
A Manual for Peace Makers Committee.
New Era in Human History.
A Challenge to Christians.
America's Asiatic Problem and Its Solution.
The Churches of America and the New World Order.
The World Alliance Directory.
America and the Orient.
The Church and Permanent Peace.

Commission on Christian Education:
Lesson Courses on International Peace and Good-will
for the Churches, 1915......................... $5.00
Outline of Course on International Peace; single copies free.
The Churches and Education for Democracy.
A Survey of Christian Education in Its Relation to Democ-
racy; by B. S. Winchester.

Commission on Evangelism: Single Copies Free
Evangelistic Work in the Churches of America.

Advance Steps in Evangelism.
Call to Prayer for a World-wide Revival.
Religious Work at the Panama-Pacific Exposition.

Commission on Temperance:
Catalogue of pamphlets sent on request.

Set of Pamphlet Literature, including social service, annual reports, and other literature describing the work for the United Churches. For the set, 25 cents.

INDEX

Lightning Source UK Ltd.
Milton Keynes UK
UKHW051437220119
335762UK00017B/143/P